DEAN SMITH

ALSO BY JEFF DAVIS:

Papa Bear: The Life and Legacy of George Halas
Rozelle: Czar of the NFL
Chicago Bears: Yesterday & Today

DEAN SMITH

A BASKETBALL LIFE

JEFF DAVIS

RODALE.

RODALE *wellness*

Live happy. Be healthy. Get inspired.

Sign up today to get exclusive access to our authors, exclusive bonuses, and the most authoritative, useful, and cutting-edge information on health, wellness, fitness, and living your life to the fullest.

**Visit us online at RodaleWellness.com
Join us at RodaleWellness.com/Join**

Rodale books may be purchased for business or promotional use or for special sales. For information, please write to:
Special Markets Department, Rodale, Inc., 733 Third Avenue, New York, NY 10017

Printed in the United States of America

Rodale Inc. makes every effort to use acid-free ♾, recycled paper ♻.

Book design by Amy King

Library of Congress Cataloging-in-Publication Data is on file with the publisher.

ISBN-13 978-1-62336-360-4 hardcover

Distributed to the trade by Macmillan

2 4 6 8 10 9 7 5 3 1

RODALE.

We inspire health, healing, happiness, and love in the world.
Starting with you.

This book is dedicated to Kris, my remarkable wife and best friend; our children, Elisabeth Davis Case and Erik Davis; grandsons Will and Charlie Case; son-in-law Dan Case; daughter-in-law Deb Davis; and Rex Lardner, a devoted follower of all sports, college and pro, and close friend since our days at NBC in the 1970s.

CONTENTS

INTRODUCTION

The Good, the Bad, and the Ugly

WEDNESDAY, NOVEMBER 20, 2013, WAS a significant day at the White House, especially for the gathered families and friends of 16 distinguished citizens whom President Barack Obama honored in a late-morning East Room ceremony as recipients of the Presidential Medal of Freedom. The Presidential Medal of Freedom is the highest civilian honor an American can earn.

President John F. Kennedy launched the award a half century before, in 1963, a few months before he was assassinated. Kennedy was honored with a posthumous medal in a special ceremony on December 6 that year—just 2 weeks after his death—by the new president, Lyndon Johnson. Johnson awarded a second posthumous medal that day, to the late Pope John XXIII. They were joined by 29 other honorees, among them architect Ludwig Mies van der Rohe; Polaroid photography inventor Edwin Land; economist and founding father of the European Union Jean Monnet; and Felix Frankfurter, the retired Supreme Court justice.

Among the 2013 honorees a half century later were former

president Bill Clinton; Kennedy's close friend and confidant 92-year-old Ben Bradlee, the longtime editor of the *Washington Post*; activist, actress, and talk show host Oprah Winfrey; late astronaut Sally Ride; late senator from Hawaii and World War II hero Daniel Inouye; former senator Richard Lugar of Indiana; activist and author Gloria Steinem; and two dominant sports figures, both born in 1931, who would come of age in the '50s as America entered the civil rights era, its time of greatest change since the end of World War II. They were 82-year-old Ernie Banks, the Hall of Fame Chicago Cubs infielder, who called the award the greatest moment of his long life; and Dean Smith, a basketball player in mid-20th-century championship years at the University of Kansas who gained renown as a coaching legend and civil rights activist at the University of North Carolina at Chapel Hill. Smith's teams won a then record 879 games in a 36-year run that began in 1961, shortly after Kennedy took office, and ended when the coach stepped down in 1997 during the Clinton administration. To break it down, Coach Smith's Carolina teams won 20 or more games in 30 different seasons, 27 of them consecutively, made 23 straight NCAA tournament appearances, reached 11 Final Fours, and captured 17 Atlantic Coast Conference (ACC) championships in addition to two national titles.

The White House medal ceremony provided a rare good day for Dean Smith, even in absentia. In his remarks, President Obama noted that Coach Smith's teams won two national championships, that he was named coach of the year "several times," that he retired as the winningest men's basketball coach in history, that he was a dedicated civil rights advocate, and that the graduation rate of his players over the years was more than 96 percent. President Obama then added his regret that the coach could not attend "due to an illness that he is facing with extraordinary courage." The debilitating illness that overhung the occasion for Smith was a particularly nasty form of the usually protracted and always fatal Alzheimer's disease.

Dean Smith was an unabashed Christian liberal who quietly but firmly supported and devoutly practiced racial understanding dating back to his childhood in tightly conservative Topeka, Kansas. A life-long Democrat, his friendships crossed party lines without prejudice or rancor. "Underneath this delightful personality is steel," said Republican Bill Bunten, Smith's best friend from Topeka through high school, college at the University of Kansas (KU), and afterward to the end of his life. "If he doesn't agree with you, he won't argue," Bunten told me the summer before Smith died. "You play together, and it works."

Another great friend from their time at Topeka High through and after their KU days was former Republican senator Nancy Landon Kassebaum Baker. "Dean was a very open person, and I admired the leadership he exhibited in so many ways, particularly the caring for athletes in the sports arena," Baker said. "That was so true in high school when he stood up for the black players who could not play and he said, 'If they aren't playing, we won't play.'

"Kansas never played Kentucky in Dean's time in school. He didn't make a big deal about it. That's the way he felt," Baker recalled. Plus, he was on friendly terms with Kentucky's coaching legend Adolph Rupp, a Kansas alum who for decades was called a racist. Rupp never signed a black player until he landed the troubled 7-foot-1 Tom Payne at the end of his career. Payne played one season, until he was dismissed for low grades and was later arrested and convicted as a serial rapist.

Like Smith, Rupp's coach at Kansas was the famed Dr. Forrest "Phog" Allen. Also, like Smith, Rupp was a substitute under Allen. In their head-to-head coaching competition, Smith's North Carolina Tar Heels beat Rupp's Kentucky Wildcats five times against two losses. Smith is the only coach at a major school whose teams had a winning record against Kentucky, a crushing 13-and-3 dominance over his career in Chapel Hill.

At Carolina, Smith personally integrated Chapel Hill restaurants and public facilities and, with Charles Scott, made integration in basketball stick at North Carolina and also the heretofore pale-skin-only Atlantic Coast Conference. As to his excellence as a coach, Smith had been a member of the Naismith Memorial Basketball Hall of Fame in Springfield, Massachusetts, since 1983. That honor came 14 years before he stepped down as coach in Chapel Hill.

Smith's pastor from the time he arrived in Chapel Hill in 1959 with his then wife, Ann, and their three children was Dr. Robert Seymour, who was just organizing the Olin T. Binkley Memorial Baptist Church, a liberal congregation. "He had a gift of being able to relate to everyone regardless of their service, regardless of who they were," Dr. Seymour said of Smith when we spoke in 2015. "The athletic record is outstanding. His legacy will live always when people talk about basketball," Dr. Seymour stated. "I think the many public references will stand up through the years. He was inspirational and universally admired."

Smith's immediate successor at North Carolina, longtime assistant Bill Guthridge, and the present coach, Roy Williams, a former Smith assistant, came to the White House to honor Smith and lend their support to his wife, Dr. Linnea Smith, who accepted the medal from President Obama on her husband's behalf.

In 1988, Coach Smith recommended Williams, his former player and assistant, to Kansas, his alma mater, as the replacement for his first Carolina point guard and friend, Larry Brown, who had led the 11-loss Jayhawks to the National Collegiate Athletic Association title that spring before the NCAA placed his program on probation for recruiting violations. Brown's UCLA Bruins went on probation after the Bruins had to vacate their 1979–80 second-place finish again for recruiting violations.

Williams would enjoy outstanding success at Kansas before answering the call in 2003 to return to Carolina at Coach Smith's behest to become head coach. Williams replaced another Smith-coached Carolina star player, Matt Doherty, who left in disappointment when his coaching stock crashed after North Carolina finished 8–20 in 2001–02, his second season, and 19–16 in 2002–03, his third and last.

The dire news of Smith's agonizingly deteriorating health became public in 2010 when the Smith family revealed that a severe illness had left the old coach disabled. It was a devastating form of dementia that his physician wife, Linnea, characterized in precise medical terminology as a "neurocognitive disorder with multiple etiologies." Dr. Smith's specific diagnosis was another way of saying her husband was afflicted with a litany of ailments—an accumulation of Alzheimer's, Parkinson's disease, and vascular dementia that would hasten any person's otherwise normal decline associated with old age, in this case, many times over.

Within a few months of the medal ceremony, Coach Guthridge, who had maintained a small retirement office in the Dean Smith Center next to his comrade and ex-boss, also would be diagnosed with dementia to add to an incurable heart condition. Ironically, Guthridge, a friend of more than 60 years whose sister in their younger days dated Smith, now faced the same inexorable fate as did his friend.

Just 24 sports figures have been honored with the Presidential Medal of Freedom. Three of them were college basketball coaches: John Wooden, whose UCLA teams won 10 NCAA titles in the

1960s and '70s; Pat Head Summitt, whose University of Tennessee Lady Vols won more than 1,100 games over 38 years before she had to retire in 2011 when she, too, was diagnosed with Alzheimer's (she died at age 64 in June 2016); and now Dean Smith, who ranks with Wooden and current Duke coach Mike Krzyzewski in a discussion of the finest men's coaches in the history of basketball. Years after he retired, Wooden gave the publisher of Smith's memoir, *A Coach's Life*, this praise for his one-time adversary in the dust-jacket blurb: "Dean Smith is a better teacher of basketball than anyone else."

In its early stages, Smith's decline was subtle, slow, barely perceptible. Signs of decline became apparent when he experienced minor memory lapses. This was especially noteworthy because it was so uncharacteristic of the man. Smith had been renowned for a virtual photographic recall of time, events, and minutely incredible, unchallenged detail. A longtime avid golfer who traveled extensively to top courses at home and overseas, the coach stopped playing the game he loved so much in 2008.

By then, his condition had become evident to friends and associates. One day, he drove to work and somehow parked his car on the patio of the Rams Club, home of the Educational Foundation, next door to the Smith Center, the huge arena where the Tar Heels practice and play their home games. The car was neither dented nor otherwise damaged, but it was clearly unsafe for Coach Smith to get behind the wheel. From that point, he had to be driven everywhere he traveled, and soon he was confined to a wheelchair whenever he left home.

"It was very sad, his last years," Dr. Seymour said. "People wanted to reach out to him only to discover he had no visible way of relating to them nor speaking."

As Tommy Tomlinson of the *Charlotte Observer* wrote in a March 5, 2014, piece for *ESPN the Magazine*, "For the past seven years, dementia has drawn the curtains closed on Dean Smith's mind." The changes were obvious to all as he suddenly went from forgetting names to not recognizing faces to often looking at friends and family with empty stares. Tomlinson noted that before Smith's death, people who knew the man well had begun to slip into the past tense when talking about him, as in *Coach Smith was*. When Smith visited the office, he no longer could watch old game footage let alone analyze it. The footage had become a meaningless blur to him. Instead, in his increasingly infrequent visits to the office, Smith passed the time rifling through golf magazines and picture books with help from his longtime administrative assistant, Linda Woods.

Many friends and acquaintances who had known Coach Smith well began to feel uncomfortable seeing him this way. By the next year, 2014, nobody could say for certain that Smith knew who he himself was, let alone recognize family members. The man whose total recall had always astounded everyone—a man who never forgot a birthday, anniversary, or special moment—now passed the days, weeks, months, and years within his own mental confinement.

It is merciful that in his last years Dean Smith did not know about nor understand the scope of the nasty storm raging outside his now insular existence within the university. Starting in 1993, when Smith still was coaching and obviously in complete charge and control of the basketball program that would win its second NCAA title (but seemingly unaware of the underside of faculty maneuvers in certain areas), the University of North Carolina began a descent into a hell that would become one of the widest ranging and most virulent academic scandals involving athletics in any school's history, one that those associated with the university fervently hoped would not lead to the "death penalty" forcing the school to shut down its program.

Two schools that did have to temporarily shutter athletics included the University of Kentucky and Southern Methodist University (SMU). Kentucky basketball did not compete in 1952–53 in the wake of a scandal that included point-shaving a tournament game in a loss to Loyola in 1949; illegally recruiting and enrolling academically unqualified student-athletes; cribbing on tests; and demoralization of the players by the coaches—namely Rupp and his 22-year assistant, Harry Lancaster. Three players—Alex Groza, Ralph Beard, and Dale Barnstable—were banned for life by the National Basketball Association for point-shaving several collegiate games. SMU's football team was shut down in 1987 for illegally buying 13 players.

The University of North Carolina was no ordinary site of academia. UNC holds a unique place in American history as the oldest public university in the country, dating from 1789. North Carolinians had been proud of the university's academic reputation and heretofore unsullied athletic program until it was dishonored by the many revelations of academic fraud that bubbled to the surface like volcanic lava. It had churned quietly since 1993 beyond outside scrutiny until it finally exploded in 2011 after nearly 2 decades in the works.

The ugly academic scandal forced the university to fire football coach Butch Davis and several of his associates. The scandal did not end there, though. It worked its way through the women's basketball program, and, worst of all for the university's image, it landed amid its proud showcase, Carolina's men's basketball program.

That's when an investigation revealed that many players, starting with Dean Smith's 1993 NCAA champion Tar Heels, had taken and passed so-called paper courses in the university's African and Afro-American Studies program (AFAM) without having to undergo the formality of attending classes, let alone in many cases of writing requisite papers or taking exams. In more than a few instances, some of those players took courses that never existed.

These practices continued through the tenures of Smith's successors Bill Guthridge, Matt Doherty, and Roy Williams, well after Smith retired in 1997. Doherty told independent investigator Kenneth Wainstein's team that both Smith and Guthridge explicitly told him he must not change the system despite "understanding that AFAM was the easiest major at Chapel Hill." During Doherty's three seasons as head coach, 42 basketball players were enrolled in the so-called paper courses. How much Smith knew about the scope of it, if he knew anything at all, was unknown before his illness and death and apparently will remain that way. No paper trail leads back to him and his time as coach, according to both Dan Kane, the Raleigh *News and Observer* investigative reporter who broke the story in 2010, and whistleblower Mary Willingham, who with coauthor Jay M. Smith wrote *Cheated: The UNC Scandal, the Education of Athletes, and the Future of Big-Time College Sports.*

At the same time, Dean Smith was not naive to North Carolina's troubles. He definitely was familiar with the problems inherent in so-called big-time college sports. He had been an integral part of the system and the way it worked since he entered college in 1949. By 1951, when he was a sophomore at the University of Kansas playing under coaching legend "Phog" Allen, regarded by many as the father of college basketball, a gambling scandal based at Madison Square Garden rocked the college game to its foundation. That scandal not only destroyed several of the foremost programs in the New York area, it severely affected such prominent powers as the University of Kentucky, coached by Allen disciple Adolph Rupp, and Bradley University in Peoria, Illinois, coached by Forddy Anderson, who later would lead Michigan State to its first Final Four in 1957.

In fact, Smith gained his promotion to head basketball coach at Carolina in 1961 at the age of 30 after a second huge gambling scandal that year led to the abrupt departure of his boss, Frank McGuire, who left the school that summer to coach Wilt Chamberlain and the Philadelphia Warriors in the National Basketball Association.

While he was active and until he descended into his dark illness more than a decade after he retired, Coach Smith epitomized the best of college athletics for more than a half century, dating back to his time as a hardworking, well-regarded student-athlete at the University of Kansas. The coaching life he would lead was assured by his relatively speedy ascendance as a junior officer in the Air Force and an assistant to Bob Spear at the fledgling US Air Force Academy before he joined McGuire as his assistant in the 1958–59 season at North Carolina. In his subsequent 36-year tenure as head coach, Dean Smith was held in the highest regard for his probity in his profession by both colleagues and the public.

1 | THE CRADLE OF COLLEGE BASKETBALL

DEAN EDWARDS SMITH WAS A child of the Kansas prairie who led a life of education and love of well-played athletic success. He was born February 28, 1931, in Emporia, Kansas, to schoolteachers, the former Vesta Edwards and Alfred Smith. Both Smiths were devout Baptists, avid readers, and followers of Emporia's most renowned citizen, William Allen White, the Pulitzer Prize–winning progressive editor of the local *Gazette*.

The Smiths' Baptist way of life was by no means harsh, nor were voices raised to effect discipline. Rather, the young Dean was friendly but not an outgoing, natural salesman. In fact, it could be argued, and still is by many, that Dean Smith was extremely secretive. In years to come, print journalists would consider him a tedious interview subject, and broadcasters outside his own world thought he was as dull as his flat, midwestern dialect.

Dean Smith certainly could be trusted to hold tightly to a friend's confidence. Qualities that might have been admirable in a secret agent or military spy were not attributes for a basketball coach who must possess a salesman's ability to make and close deals. Somehow, he developed a certain ability to sell athletes and their parents on his qualities despite the inner doubts that had to run counter to his natural instincts. He had to be able to pitch himself to succeed as well as he did to land the many great athletes he would coach, develop, and continue to remain close with long after they finished their college careers under his tutelage. As Frank Deford put it in a 1982 *Sports Illustrated* profile, Dean Smith was a man who acted as if he always was no younger than age 62.

Actually, Dean had barely turned 3 when his father, Alfred, coached the Emporia High Spartans to the 1934 Kansas state high school basketball championship. The senior Smith took a bold, unprecedented step that season when the first black player at a white school in state history joined his team. Paul Terry, a 10th grader, played guard and was the sixth man, first player off the bench. Terry performed under heavy pressure, and as Dean Smith noted in *A Coach's Life*, written with John Kilgo and Sally Jenkins, Terry, a lifelong resident of Emporia, admitted in a 1982 conversation with Smith that "I took some verbal abuse from fans and other players."

The abuse intensified and grew ugly as the season wore on toward the finish. Before Dean's father took his Emporia team to rival Chanute, he got a telegram from that school's principal. "Leave the Negro boy at home, or don't come," the writer of the telegram ordered. Coach Smith ignored the wire and apparently said nothing to anybody else, including Terry, who came out with his teammates onto the Chanute floor. The star at Chanute was Ralph Miller, a future Kansas All-America football and basketball player and, later, with 657 wins, a Hall of Fame basketball coach who developed great integrated teams at Wichita, Iowa, and Oregon State.

When tournament time came, state officials went to Coach Smith and literally laid down the law, a law in Kansas that legalized racial segregation. A devastated Paul Terry had to stay at home while his white teammates went on to win the Class A state championship, beating Wichita East 22–15 in the Topeka High School gym. Thanks to Alfred Smith's discussions at home and lessons to his young son in his formative years, Terry's crucible shaped Dean Smith's future and desire to change that reality forever. "He never got another chance to compete at the top level again," Dean Smith wrote years later concerning Paul Terry. After high school, Terry went to Kansas State Teachers College in Emporia, earned a degree, and opened a dry-cleaning business that enabled him to support his wife, Odessa, and their eight children. Five Terry children received graduate degrees, one a doctorate. Three of Paul and Odessa's sons played college basketball.

Dean Smith wrote in his memoir that in 1974, Terry's son John, who was playing basketball for the University of California, Berkeley, came with the team to Chapel Hill to face North Carolina. Before the game, Coach Smith walked over to John Terry and introduced himself as the son of his father's coach at Emporia High. To Dean, "it was a moment worth reflecting on," as he grew to realize that life's realities extended far beyond Emporia, Kansas.

Innovation, devotion, and learning were second nature to Dean Smith. He was taught the history of Kansas basketball in early childhood, Alfred impressing on his son the significance of the game and the story of James Naismith, the man who literally invented it. Dean learned that Naismith nurtured the game as he made the University of Kansas in Lawrence his base of operation from the time he arrived on campus in 1898 and organized a new basketball team. And the elder Smith told young Dean many times that Kansas coach Dr. Forrest "Phog" Allen, as Naismith's protégé and athletic heir, was the most important coach in college basketball.

A first-time out-of-area visitor to Lawrence, Kansas, heads there thinking it will be a more settled version of the flat prairie that describes much of the state. Nothing could be more untrue. This city of 87,000 is built on a series of hills in northeastern Kansas. As it happens, the highest point on Mount Oread is called the Hill, site of the unique campus that became the University of Kansas. Nobody in that part of the country would ever call the school the U of K or UK. Everyone, regardless of affiliation throughout the state, and its Big 12 rival schools call the place by no other name than KU. Its in-state rival, Kansas State University, was founded as a land-grant college in Manhattan in 1863, leaving Lawrence and Emporia to battle for the legislature's blessing as home of *the* state university of Kansas.

KU was founded after the Civil War in 1865, when Lawrence offered the inducement to beat out Emporia. Lawrence simply could offer more land (40 acres) and enough cash ($15,000) as an endowment start-up. KU now covers 1,100 acres and has some 19,000 undergraduates and 7,500 grad students on campus. Besides the hills, two geographic markers on campus are dedicated to two names synonymous with the game they made famous.

Markers honoring basketball's inventor, James Naismith, are prominent in this campus area. There's Naismith Drive and Naismith Hall (a private dorm), and inside the Allen Fieldhouse, named for the coach who made KU the cornerstone of college basketball, the basketball floor at 1651 Naismith Drive is proudly named the James Naismith Court. These distinctions were well earned over decades of service to the school.

In the extremely bitter winter of 1891 in Springfield, Massachusetts, James Naismith, a Canadian émigré and Presbyterian minister at the YMCA International Training School, who had left his job as the first athletic director at Montreal's McGill University, was summoned by his boss to solve a problem. Dr. Luther Gulick gave Naismith 14 days to come up with a viable idea to give his boys cooped up in heavy snow and cold a chance to blow off some steam. Naismith, a physical education instructor who never preached and who specialized in wrestling, took a look at the gymnasium, noted the layout, and devised a plan.

Naismith analyzed the most popular team games of that time and learned that all were built around some sort of ball: rugby, soccer, football, hockey, lacrosse, and baseball. He quickly decided that the hard solid baseball, lacrosse ball, or hockey puck that traveled at high speeds were too dangerous at close quarters. Rugby, soccer, and football had the most physical contact, especially when running with the ball. Lacrosse, a game that originated some 400 or so years earlier in the St. Lawrence Valley among Native tribes, was played, like hockey and baseball, with a stick. It became popular in certain pockets of the United States by the 20th century, especially so in New England, Long Island, the Mid-Atlantic states from Maryland to the Carolinas, and pockets of the Midwest.

Naismith did not want the players in his new game waving sticks in close confinement. Also, being indoors did not work with those high-speed, physical-contact sports. Naismith knew he needed a bigger and softer air-filled version of a soccer ball that would be easy to handle and pass. With his final, major idea, this ball could be aimed in an arc at an unguarded goal high enough off the ground to be over the players' heads that they could not leap up and catch nor bat away the ball.

To that end, Naismith got a hold of a ladder and two wooden peach baskets. He ordered a worker to attach one basket to a railing guarding the gallery that circled the gym. Then he had the man hang the other basket on the railing at the opposite end of the floor. The height of the baskets above the heads of the players forced a "shooter" to lob the ball or arc it toward the goal. The height itself is not mentioned in the original rules. It measured about 10 feet thanks to necessity and an architectural quirk in the Springfield Y gymnasium. When Naismith had the peach baskets attached to the railing that circled above the gym court, it measured 10 feet high. That looked right to Naismith, who decided 10 feet would become the official uniform height. That standard has held to this day.

How Naismith came up with the name for his game is conjecture, but this much is known. He called the game "Basket Ball," and the moniker has stuck.

The first game was played in December 1891, nine to a side. After seeing what he had created, Naismith wrote 13 rules that formed the basis of his game. No running, passing only, no dribbling, and no kicking the ball. Officials called fouls on players for too much "rough" play. After each "basket," the official climbed a ladder, retrieved the ball from the peach basket, and tossed it at the center jump circle. The game lasted 30 minutes and was played in two halves with a running clock and a 5-minute break at halftime while the clock still ran. Rules changed as quickly as the game kept developing. Dribbling was allowed to supplement passing. Eventually, all high school, amateur, international, and professional games would be played in quarters: 8 minutes in high school; 10 in amateur; 12 in the pros. Unlike soccer, in which time to play is more or less a suggestion, basketball time is displayed on what became a scoreboard for all coaches, players, and spectators to see. With the exception of a 3-year period in the early 1950s when colleges played in 10-minute quarters, college basketball has been played in two 20-minute halves, a link to its origination.

The game evolved immediately with the adaption of practical rules changes. By 1903, metal hoops draped with open-bottomed nets replaced the peach baskets and the need to stop play to retrieve a made basket. In time, custom-made round leather basketballs (with laces in the early years) replaced the soccer balls. The court's dimensions, not mentioned in the original rules, became a rectangular 94 by 50 feet and were lined with boundaries, jump circles, and "foul" lanes. In time, each team would be limited to five players a side during play to keep the floor from getting clogged. In the beginning, in case of fouls, the clock was stopped as each team designated a single player to shoot all foul shots, also called free throws. Substitutes would replace players on the floor at the coach's discretion.

Naismith's original 13 rules were purchased at auction from Sotheby's in 2010 by KU alum and philanthropist David G. Booth and his wife, Suzanne, for $4,338,500. The rules are now on permanent display at the DeBruce Center, adjacent to the Booth Family Hall of Athletics at the northeast corner of the Allen Fieldhouse.

The game was introduced and spread internationally by the YMCA movement, and it became immensely popular right away. From its New England origin, it moved to New York and Philadelphia, then moved like a wildfire through the country. Naismith left Springfield in 1895 to study medicine in Denver while working as physical education director of the local YMCA. On his journey west, he spread word of his game to various YMCAs, particularly in Ohio, Indiana, and Illinois. Soon the game took root and spread everywhere, from farms to country towns to cities, because it was and is a game that can be played indoors in bad weather and outdoors in nice weather, and equipment is minimal. By the 21st century, basketball would be played around the globe in organized and pickup games. Today, basketball is avidly followed by an estimated 300 million people, according to Sporteology.com. Only soccer and cricket are more popular.

In 1898, Naismith, now known as "Doctor," returned to the University of Kansas in Lawrence, but never to practice medicine. He instead served as a chaplain and physical education instructor. In short order, he became the school's athletic director and its first basketball coach. At the turn of the 20th century, Kansas teams played a schedule composed of opponents few people would recognize today. Most opponents were teams from area YMCAs plus such colleges as nearby Baker University, William Jewell College, and Haskell Institute, an American Indian college located just a few blocks east of the KU campus in Lawrence. The lone exception was future conference rival Kansas State in Manhattan, 80 or so miles to the west. Despite KU's better than 2-to-1 dominance (190–93 through 2015–16), this rivalry has thrived and burned hot through their mutual existence in the Missouri Valley, Big Six, Big Seven, Big Eight, and Big 12 conferences.

Over the next decade, Dr. Naismith would go 55–60, the *only* coach in KU history with a losing record. But he would find a loyal disciple and lifelong friend in Forrest Clare Allen.

In 1904, Forrest Allen, a bright and ambitious 19-year-old student-athlete from Independence, Missouri, enrolled at the University of Kansas. Allen, who in his youth lived down the street from future president Harry Truman, came to school as its best basketball player. In that formative era of basketball, the best player on a team was designated by his coach as the sole free throw shooter under the rules of that time. Allen also arrived with the colorful nickname "Phog," courtesy of a local sportswriter named Ward "Pinhead" Coble. When Coble heard the boy's loud, penetrating calls as a baseball umpire that reached all corners of the ball field, he tagged him with the name "Phoghorn," which in short order was shortened to "Phog." Ironically, everyone, players included, who knew Allen after he became an osteopath called him "Doc." Phog was the tag the sportswriters gave him.

Allen became a basketball coach in his sophomore year at KU when, while playing for Dr. Naismith, he took on a moonlighting job coaching Baker University's Wildcats. He led them to an 18–3 record in 1905–06 and a perfect 14–0 mark in 1906–07. Before he accepted the Baker job, Dr. Naismith told Allen that "you don't coach basketball, Forrest. You play it." Allen respectfully disagreed with the inventor and would go on not only to coach the game but also to be called the Father of Basketball Coaching, much to his mentor's delight.

By 1907, Dr. Naismith realized that his 22-year-old protégé was so athletically gifted and charismatic and had such unique organizational skills that he named him his coaching successor at Kansas for the 1907–08 season. Now a college senior, young Allen responded by leading the Jayhawks to an 18–4 record. In his second job that year, Allen coached Baker to a 13–6 record, his third and last season there. Then, in 1908–09, Allen pulled another double-duty coaching chore. He led the Jayhawks to a 25–3 record while moonlighting as coach at nearby Haskell Institute, the Native American college, and guiding them to a 27–5 mark.

After the season, Allen quit his coaching jobs at both KU and Baker and enrolled at a Kansas college of osteopathy, where he earned a DO degree in osteopathic medicine in 1911. An osteopath not only may prescribe medications; that individual is also trained to believe in hands-on treatment using manipulation and massage to treat ailments. Dr. Allen would gain a widespread reputation among athletes as a strong-handed "healer," especially caring for those with sore knees, ankles, and backs. In 1912, he moved to Warrensburg State Teachers College (now the University of Central Missouri), where he coached football through 1917 with a 29–17–2 record and basketball through the winter of 1919. His teams went 84–31 before he returned to Lawrence with the nickname "Doc" to become athletic director and football coach when Dr. Naismith told him he wanted to devote himself full-time to teaching.

That fall, Doc Allen's Jayhawks went 5–2–1 on the gridiron, his only season as KU football coach. His duties as basketball coach and as athletic director would consume his time. Just one game into the

1919–20 basketball season, Coach Karl Schlademan walked into Allen's office and told the new athletic director he wished to devote his full attention to his track-and-field team. Doc Allen took over the team and this time remained in charge for the next 37 years, doubling as athletic director until 1937.

The Jayhawks accomplished nothing of note the next two seasons but suddenly broke out in the 1921–22 season, going 16–2 to tie for the Missouri Valley Intercollegiate Athletic Association championship. The Jayhawks won the title again the following season, with a 17–1 record. In 1936, the Los Angeles–based Helms Athletic Foundation retroactively named those two Kansas teams back-to-back national champions.

A substitute on Phog Allen's two Helms championship teams was Adolph Rupp. The son of a farmer from Halstead, Kansas, Rupp learned his basketball lessons well from both Allen and Naismith, who by then was serving as an assistant to his protégé. Upon graduation in 1923, Rupp became a high school coach, but not of the game he loved and wanted to teach. After 2 years as a wrestling coach in Marshalltown, Iowa, he led his team to the Iowa State wrestling title. That championship gave Rupp the break he sought.

In 1926, he moved to Freeport, Illinois, a town along the Wisconsin border largely settled by German immigrants. Freeport was the site of the second of seven debates on slavery in the 1858 Senate campaign between Republican challenger Abraham Lincoln and Democratic incumbent Stephen A. Douglas, who would win that race. The town became so well known for the popular pretzels produced at the local Billerbeck Bakery that it was called the Pretzel City. The Billerbeck Bakery went out of business early in the 20th century, but its name lived on as the nickname for the high school's athletic teams.

The Pretzels' biggest athletic star in the early years of the century was Glenn "Pat" Holmes, who captained the team to the Illinois high school championship in 1915, then, in 1926, coached the Pretzels to the state championship, making him the only person in Illinois high school history to play for a state champion then coach another team to a state title. That accomplishment caught the attention of the people at prestigious Oak Park–River Forest High School on Chicago's western border. Holmes moved to Oak Park, hometown of famed architect Frank Lloyd Wright, the writer Ernest Hemingway, and his high school football coach Bob Zuppke, who moved on in 1913 to a Hall of Fame career at the University of Illinois. Holmes's departure left Freeport's coaching slot open, which Rupp filled the next school year in his first varsity coaching job.

From 1926–30, Rupp taught history and economics as his Pretzels continued Holmes's winning tradition, going 66–21. Rupp also started a black player. He was William Mosely, the first African American to play basketball at the school and the second to graduate from there. When Rupp's 1928–29 Pretzels finished third in the state basketball tournament, University of Illinois coach J. Craig Ruby took notice of how well the young coach had prepared his team.

A year later, Ruby spoke at Freeport's team banquet. Ruby was a close friend of Rupp's college coach, Phog Allen. So Ruby took Rupp aside to tell him that the Kentucky job was open and that he should apply and likely would get it. On Ruby's recommendation, Kentucky hired the 29-year-old Rupp for the 1930–31 season, and he began his historic renown as the Baron of the Bluegrass and the winningest coach in college basketball history during his tenure, with 876 victories over the next 42 seasons, a record that lasted until Dean Smith caught and surpassed him late in the 1996–97 season.

The Rupp name is as beloved in the Commonwealth of Kentucky as it is despised in many other places because of his career-long refusal to enroll black players until that single year with troubled

Tom Payne, well after his fellow KU alum Dean Smith reached out to integrate North Carolina and the Atlantic Coast Conference. That refusal was ironic, because Rupp's Kentucky successors have built their teams around black players for decades since Rupp's departure and subsequent death in 1977 at age 76.

When Allen published *My Basket-ball Bible* in 1924 at age 39, his position was established as the Father of College Basketball. From 1921–22 through the 1926–27 season, Allen's Kansas teams won 97 games and lost just 11, as they captured six straight Missouri Valley titles.

Basketball's rulebook has been rewritten and tinkered with countless times over the years. One of the most bizarre experiments was conducted in 1927, when someone on the rules committee pushed through abolition of the dribble, a move that would have destroyed not only the movement inherent to the game but the game itself. A furious Allen gathered the nation's college basketball coaches that April at the Drake Relays in Des Moines, Iowa, and raised the roof. They protested so loudly and firmly as a unified group that the basketball rules committee backed off and eliminated that change, to everybody's relief and delight. From that success with his peers, Allen led the formation of the National Association of Basketball Coaches (NABC), whose contributions have been vital to the progress of the game.

In 1927, the old Missouri Valley Conference broke up and Kansas, Kansas State, Missouri, Oklahoma, Nebraska, and Iowa State left to form the new Big Six Conference. Allen and Kansas dominated basketball. From 1907–08 to the end of his coaching career in 1955–56, Allen-led Kansas teams won 24 conference championships.

The quality of Allen's coaching tree was as impressive as any in the history of any sport. Besides Rupp, Allen-trained coaches included Arthur "Dutch" Lonborg, the successful coach at North-western from 1927–50; Dean Smith of North Carolina; Frosty Cox of Colorado; Ralph Miller of Wichita, Iowa, and Oregon State; Allen's successor at Kansas, Dick Harp; and Naismith Hall of Famer John McLendon, who went to Kansas but was barred from playing there by the segregation rules that would prevent Kansas from fielding its first black player until 1951. Dr. Naismith and Allen befriended McLendon, who polished his knowledge of the game under their tutelage. In 24 college and pro seasons, McLendon-coached teams won 496 games. Although he loved the running game and was one of the first coaches to employ the full-court press, McLendon is credited with inventing the slowdown/stalling four-corners offense that Dean Smith would refine and popularize at North Carolina.

After years of pushing for basketball's inclusion in the Olympic movement, Allen succeeded in getting the game included in the 1936 Berlin Games. Twenty-one countries participated in brutal conditions. The basketball games were played outdoors in a tennis stadium on a clay court with no seating and room for just 1,000 standing spectators. To compound the difficult situation, a heavy rain fell during the gold medal game as the United States team edged Canada 19–8. The highlight of the basketball competition came when Dr. Naismith presented the teams with their medals: gold to the United States, silver to Canada, and bronze to Mexico. Three years later, Dr. Naismith, the inventor of basketball, died of a cerebral hemorrhage at the age of 78. He was buried next to his first wife, Maude, in Memorial Park Cemetery in Lawrence.

Phog Allen had been responsible for so much in the rules and organization of college basketball. The key rules change that opened the game to quickness, speed, and excitement was the abolition in

1938 of the game-slowing center jump after every basket. Allen coached Kansas to a pair of NCAA berths in the early years of the tournament, most significantly in 1940 when the tournament badly needed a jolt.

The first NCAA tournament finale was held at old Patten Gymnasium on the Northwestern University campus in Evanston, Illinois, thanks largely to the efforts of Allen's disciple Dutch Lonborg. The first ever NCAA tournament opened at the Palestra on the University of Pennsylvania campus in Philadelphia on March 17, 1939, as Villanova beat Brown 42–30 and Ohio State topped Wake Forest 64–52. The next night, Ohio State routed Villanova 53–36 to advance to the championship game. Two nights later, at the old California Coliseum in San Francisco, Oregon beat Texas 56–41 and Oklahoma defeated Utah State 50–39. On March 22, Utah State beat Texas 51–49 in the third-place game before Oregon advanced to the finals in a 55–37 rout of Oklahoma. The tournament got virtually no publicity, and the gym on the Northwestern campus was so small, cramped, and dingy that nobody cared to attend until the university literally papered the house with free tickets to boost attendance to 5,000.

Then four things happened. Oregon beat Ohio State 46–33 to win the first championship. The tournament lost money, $2,531, for the only time in its history. Northwestern immediately tore down its gym; built its massive, world-class Technological Institute on that land, which opened in 1940; and moved its home games for the next decade to Evanston High School while it haggled for years over building a new campus facility until at last it opened McGaw Memorial Hall in 1951. And Phog Allen took charge to save the tournament.

In 1940, once again, only eight teams would get into the field, and Allen promoted it widely, even reaching into his own pocket. Plus, he created interest. He got Kansas City to host the Western Region of the tournament. Then Doc Allen got lucky. In that era, when a team was required to win its conference to get into the tournament, Kansas had to beat both Oklahoma and Missouri in a unique playoff situation to get there—and they did. Then, playing all their games in Kansas City, KU played a pair of great, crowd-attracting games to generate excitement in a tough push to the championship game. Kansas beat Rice 50–44 in the quarterfinal, then escaped defeat to favored USC when the Trojans' Jack Morrison's last-second shot from midcourt bounced off the rim, to give KU a 43–42 win.

Allen's luck continued when the Indiana Hoosiers, the other school in the country as basketball crazy as Kansas, met the Jayhawks in the final at the Kansas City Municipal Auditorium. Coached by John Wooden's boyhood friend Emmett "Branch" McCracken, Indiana had an easy time getting through the Eastern Region on March 21 and 22 at Tony Hinkle's Butler Fieldhouse in Indianapolis. The Hoosiers routed Springfield College 48–24 in the quarterfinals and encountered little trouble in the semis the next night when they defeated Duquesne 39–30 in the semis.

Then, in a brilliant pregame move before the final on March 30, Allen convinced the NCAA to pay tribute to James Naismith, the game's inventor, who died the previous November.

Playing before 10,000 mostly partisan fans, Kansas may have had the backing of the crowd but Indiana had the better players and McCracken's Hurryin' Hoosiers, led by Marvin Huffman, literally ran the Jayhawks into the ground, winning their first of five NCAA championships with ease, 60–42. Kansas made the tournament once more in 1942, when Colorado beat them 46–44 in a first-round game in Kansas City. That began a decade-long tournament drought.

When they finally qualified again in 1952, they captured their first NCAA tournament championship. Contributing to the title run was a seldom-used junior guard named Dean Smith who, thanks to his father, had learned his lessons well in all facets of sport, attaining his first ambition: to represent the University of Kansas in a major sports competition that he hoped would lead to a coaching career in the big time. As a player on a national championship team, this was the beginning of a whole lot of winning for the kid from Emporia.

2 | LESSONS FOR A COACH'S SON

BY THE TIME HE TURNED 9, in 1940, young Dean Smith had a firm grasp on his own Democratic political leanings, notably that his beliefs ran counter to his parents, who were born-and-bred die-hard Kansas Republicans. That year, almost every adult young Dean knew was wild about Republican standard-bearer Wendell Willkie and his bid to prevent President Franklin D. Roosevelt from winning a third term as president. Finally, the intrafamily tension broke during a hot summer weekend drive to the Ozarks. Young Dean sweltered in the backseat as his father and a driver friend carried on a nonstop conversation about Willkie. "I couldn't take it anymore," Dean wrote in *A Coach's Life*. "I burst out and said, 'I hope Roosevelt wins!' That set off a horrified reaction in the car." Fortunately for Dean, his parents did not hold his Democratic beliefs against him.

As he grew older, Dean Smith learned other life lessons from his father that he would later apply in his own coaching situations. In 1942, on the eve of an important game with large Wichita Plainview, Emporia High held a big all-school dance. Coach Alfred Smith, aware that many of his players wanted to go, told his team members that if they attended the dance, they had to honor his curfew. He told the players they had two choices: Play or not play the big game. Apparently, several players felt the curfew was ridiculous and decided to ignore their coach.

The next morning, when Coach Smith gathered his team, he asked who missed the curfew. That was an era when young people would face an adult's questions with truthful answers, and several team members admitted they had stayed out after curfew. Four of them were starters. True to his promise, the coach suspended the young rebels, and they missed the trip. Both 11-year-old Dean and his 14-year-old sister, Joan, could not fathom what their father had done, let alone his thinking.

Playing with a lineup of reserves, Emporia somehow came out of Plainview with a one-point victory. His father may have been strict, but he considered his rules simple and worth following, and his players honored them and their mentor.

This situation confirmed Alfred Smith's long-held belief that a team wins consistently by playing as a team and that a team can lose one or two players and still win by dedicating themselves to a common goal. "It took sacrifice, unselfishness, and discipline," Dean Smith later wrote. "Young people can do marvelous things when responding to a formidable challenge."

When it came to team play, the elder Coach Smith taught Dean another lesson that became a noteworthy principle of his coaching mantra. "I would be credited years later for the practice of having a scorer point to the passer to thank him for the assist," Dean Smith wrote. "But the germ of that idea came from watching my father coach and listening to his dinner table conversation." Alfred Smith strongly believed the assist man deserved credit for his play and preached it so constantly that Dean took it to heart and would instill in his Carolina teams the reactive habit of pointing to the individual who passed the ball—the assist man—after scoring the field goal.

Emporia in World War II was typical of so much of small-town America. Boys who had been local sports heroes joined the service and went off with their friends and neighbors to fight the Axis powers. The local American Legion building downtown features a glass wall etched with the names of 150 townsmen from the Emporia High School classes of 1937, '38, and '39. Dean Smith knew many of them and regarded them as heroes. About a third of the boys named on that wall died in combat.

One of them was US Army Air Corps Lieutenant Jack Snow, a bombardier, who had played for Alfred Smith at Emporia. In the late spring of 1943, Snow came home on furlough from the Aleutian Islands in western Alaska. He dropped by the Smiths' house, where Dean recalled that Snow and his father talked for a long time before the young man left to return to combat. A few weeks later, word reached Emporia that Lieutenant Snow had been killed in combat in the Aleutians on July 6, 1943. That news so affected 12-year-old Dean that he wrote about it decades later, well after his own honorable service as an officer in the US Air Force and his subsequent opposition to the Vietnam War in the mid- to late 1960s. It also affected the way he handled issues on military service in private teaching moments at the University of North Carolina.

As much as he loved basketball, young Dean's favorite sport was baseball. He was a leader on the diamond, of course, playing the leadership position, catcher. By the time he turned 14, a now physically matured Dean stood 5 feet 10 inches, a self-admitted early bloomer. In due time, he realized he had reached full growth. Dean, a natural right-handed batter as he was a golfer when he took up the game, practiced switch-hitting from both sides by hitting a baseball strung from a rope attached to his basement ceiling. He believed that switch-hitting would give him an advantage: As most players in high school throw right-handed, he would hit more from the left side, and he would become a better player. He had no way of knowing at that time that the New York Yankees' great center fielder was taught to become a switch-hitter by his father to the point where he demonstrated nearly indistinguishable power from both sides of the plate.

Regarded as something of an athletic prodigy, Dean Smith, no Mickey Mantle for certain, became the youngest Emporia boy to that time to make the local American Legion team. He and his friends played baseball every day, all day long.

Dean's rabid love of baseball landed him in a jam at home, though. His father was a solid Baptist, and the family spent upwards of 4 hours in church on Sundays. It started with an hour of Sunday school, then the regular service in late morning, and culminated with 2 more hours of church services and youth group on Sunday evenings. Also, the family held a "short devotional period" before evening dinner.

One Sunday in the early summer of 1945, Dean's American Legion team had to make a 97-mile bus trip to Abilene. Defying his father, the boy sneaked out a side door and made the trip. On the drive home from church, Alfred heard enough about Dean's rascally behavior from an irate neighbor, who rode Alfred so sharply that he turned on a baseball broadcast on the car radio to shut him up; however, the neighbor, who considered playing baseball on Sunday a mortal sin against Baptist teachings, then admonished Alfred for listening to the ballgame. Dean feared the worst when he got home. But instead, his father had cooled off by that point and offered a compromise, which the boy was all too glad to accept. He said that Dean could play ball on Sundays if there was no conflict with church. "When there was a conflict, I had to choose church," the chastened Dean wrote later in *A Coach's Life*.

A personal crisis for Dean occurred over Fourth of July weekend that same summer. Dean caught both ends of a doubleheader playing alongside a boy named Shad Woodruff, whom he called "the best athlete in town." On the way home after the second game, Woodruff complained that he didn't feel well. Within minutes, he had to be rushed to the hospital, where he was diagnosed with an attack of bulbar polio, lethal in that era before the Salk and Sabin vaccines basically ended the disease. Dr. Jonas Salk's serum injections were introduced to the general public in 1955, and Dr. Albert Sabin's oral vaccine became accepted for general use in 1963 after several years of testing. In the Woodruff case in Emporia, back in 1945, the boy died within 4 days of contracting the disease. The grieving Dean gathered all the newspaper clippings he could find about Shad, cut them into squares, and pasted them into an album, which he took to Shad's parents. He stayed in touch with them until they both died years later.

Baseball still was America's national pastime in the 1940s. Dean and his friends closely followed the daily doings of the major leagues and high minors in the newspapers. He paid special attention to the nearby New York Yankees Triple A team, the Kansas City Blues, as they fed players such as future Hall of Fame shortstop Phil Rizzuto and his double-play partner, second baseman Jerry Priddy, to the big club in the Bronx. The favorite major league team for the Smiths and most boys in that part of the Midwest and Southwest was the St. Louis Cardinals, in those days the westernmost team in the National League, with its American League counterpart, the Browns.

By the late 1940s, Dean became "captivated" with the star-filled Brooklyn Dodgers after they broke organized baseball's color line. His special favorites, in the order he listed, were second baseman Jackie Robinson, shortstop Pee Wee Reese, first baseman Gil Hodges, center fielder Duke Snider, right fielder Carl Furillo, and catcher Roy Campanella.

Like his father, who years later would share his Cardinals loyalties with the close-by Kansas City Royals, an older Dean befriended the late George Steinbrenner and his daughter Jenny and became a New York Yankees fan from the 1980s on.

Alfred Smith took his family on the train in 1945 to the magnificent Union Station in St. Louis to see the Cardinals play at Sportsman's Park. It was as decent a team in that final war year that the Cardinals could field while their best players—hard-charging Enos Slaughter, popular young hitting star Stan Musial, captain and premier center fielder Terry Moore, and shortstop Marty Marion—were away in service. The Cardinals finished second in the National League, three games behind the Chicago Cubs, who won their last pennant before they began a 71-year run of sad and often comedic frustration and futility.

Baseball certainly was young Dean's game, and he was positive his athletic future lay there. He was too young and overwhelmed by baseball fever to know that his father had grown restless with his teaching career and, as the war was winding down, was looking for a chance to make more money. That trip to St. Louis got the family to a ballgame, of course, but Alfred had also scheduled an interview with the American Red Cross during the visit. It was the start of a job hunt, and he finally landed a good one in 1946 with the Veterans Administration, a department of high activity after World War II as the VA reoriented returning servicemen to civilian life. "In those days, a teacher made $3,500 a year. So he came in here and took a job with the Veterans Administration," Bill Bunten said in the summer of 2014. Bunten would serve Topeka for decades as a state legislator and two terms as mayor. "Vesta, his [Dean's] mother, was a teacher also."

Alfred Smith's 14 years as a high school basketball coach ended, of course, with his career change. With that 1934 state championship, his tenure at Emporia had been a huge success. Now, in 1946, he was assigned to the VA office in Wichita for several months of training. Thus as Dean returned to school for his sophomore year, he knew the end-game in Emporia had begun. As a final gesture, Alfred made time to coach Dean's ninth-grade basketball team so they could share that father-son memory.

While Alfred prepared for his new assignment with the VA in Topeka, everyone in Emporia could see that Dean had developed into a fine catcher for the high school team. His favorite battery mate was an all-state pitcher named Dick Hiskey, who graduated in 1947 and went away to college. Coincidentally, in 1958, Dean would meet up with Hiskey again on the North Carolina campus, where Hiskey was a young professor of chemistry and Dean had become the brand-new assistant basketball coach under Frank McGuire. They saw much of each other in the ensuing years, as Hiskey in 1980 became the university's faculty chairman of athletics while Dean was developing Final Four teams.

By the end of Dean's sophomore year at Emporia High in 1947, Alfred had finished his training in Wichita and packed up the family and household goods for the move to Topeka, the state capital and railroad center 60 miles away, through the rolling prairie of northeastern Kansas. For 16-year-old Dean in the summer of 1947, apprehension ruled as it does for any normal teenager who is about to move away for the first time. Dean was leaving behind his friends in the only town where he had ever lived and the cozy ease of being a big wheel in the 600-student Emporia High. Worst of all, older sister Joan, whom Dean considered his best friend, would not travel to Topeka with the family, as she was starting college at Emporia State. He would start a new life in Topeka High School, one of the largest and best public high schools in the state of Kansas, where he adjusted quickly thanks in large part to athletic participation, helping him make a large number of enduring friendships.

Topeka High had African American students within its doors

from its 1871 opening in the original building, but it was not as integrated as the term suggests. Topeka High boasts many famous graduates, among them Herbert Hoover's vice president, Charles Curtis; the supreme tenor saxophonist Coleman Hawkins; psychiatrists Drs. Karl and William Menninger; and class of '58 member David Ebel, who became a federal judge in the 10th Circuit Court of Appeals in Denver.

Topeka's population by 1947 was pushing 75,000, and its high school was filled nearly to overflowing with its 2,700 students and a stellar national reputation among educators. The fourth floor of the original Topeka High School, built in 1871, was condemned as a firetrap in 1924, and construction on the present campus began in 1928. The 278,000-square-foot, three-story Gothic-style structure that cost $1.8 million in pre-Depression dollars opened in 1931, the highest cost for a public school to that date west of the Mississippi River. The immaculately kept school grounds cover a city block just west of the Kansas statehouse–capitol building complex in downtown Topeka.

One of the first people Dean met in school was senior Bill Bunten, who quickly became his best friend. Their close friendship endured and continued to grow through high school, during their college days at KU where they were Phi Gamma Delta fraternity brothers, and onward through their lives and careers: Dean, politically a Democrat, as basketball coach at North Carolina, and Bill, a Republican legislator in the Kansas house and senate before serving two terms as mayor of Topeka. The boys clicked immediately when they met early in the 1947–48 term, finding a common ground on the basketball court. "I met him when he played football. I didn't," Bill Bunten said when we talked at his Topeka home in the summer of 2014.

"We played six-man football where I went to school," Bill Lienhard, another of Phog Allen's basketball recruits and a 1952 Olympic team member, recalled 62 years later. "Dean was a good football player at Topeka High School."

"He was a very likable person," Bunten said. "He became the starting quarterback on the team as a junior, and that put him in with the stars at school. We lost only one game. We tied two other games as well."

The loss came at Lawrence/Dumont Stadium in Wichita against Topeka's top rival, Wichita North. Smith's coach, D. L. Erwin, let him call his own plays, the norm in the '40s when scores of college and high school teams switched from their ground-oriented single-wing attacks to the passing-friendly T formation with its many variations, popularized by George Halas's Chicago Bears and his cohort and coaching comrade Clark Shaughnessy. The score was tied 7–7 with 30 seconds left when Dean called a pass play and threw for what he hoped would be a touchdown. "I looked for our great end, Adrian King," Dean wrote in *A Coach's Life*. Instead, a Wichita North defender intercepted and ran it back for the winning touchdown and a 14–7 final score.

"In the paper they didn't say it was Dean Smith who threw the intercepted pass," Bunten said. "They had the wrong guy. Dean always was fortunate, I guess." In that era before state high school football playoffs, the newspapers at the end of the season named Wichita North the 1947 Kansas state champions. Topeka was ranked third.

By then, Dean and Bunten had gotten a head start on the basketball season. "We started playing basketball one-on-one late in the football season," Bunten recalled. "We had a garage with a basket on it and we also went to a church that had [an indoor] court. We'd play one-on-one until we were exhausted. That paid off a little later when

we played organized basketball. We had a real good team and reached
the semifinals of the 1948 state tournament."

The '48 tournament featured 16 regionals around the state, and
the winners of each came to Topeka for the finals. "They played in
our Topeka High gym," Bunten said. "They put up bleachers at the
end to take care of the crowds. I got my picture in the paper during
that tournament, and it said Bill *Benton*. In the second game, we
played Shawnee-Mission, some of whom went on to play college ball.
We were stalling and holding the ball. With about 10 seconds to go,
I dribbled the ball off my foot and it rolled between Coach Daven-
port's legs. I'll never forget the look on his face. Shawnee-Mission got
a shot but didn't make it, and it came out okay."

Dean, a junior, had moved up to the varsity team after the first
semester when one starter graduated. "He and I started together. As
seniors, we had the tallest guy at 6-foot-3," Bunten said. "Dean was
a very good player in high school, adhering to a common goal."

Beloit stood in the way of Topeka's chance at the 1948 state title.
"I played against Dean in the semifinals at Topeka," future Kansas
teammate and "Fiji" (Phi Gamma Delta) fraternity brother Bill Hougland said. "We beat them to knock them out of the state tournament."

Lawrence defeated Beloit for the AA title, but Topeka came back
to gain a trophy. "We won the consolation game to finish third in
AA," Bunten said.

Topeka High finished third in that 1948 tournament. "To this
day, Bill loves to parade around with a newspaper headline that reads
'Bunten Man of the Hour. Smith on Time Too,'" Dean wrote.

Bill Hougland would play for Coach "Phog" Allen on the 1952
Olympic gold medal team in Helsinki, and he came back again in
1956 when he was working for Phillips 66, carrying the American
flag into the Melbourne Cricket Ground, the Olympic Stadium in
Australia, as the USA team led by University of San Francisco's Bill

Russell and K. C. Jones defeated the Soviet Union 89–55 in the gold medal game. Hougland joined Koch Industries, where he eventually became president of Koch Oil until he retired in 1991.

Bunten also boasted that that he and five other friends would routinely pile into the Bunten family Buick Roadmaster for rides around town. Another one of their friends was Nancy Landon, daughter of the former Kansas governor and 1936 Republican presidential nominee Alf Landon, whom Franklin Roosevelt overwhelmed 523 to 8 in the electoral college to win reelection to the second of his four terms. As an adult, Republican Nancy Landon Kassebaum became a US senator and later the second wife of former Senate majority leader Howard Baker of Tennessee.

According to Bunten, Dean took Nancy to Topeka High's junior prom. "Bill likes to tell that story," Nancy said. "Dean and I were friends enough that if neither of us had a date, we were happy to accommodate, going to party or something. It was friendship. Bill loves to embroider that story, and I say, 'Bill, you don't remember. You weren't there.'"

Bunten left for KU in the fall of 1948 as his buddy remained behind in Topeka for his senior year. Dean had one more mission to accomplish in his Topeka school days before he left for the University of Kansas himself. As previously noted, Topeka High had black students but wasn't integrated in athletics. The nickname of teams for the white students was Trojans. The black teams were called the Ramblers. Believing a truly integrated team would win the state tournament, Smith wanted the Ramblers' players, especially his friend Jack Alexander, to join up with the Trojans and become a single school team. In 1949, Smith, a senior who, in the words of Bunten 65 years later, "hated discrimination and believed in equality," approached Topeka High principal E. B. Weaver and asked him to integrate the team. The school board denied his request. The status quo would prevail for one more year as athletic integration came to Topeka High athletics in 1950, the year after Smith graduated.

By the mid-20th century, Topeka High School was ahead of other schools in the state in race relations. It had been integrated since the school opened in 1871 but still had separate athletic teams for blacks and whites, as Smith failed to change during his high school days. Junior high schools in the capital city had been integrated since 1941. But, by 1951, even with segregation still practiced in the elementary (grades one through six), change was gaining momentum that no longer could be stymied.

That year, 13 black parents, with the backing of the Topeka NAACP, filed suit against the local board of education. They wanted to enroll their children in the closest neighborhood schools to their homes, within walking distance. So they filed their suit in the name of Oliver L. Brown. Mr. Brown was the only male among the plaintiffs for political and legal reasons. He was a welder at the Atchison, Topeka, and Santa Fe Railway's maintenance and repair shops in town, an assistant pastor at his local church, an African American, and father of third grader Linda Brown. Linda had to walk six blocks to her segregated school's bus stop, then ride another mile to the school.

The three leaders of the Topeka NAACP who drove the case were chairman McKinley Burnett; attorney Charles Scott, a close friend of Brown; and Lucinda Todd. Scott and other lawyers involved believed that Brown's presence on the suit as the lead plaintiff would be better received by the all-male US Supreme Court, where they hoped to get the positive result they sought.

When the local federal district court turned back the suit, the NAACP, now represented by powerful attorney and future Supreme Court justice Thurgood Marshall, took the case to the US Supreme Court, led by Chief Justice Earl Warren. On May 17, 1954, thanks to

Warren's persuading potential dissenting justices Robert Jackson and Stanley Reed to join the others in striking out the 1896 decision *Plessy v. Ferguson* that had legally sanctioned segregation, the high court struck down school segregation in a unanimous 9–0 decision. The opinion, though, made enforcement extremely difficult, especially in the South, due to three words courtesy of Justice Felix Frankfurter, who said the states should end segregation with "all deliberate speed."

On Thursday, May 15, 2014, nearly 60 years to the day of that landmark decision, Topeka High School honored Dean Smith in a special all-school assembly in the school's Hoehner Auditorium. The coach was too ill to travel and attend. With Smith's school pal Jack Alexander in attendance among others who knew the coach, Bunten unveiled a special plaque that would become a permanent display in the front entrance to the school. The 84-year-old got the idea for a plaque after President Obama honored Smith with the Presidential Medal of Freedom in November 2013.

Bunten went to local sculptor Tim Degginger, who had designed and crafted several other objects of art for the school, including the life-size statue outside the building of the school's symbol, the Trojan. Degginger returned a short time later with the design for a 30-by 38-inch black metal plaque with an embossed bronzed likeness of Smith adorned with the Presidential Medal of Freedom and a list of his accomplishments. Degginger told Bunten it would weigh 200 pounds and cost $13,000.

Bunten, who knew what to do and where to go, hit the phones. Many of those he called were longtime KU Phi Gamma Delta fraternity brothers of his and Smith's. Among them was their close friend Gil Reich, a retired insurance executive who was an All-America football player and basketball teammate of Smith's on the 1952–53 NCAA runners-up. "Bill called me, and we took all of

1 day to round up the contributors," Reich said when we met at his Barrington, Illinois, home the summer after the installation ceremony at the high school.

Bunten said the plaque was meant for current and future students to understand Smith's lifelong contributions and accomplishments. Most important, though, Bunten said, "We want it to serve as an inspiration for current and future students at the school, that they, too, can achieve great things in their lives."

Alexander told *Topeka Capital-Journal* reporter Phil Anderson that he felt Smith's spirit inside Hoehner Auditorium that day. "Dean is a wonderful, wonderful human being, one of the most humble people that you'll ever run into," Alexander said that day. "Had he been here today, he'd have been sitting in the last seat in the last row, ready to run as soon as all of this took place."

Aware of Bunten's success at funding the Smith plaque, Nancy Landon Baker called him shortly after at his home in Topeka. "She had the idea of the scholarship in Dean's name, and fool that I am, I took over the job of fund-raising," Bunten said. "Nancy made the first contribution and turned me loose."

"The high school gave the first two at the end of the past school year to a young man and girl. A lot of people who contributed knew Dean at Topeka High or KU," Baker said.

"Gil Reich contributed to both the plaque and scholarship," Bunten said. "We raised several thousand. We got it endowed."

"Yes, we raised $50,000," Baker added.

"The scholarship kids have to get good grades and be active in school," Bunten said.

"Dean played football, basketball, and baseball in high school. He enjoyed it and worked at it," Baker said. "That's why the scholarship made it fun to see the young people win. The coaches and administrators select the winners. [The 2016 male winner] is going to Ottawa Community College in basketball. [The female winner] is in tennis at Washburn [University]."

In his senior year at Topeka High, Dean Smith, a brilliant mathematician, was one of 13 students enrolled in a special class. Twelve of them got A's and, as he noted in his memoir, he earned the only B. Many of his classmates in that group went to Ivy League schools. Columbia University wanted Smith for its School of Education, but he didn't want to go so far from home.

When Dean was 3 years old, his father went to Lawrence to finish his master's degree at KU, and he sent Dean a picture postcard of Memorial Stadium. "I hope to see you running down the field here one day," Alfred wrote. He showed Dean the card 10 years later and, by then, the boy was hooked on Kansas; however, in early 1949, when it came time to decide on a college, KU's legendary coach Phog Allen was cool on Dean.

Tex Winter, then assisting Jack Gardner at Kansas State before starting his long career as an esteemed college and professional coach, saw qualities in Dean that he wanted, and after a daylong visit, was interested in the young man. To lure him, Winter offered an academic scholarship with a chance to sell football programs on the side. Dean decided to sit on the offer and see what he might be able to get from KU.

He called Phog Allen's assistant, Dick Harp, who understood Kansas State's desire to land him. Harp told Dean that KU could match Kansas State's offer. But Kansas was Kansas, and that's all it took for the young man to say yes and sign up to play for the legendary Phog Allen, the protégé of basketball's inventor, James Naismith, in the Cradle of College Basketball.

3 | DESTINED
TO COACH

FRESHMAN DEAN SMITH ARRIVED ON the KU campus in the fall of 1949 with a full agenda, high hopes, and his best friend Bill Bunten there to greet him and teach him the ropes both in the classroom and on the social fields of play. "Dean did play football in college as a freshman," Bunten said. "We pledged the same fraternity. We had a lot of good players from Kansas, especially around Kansas City, and several became our Phi Gamma Delta fraternity brothers."

"My football career was short-lived," Smith recalled in *A Coach's Life*. He was the third of six quarterbacks on the freshman team, and he also played some safety. Mondays traditionally were the days when the varsity installed its game plan and tested freshmen toughness in bone-crunching scrimmages. In one Monday scrimmage, Dean read a trap play, and star fullback Forrest Griffith, who had played in the 1948 Orange Bowl and who would go on to play 2 years with the New York Giants, broke free. Dean threw his 5-foot-10-inch, 155-pound body at the charging bull-like figure. Several minutes later, he came to his senses after head coach J. V. Sikes ordered someone to help the young man off the field. After the season, Smith recalled, he went to see Coach Sikes for an evaluation. "You might be sixth by spring practice," the coach said before he added, "Doc Allen thinks you could end up second string in basketball. So, for your sake, maybe you should concentrate on that." That settled it. Dean Smith would stick to basketball, and baseball in the spring.

Almost immediately, Smith was positive he made the correct decision. In Coach Allen and his "invaluable" assistant, Dick Harp, Smith knew he was on track for his coaching future. "I had met two of the most interesting authorities the game has ever known," Smith wrote. "It was impossible to play for these men and not learn something." Most important, this was a glorious time for Kansas basketball and the Allen-Harp combination, as KU would win the 1952 NCAA title, finish second to Indiana by two points in 1953, and play a dominant part in the Olympic basketball movement.

"Dean was a role player. He wanted to be a math teacher and a coach like his dad was in high school," Bunten said of his best friend. "It started in earnest in his junior year, when he helped Dick Harp coach the freshman team. Freshmen couldn't play varsity then."

By then, Phog Allen had slowed somewhat and no longer was a one-man gang doing everything for KU and the game itself, as he had been since the early years of the 20th century. He now concentrated on the starters and firing up the team with his pep talks. "Dick Harp developed us," Bill Lienhard said, describing the methods that turned out to be the making of a future coach, his young teammate and fraternity brother from Topeka. Harp was busy assisting Allen and was still responsible for the freshmen. Harp realized from the beginning that Smith knew the game and, more important, had a feel for what should be done. "Dick took Dean under his wing and, by Dean's junior year, had him install the plays for the freshmen and the scout teams," Lienhard said. "Then Dick put in the offense and Phog pumped us up before the game."

The big talk on campus when Smith arrived in Lawrence was

Phog Allen's prized 6-foot-9 sophomore center, Clyde Lovellette, from Terre Haute, Indiana. Allen signed Lovellette after an all-out recruiting battle with Indiana's Branch McCracken. Lovellette was the most agile big man the game had yet seen, skilled in all facets, and an excellent shooter, inside and out. With a deadly, unstoppable hook shot, accurate pillow-soft jump shot, and long-range one-handed set shot, Lovellette had his way with opponents. He would take big men outside where they were lost and move inside to use his size advantage against smaller, slighter opponents.

Lovellette was the finest player Allen had ever lured to Lawrence since the start of his coaching career in 1907. As an individualist, Lovellette was well ahead of everyone else in that era: The game was undergoing its major transition to the modern era, from the non-jumping flat-footed game of weaves, patterns, and two-handed set shots with an occasional hook to the wide-open style with jump shots and drive moves around the hoop that signaled the big changes that would open up the game.

Lovellette became the most sought-after player in the country as a junior after he scored 25 points in the 1947 Indiana state championship game, where his Terre Haute Garfield team lost to Shelbyville and its two black stars, the tournament's leading scorer Bill Garrett and Emerson Johnson, 68–58. By the summer of '48 a year later, Allen was sure he had him locked up, but he was taking no chances, aware that his old rival Branch McCracken, who had Garrett on campus, was equally hot on Lovellette's trail. The persuasive Allen told Lovellette he was the key to building a championship team that, in 1952, would win the NCAA and that he would go on to the Olympics in Helsinki that summer.

Doc Allen so feared McCracken that he drove alone in his big car to Lovellette's house in Terre Haute, watched him pack, helped load his luggage and gear for school, and drove him to the Kansas campus in Lawrence some 447 miles to the west before McCracken could stop him. Then, like every other freshman athlete in those days, big Clyde had to sit, wait, and make his grades before he could play his first varsity game in late 1949. Lovellette lived up to the hype his sophomore year, as he averaged 21.8 points a game.

First, as always at tournament time, came the 1950 renewal of the National Invitational Tournament (NIT) while Kansas waited in Lawrence and practiced for their appearance in the NCAA West Regional in Kansas City, starting March 23.

The NIT was a more prestigious and important tournament in those days than the NCAA. Both events were played in back-to-back weeks in New York's Madison Square Garden, as they had been since the NCAA moved to New York in 1943 because of wartime travel restrictions. Realizing the unparalleled exposure in the media capital of America in the most famous arena in the country, the NCAA then decided to make New York its permanent tournament home.

Before March 1950, no team had ever pulled a double, winning both the NIT and NCAA tournaments. Interest in college basketball that season was focused mostly on the Midwest, where Bradley University had been ranked at the top of the wire service polls week after week with Big Ten champion Ohio State second, followed by the likes of Kentucky, Holy Cross, North Carolina, and, in their first lofty ranking in the season's final poll at number seven, UCLA and third-year coach John Wooden. Kansas, at 14–11, was ranked 19th going into the tournament after a late-season surge that saw them tie for first place in the Big Seven Conference at 8–4 with Kansas State and Nebraska.

In the East, the City College of New York Beavers (CCNY), at 17–5, finished the regular season unranked and ignored by all but the NIT committee. Then, thanks to their famous coach Nat Holman, they got the proverbial stickpin and corsage to join the NIT dance at the Garden as the 11th seed in the 12-team field. Coach Holman, now 53, had become a legendary New York City basketball player in the game's early years when he starred as its first true point guard in the '20s for the ballyhooed Original Celtics barnstorming team. While he traveled, Holman began his day job as coach of CCNY at age 23 in the 1919–20 season. Now, in March 1950, 31 seasons later, Holman knew that his CCNY bunch—composed entirely of New Yorkers—had developed into a superior unit, the best he had ever coached.

Holman, a stickler on fundamentals, stressed smart, disciplined teamwork in all facets of the game. His players got position, boxed out to control the backboards, and ran the fast break in coordinated lanes. Their offense featured minimal dribbling and passes to the open man, and they were committed to playing tight, man-to-man defense. Holman's 1950 team started two blacks, Ed Warner and Floyd Layne, augmented by four interchangeable Jewish athletes: center Ed Roman; slick ball handler Irwin Dambrot, a pre-dental major; Alvin Roth; and first-off-the-bench guard Norm Mager. Their goal by this point in the season was simple: to pull off an unprecedented double in college basketball history—victory in the NIT followed by a title in the NCAA tournament.

The top-ranked Bradley Braves from Peoria, Illinois, were City College's main obstacle. Bradley's All-America stars were center and leading scorer Paul Unruh, a 4-year starter who averaged 20 points per game in his senior year, and Gene "Squeaky" Melchiorre, a lightning quick 5-foot-8 guard who ran Forddy Anderson's fast-moving offense with clever give-and-go passes and pick-and-rolls, working off the high post as a scorer and assist leader. On defense, Melchiorre was pickpocket slick. Bradley's game calls were handled by a brilliant, quick-witted radio announcer from WMBD in Peoria, 34-year-old Illinois native Francis "Chick" Hearn.

Hearn's calls already were chock-full of the colorful descriptive phrases he would later employ, augment, and popularize through his long run with the Los Angeles Lakers, from "dribble-drives" for lay-ups to "air balls" on misses that did not "draw iron" (hit the rim), "slam" dunks, and "the popcorn machine," that tight area of physical play where bodies bounce off each other near the basket.

The public at large knew the Beavers were legitimate when they opened in the Garden on March 11 with a 65–46 rout of defending NIT champion San Francisco. It was Coach Pete Newell's last game with the Dons before he moved eastward to Michigan State, which had just joined the Big Ten. Three nights later, Holman's CCNY Beavers and Adolph's Kentucky Wildcats got into it before the game when Rupp cut loose with a racist and anti-Semitic diatribe that infuriated CCNY, remarking that he'd never coach a team with "kikes" and "blacks." It only got worse prior to the opening tipoff, when several Kentucky players refused to shake hands with City's black and Jewish players. That lit a bonfire under CCNY, who scorched twice-defending NCAA champion Kentucky in the quarterfinals, 89–50, a 39-point shellacking. Rupp and his Wildcats were sent home to Lexington in a disgrace that so dismayed the Bluegrass State that the Kentucky legislature ordered the flag over the capitol to be flown at half-mast. The Beavers then easily handled Duquesne 62–52 in the semifinal.

Meanwhile, top-seeded Bradley only had to play three games to advance through the field. Syracuse fell 78–66 to the Braves in the quarterfinals. St. John's went down 83–72 in the semis, setting up the title game against CCNY on Saturday, March 18.

Bradley took a 29–18 lead with 6 minutes to go in the first half. Then, when CCNY's Coach Holman inserted Norm Mager into the game, the Beavers ended the half with a surge to go into halftime with only a three-point deficit and the momentum. That carried into the second half, as the Beavers pulled away and won the game and NIT title 69–61 behind Most Valuable Player Ed Warner.

The teams had to gather again the following week for the NCAA. Out in Kansas City, Doc Allen brought his well-rested Jayhawks to the Kansas City Municipal Auditorium to face the NIT runner-up Bradley Braves in the tournament opener. In a battle to the finish, Bradley outlasted KU 59–57 despite Lovellette's outstanding performance. Allen's prized big man was blossoming into a top-tier talent. Over the next two seasons, he would twice lead the nation in scoring and be named first team All-American.

In the East Region at the Garden, CCNY slipped past the Big Ten champion Ohio State Buckeyes 56–55 on March 23, as Floyd Layne took charge with a 17-point performance. The Beavers now had knocked off top-ranked Bradley in the NIT finals and number two Ohio State in the NCAA. Next came Everett Case's number five North Carolina State Wolfpack, who went down in the semis 78–73 as Ed Roman led the way.

Back out West, Bradley knocked UCLA and John Wooden out of the tournament in the quarterfinals 73–59 before they had to squeeze past tough Baylor 68–66 for the right to meet CCNY again for a repeat title game, this time, the NCAA. That game ended in controversy when Bradley's Squeaky Melchiorre intercepted a CCNY pass and took off in a flash for the potential winning basket. At the hoop, Melchiorre collided with CCNY's Irwin Dambrot. No whistle. Dambrot grabbed the loose ball and fired a perfect pass downcourt to Norm Mager for the clincher, as CCNY won 71–68. Many people who saw the game live and on television thought Dambrot got away with a foul against Melchiorre. More than 6 decades later, a corporal's guard of Bradley followers still bemoan the "non-call" that never will be made. Dambrot was named the tournament's outstanding player.

All the memorable action that transpired those 2 eventful weeks in New York unraveled the following winter. The game of college basketball imploded in mid-January 1951 when Manhattan College star Junius Kellogg told New York police he had been approached by a former teammate who offered him $1,000 to shave points or ensure a loss to DePaul at Madison Square Garden. The scandal broke open on February 18, 1951, eventually snaring 32 players from seven schools. Named as taking bribes to shave points or dump games were seven members of CCNY's 1950 NCAA and NIT championship team. They were Irwin Dambrot, Ed Warner, Ed Roman, Norm Mager, Floyd Layne, Herb Cohen, and Alvin Roth. CCNY shut down its basketball program for 2 years and left Division I when it resumed play. Holman retired as soon as the scandal broke. He was not then nor ever would be implicated in the mess. After the scandal, the NIT continued, but its prestige was and remains diminished.

Long Island University of Brooklyn, a basketball power since the NIT's founding in 1938, not only ceased its participation in major college basketball, it shut down its entire athletic program for 6 years and, despite earning sporadic berths in the NCAA tournament over the years, has never returned to the big time. LIU's star, All-America Sherman White, perhaps the best player in America, served 9 months of a 1-year sentence in New York City's infamous Rikers Island prison facility. The LIU Blackbirds' famed coach was the innovative Clair Bee. Bee dreamed up the 1-3-1 zone to stop big men and the 3-second rule to unclog the foul lanes. The prolific Bee wrote basketball instructional books and a series of sports books for younger readers, the Chip Hilton series. After LIU closed up shop, Bee coached the NBA's Baltimore Bullets for two unsuccessful seasons before retiring. He gained a close friend in the persona of then Indiana coach Bob Knight, who valued the old coach's counsel and advice in much the same way Knight befriended and listened avidly to Pete

Newell. LIU resumed Division I basketball in the 1980s. The Black-birds reached the 2011 NCAA tournament, losing to North Carolina 102–87 in a first-round game in the East Regional.

Manhattan College, New York University, and University of Toledo also were involved in the scandal. Another shocker followed in July 1951, when five Bradley players, foremost among them All-America Gene Melchiorre, admitted they took bribes to hold down scores but not lose in two games: St. Joseph's in Philadelphia in 1951 and Oregon State in Chicago Stadium. Paul Unruh was not one of the players involved.

By the time of the revelation, the Baltimore Bullets had made Melchiorre the first player selected in the 1951 NBA draft. When the point-shaving led to his indictment and a suspended sentence, NBA Commissioner Maurice Podoloff banned Melchiorre and all other convicted bribe takers for life. Thus, Squeaky Melchiorre became the only number one NBA draft choice who never played a single minute in an NBA game.

Speculation that more players were involved in the scandal had been flying like shrapnel in a combat zone for months. Most of it focused on Kentucky's number one–rated college basketball program in Lexington. That led Kentucky coach Adolph Rupp, Phog Allen's one-time Kansas disciple, to proclaim that his team was clean and in the clear. "They can't touch my boys with a 10-foot pole," Rupp crowed.

Rupp appeared to have navigated the storm without smashing onto the rocks as his Wildcats rebounded from the CCNY rout to win the 1951 NCAA title behind 7-foot center Bill Spivey. They almost didn't make the finals but got new life in the Final Four semifinals at Madison Square Garden when Illinois All-America Don Sunderlage missed two easy shots, one a layup, in the late going and Kentucky came away with a 76–74 victory. In the final at

Minneapolis, Spivey was named Most Outstanding Player of the tournament when Kentucky beat Kansas State 68–58.

Rupp's proverbial 10-foot pole came down on Kentucky like a sledgehammer on October 20, 1951, when New York District Attorney Frank Hogan arrested three Kentucky star players from their 1948 and 1949 NCAA championship teams, Alex Groza, Ralph Beard, and Dale Barnstable, and accused each man of accepting $500 bribes to shave points against Loyola of Chicago, who beat Kentucky 61–56 in a 1949 NIT game at the Garden.

Groza and Beard were members of the 1948 Olympic basketball gold medal team. After they won the 1949 NCAA championship, they joined three other Kentucky and Olympic team members to form the NBA's new Indianapolis Olympians franchise. In a sad, ironic note, both Groza and Beard had famous professional athletic brothers. Alex Groza's was Cleveland Browns future Hall of Fame tackle and placekicker Lou. Ralph Beard's brother was well-regarded professional golfer Frank. NBA Commissioner Podoloff barred Groza, Beard, and Barnstable from the league.

It could only get worse, and it did when indicted Kentucky players Jim Line and Walter Hirsch accused Spivey of shaving points in the 1950 Sugar Bowl holiday tournament in New Orleans. Spivey denied all when he testified to a New York grand jury on February 16, 1952. The university expelled him though on March 2. He went to trial for perjury but escaped conviction by a hung jury that resulted in a mistrial. Commissioner Podoloff stuck to his decision and would not allow any of the figures named in the scandal to play in the NBA.

Unlike any other big-time athletic program that had undergone the scandal, Kentucky endured. Adolph Rupp literally rebounded as his Wildcats thrived and continued to rule college basketball and were accorded royal treatment at home. After the scandal, the

Southeastern Conference barred them from play in 1952–53, and the NCAA followed, ordering other non-SEC schools to not schedule Kentucky, creating the first "death penalty."

The very next season, Rupp's Wildcats, led on the floor by seniors Cliff Hagan, Frank Ramsey, and Lou Tsioropoulos, went undefeated, 25–0, but NCAA rules of the time barred them from postseason play because the three named stars were graduate students that season. Rupp did not want to endanger his perfect record without them and turned down any postseason bids. Nonetheless, he claimed a national championship. Now, in the 21st century, 41 jerseys hang from the rafters of Rupp Arena. Among them are Alex Groza's number 12, Ralph Beard's number 15, and Bill Spivey's number 77.

Phog Allen had warned of trouble. He took charge.

4 | KU JOINS THE ELITE

DEAN SMITH AND MOST OF his basketball teammates signed up for ROTC when they returned to school in the fall of 1950. The Korean War had broken out on June 25, and under the terms of their agreements they would be able to serve as junior officers and give back 2 years to their respective branches of service after graduation. Smith chose the Air Force, which turned out to be a decision that would set a positive course for his memorable coaching career at North Carolina. Finished with his football fling, Smith, a math major and solid B student who had been training to become a high school teacher at the prodding of his father, concentrated on his courses while he continued to work on his games in basketball and baseball.

When Smith and his Phi Gamma Delta brothers, the "Fijis," returned to school a year later, after the gambling scandal of 1951 had rocked college basketball, they landed an outstanding pledge class in fraternity rush. Prominent among them was a junior transfer who had come to the University of Kansas (KU) as an academic and athletic star fresh off the Plain at West Point. He would be recognized as one of the truly great athletes in KU history.

Gil Reich was no ordinary former cadet. At West Point, cadet Reich was on track to become an influential Army officer, perhaps attaining a rank as high as chief of staff. Reich was a special cadet, not unlike future Heisman Trophy winner, Vietnam War hero, and Brigadier General Pete Dawkins, who ran Citigroup Private Bank after he left service for an unsuccessful run as a Republican for the US Senate from New Jersey. Reich was a two-sport star, a superb basketball player, a guard, and in football a superb two-way talent as an All-America defensive back and backup quarterback behind Coach Earl Blaik's son, Bobby. Reich's position coach at quarterback was none other than Colonel Blaik's top assistant, Vince Lombardi. Army was the preseason favorite to win the national championship.

Suddenly, on August 3, 1951, the earth on the Plain moved in a massive upheaval. After an uneasy summer of meetings and internal investigation at the US Military Academy, 90 West Point cadets—37 of them members of the football team, including Reich—were expelled. The preferred euphemism that year for public consumption was "cribbing scandal." Those two grim words described an irrevocable violation of the academy's honor code that not only forbade academic cheating but also called for a cadet's dismissal if he knew about cheating and did not report it nor identify any violator whom he knew had cheated. Reich was no cheater, but he knew several who were. And he paid the price for not revealing his knowledge.

Reich, who ranked third in his cadet class after 2 years, was on track to become a top officer in the Army. "He would have been a general, a great one," said Ernie Accorsi, the retired general manager of the New York Giants, who got that assessment years before from Lombardi himself. Accorsi, a career National Football League executive who grew up in Hershey, Pennsylvania, close to Reich's hometown, was 8 years old when his father took him to Harrisburg to see a late-season high school game. He never forgot Reich. "He was an A student from Steelton, Pennsylvania," Accorsi said. "I met Vince Lombardi once late in his life, and I told him the first football game I ever saw was in 1949 when I saw Reich's Steelton team beat William Penn." Steelton and William Penn were the number one and two powers around Harrisburg.

"Let me tell you something about Gil Reich," Lombardi replied to Accorsi. "He's one of the greatest football players I ever coached, and he's an even better man."

Reich's closest friends from KU confirmed Lombardi's strong endorsement. "They expelled just about all the members of the football team not because they cheated, but because they didn't tell on somebody else who was cheating," said Bill Bunten, Smith and Reich's fraternity brother, in the summer of 2014. "So they just kicked them out."

Reich did not turn in anyone, especially his roommate and close friend, Al Pollard, a preseason All-America fullback whom Gil knew had gotten tests in advance. It took years for the Army to reveal how it worked. Classes in a course, say military tactics, were divided into two sections. If a test was given on a Monday, that *same* test would be administered the next day, identical in every form. It was part system, part lazy instructors. All of it was wrong for all concerned.

West Point still has not relegated the Cadet Honor Code to the trash heap, but it has amended it for the better and made it more practical. Wrongdoers no longer are subject to automatic dismissal on the first go-round as they were in '51 when a cadet told hard-nosed Corps Commandant and Head of Tactics Colonel Paul D. Harkins that a sizable group of cadets, many of them on the football team, were involved in a cheating ring. Colonel Harkins made it plain throughout the summer of 1951 that football did not fit into his vision of the US Military Academy. That brought him into direct conflict with football coach Colonel Earl Blaik, who called Harkins a black-and-white man with no shades of gray. Harkins, who served as General George S. Patton's deputy chief of staff with the Third Army in World War II, earned another shrewd, unwanted enemy in Blaik's mentor, the honored General of the Army Douglas MacArthur, who would watch the proceedings and wait.

Colonel Blaik's son, Bobby, was one of the cadets who took the fall. Like Reich, the younger Blaik did not act despite knowing that cadets had been cheating. Just over a decade later, Harkins would become the much-despised predecessor to General William Westmoreland in his role as commander of Allied Forces in Vietnam, who had tackled the unenviable job of selling the American people on the notion that everything was positive and hunky-dory in execution of that impossible war in that incredibly corrupt country.

Former cadet after former cadet gained redemptive opportunity at other colleges and universities. No sooner did Reich, who had important people in his corner, get dismissed at West Point than he got a call that the University of Kansas would become his new college address.

"Chancellor Franklin Murphy got Gil in here," recalled former basketball star Bill Lienhard in the summer of 2014. "Murphy said it was wrong what happened to Gil at West Point."

"Warren Woody really pushed for Gil," said Bill Hoagland, Lienhard's running mate on the NCAA title and Olympic teams. Woody was an influential KU alumnus from Chicago who owned a large ranch near Lawrence.

"In 1951, I arrived in Lawrence, Kansas, from Harrisburg," Reich told me when we talked. "I had gone through a nasty situation that got out of hand." That "nasty situation" was the so-called cribbing scandal. "I knew a gentleman from Harrisburg named Tate Woody who had a brother in Chicago named Warren. Both were managers with a big insurance company called the Equitable."

Warren Woody played football at Kansas in 1916 and 1917, served in World War I, and returned to finish his studies at KU in 1920. He became head coach at Sterling College in central Kansas for three seasons, then began his career in Chicago with the Equitable. In Harrisburg, Taft Woody told his brother about Reich after seeing him play high school sports in Steelton. Bethlehem Steel owned the mill there. "I was told as a kid that the steel they produced was used to build the Golden Gate Bridge," Reich said. "Right next to my hometown is a famous island called Three Mile Island."

Three Mile Island is the home of a large nuclear power plant where Unit 2, owned by First Energy Company of Akron, was severely damaged in a 1979 accident and closed for good. It became a symbol and reminder of the potential good and the fearsome dangers of nuclear power.

"I had to sit out a year after the transfer to KU from West Point," Reich said. "I majored in engineering at Kansas. Some of my future teammates were in Phi Gamma Delta fraternity, the Fijis, and Dean Smith was one of them."

Several of the KU Fijis who rushed Reich also hailed from the Chicago area. Warren Woody Jr., son of the Equitable man, went to New Trier High School in Winnetka. Charlie Hoag (an All-America running back in football and a basketball mainstay) came from Oak Park. Frank Sabatini also was from Oak Park. He played football at Fenwick High School with 1953 Heisman Trophy winner Johnny Lattner.

Bill Hougland from Beloit, Kansas (the star guard on the basketball team whose high school knocked Dean Smith's Topeka out of the 1948 Kansas AA tournament), was another who rushed the former cadet. "These guys convinced me to rush and live in the Phi Gam house," Reich said.

"Warren Woody Sr. sent a lot of players to KU," Bill Bunten recalled. "He recommended to Gil that he come here, and when he got out he would have a job waiting in Chicago. I think Woody was the top guy in Chicago in Equitable. At KU, Gil was going to play football and also basketball. They got room and board, tuition, and $15 a month for laundry and snacks. It's not like they do it today. All of those guys who came down here went out into the world and did well."

"Dean was right there from the beginning," Reich said. "I was a pledge and got to know Dean pretty well. He was an upperclassman, an active, even though we were the same in age in the class of '53. But he, of course, was there ahead of me."

The early '50s were a period of heavy pledge hazing in fraternities, and Reich was not pleased about undergoing that treatment again. "I had a very difficult time, so to speak, accepting this pledge treatment. I had a heavy dose of Beast Barracks when I was a plebe at West Point. I went through that and survived," Reich said. "I rebelled a bit having to undergo that again. Dean, his best friend from Topeka, Bill Bunten, also a Phi Gam, and I became close.

"I was a quarterback and defensive back and practiced with the football team although I could not play that year, 1951–52. Dean was a student, but he helped coach the substitutes, the scout team for the varsity. We had fraternity touch football that year when I was ineligible. He was on the basketball squad," Reich recalled. "We played intramural volleyball. He was a great retriever. He was a good athlete, as was I. He was very versatile. I was 6-foot-1. He was probably 5-foot-10. He was a very good player in high school football and basketball. His best game was baseball, where he was a catcher on KU's baseball team.

"Dean was a prospect, possibly major league," said Reich. "Fortunately for him, he didn't sign, and the rest of the story for Dean was how he got into coaching. Air Force Academy, then North Carolina." Reich and Smith became extremely close friends for life.

One day Smith told Reich, his new pal and fellow Fiji, that he wanted to test him on the basketball court. "I'm the best one-on-one player on this campus," Smith told Reich.

Gil accepted the challenge and countered with one of his own. "I'll show you who's the best one-on-one player on this campus."

"I'll never forget that first time we played one-on-one basketball. I shocked him because I could defend him," Reich said, chuckling at the memory. "He was the best defender on the Hill. He found out I had pretty quick hands and feet, too." Like most series of one-on-one contests between friends, they kept any results in their heads, not bothering to write them down, ending up basically even.

"How I got Phog Allen's attention was through Dean Smith," Reich recalled. "I was I ineligible that [1951] football season as a transfer. Dean didn't have to play basketball or practice in the fall. We used to go up to Robertson Gym, put our sneaks on, and play one-on-one. He found out there was another guy who could play one-on-one. And so he reported all this to Phog Allen. After the football season the next year, Phog Allen wanted me to come on and be on his basketball team. He was hurting for experienced players, because that whole Olympic basketball team had graduated. Dean didn't play on that Olympic team. He was a reserve on the national championship team."

By the start of the 1951–52 season, Coach Allen believed this Jayhawks team was the best he had ever coached, with such players as All-America football halfback Charlie Hoag, Bill Hougland, Bill Lienhard, the Kelley brothers (Dean and Al), Bob Kenney, and John Keller, plus versatile reserve Dean Smith. The parts were solid. Everything was in place since he had this bunch; all of them had been with him from the beginning of college, trained and developed by Dick Harp. Back for his senior year was the best individual player in the country, 6-foot-9-inch center Clyde Lovellette.

The only guy missing from the mix was graduated 3-year starter and point guard Jerry Waugh, who later would serve Kansas as associate athletic director and golf coach. "I always say I've missed only two major events in my life," Waugh said. "The Battle of the Bulge because I joined the Army too late, and our 1952 national championship because I graduated the previous spring."

As for the head coach, Dean Smith in retrospect found Doc Allen to be quirky in his methods and teaching, often unintentionally funny. A case in point was the time Allen got off the team bus after a postgame meal to dispute a restaurant bill. When Allen came back outside, he mistakenly boarded a city bus. Dick Harp leapt from his seat and sent a team manager to flag down the city bus carrying Allen. While the manager was gone, Harp admonished the players who were laughing so hard it brought tears to their eyes, and he warned them never to speak about this to any outsider without heavy consequences.

Like his teammates, Smith grew weary of Allen's decisions to conduct tedious drills in extra-long practice sessions. In time, though, Smith admitted that the coach's endless drills on fundamentals, from footwork to passing to positioning and defense, made Kansas better in the basics than anyone else they ever faced.

A constant that occupied Phog Allen's thoughts from the time Smith arrived on campus was an obsession with raising the basket height to 12 feet from the 10-foot standard. "He believed it would make big men less dominant and force them to develop into better all-around players," Smith wrote in *A Coach's Life*. Smith countered in that book that "raising the baskets would actually *emphasize* the big man, since more shots would be missed and rebounding would become even more important." The 12-foot-high basket remains an idea whose time has not come, nor is it likely that it ever will.

Smith was one of 11 lettermen on the 18-man team in the 1951–52 season. He saw little action that season, coming off the bench late in a game if appearing at all. The only memorable rules change that year did away with the traditional two 20-minute halves in favor of four 10-minute quarters. With only three defeats, KU entered the NCAA tournament ranked number eight in the AP writers' poll and number three in the UP coaches survey. Kentucky and Illinois were ranked 1–2 in both polls.

Led by All-Americas Cliff Hagan, Frank Ramsey, and Bobby Watson, Kentucky was favored to win its fourth title in 5 years and showed why in the opener of the 16-team tournament, when the Wildcats opened with an 82–54 rout of Penn State. But Adolph Rupp's Wildcats had to face clever Frank McGuire and St. John's in their regional final at Reynolds Coliseum in Raleigh, North Carolina. McGuire's Redmen, led by Bob Zawoluk's 32 points, stunned Kentucky 64–57 to advance to the Final Four in Seattle.

Kansas barely squeaked past Texas Christian in their regional opener in Kansas City, 68–64, but handled St. Louis University in the next round with an easy 74–55 victory as Clyde Lovellette scored 44 points, to this day the most points a Jayhawk player has ever scored in an NCAA tournament game. At the University of Washington's Hec Edmundson Pavilion in Seattle, St. John's upset Illinois 61–59 to advance to the championship game against a Kansas team that walloped Santa Clara 74–55 in their own semifinal. Smith played only 3 minutes in that game and failed to score, just as he did in closing out the Jayhawks' 80–63 title game victory over St. John's. Lovellette opened the scoring in the title game with a free throw, and the referees exercised their whistles, tooting 60 foul calls, virtually nonstop, or 1.5 whistled fouls every minute. By the final buzzer, Lovellette had wrapped up the Most Outstanding Player award by

ringing up 33 points, a title game record. He would also smash the
existing four-game tournament scoring record, which had been 85
points, when he totaled 141 in a four-game display Phog Allen called
the greatest performance in basketball history. That, of course, like
so many basketball scoring records, would be exceeded many times
through the coming years. Today, Michigan's Glen Rice holds the
record for total points in an NCAA tournament with 184 in 1989.

"Dean was a good player, a journeyman," said teammate Bill
Hougland, an Olympian in both the 1952 Games in Helsinki and the
1956 Games in Melbourne. "He got in at the end of the national finals."

When the newspapers came out, Smith, who did not score or
commit any fouls, saw he was not listed in the lineup. He was furious.
He looked at the Kansas scorebook and wrote to the NCAA to get a
correction in his favor. "He complained so much," said Max Falkenstien, who started calling KU games on the radio during World War II,
"because he played the final 30 seconds, which was not listed in the
NCAA's official box score. He got his way, of course, and eventually
got listed in the sanctioned statistical breakdown as 'Smith, g 0 (field
goals) 0 (free throws made) 0 (free throws missed), and 0 (personal
fouls).' All he wanted was recognition for his work, and he got it."

Smith joined his Jayhawk teammates for the Olympic Trials. The
Caterpillar AAU champions from Peoria, Illinois, beat Kansas
62–60. The Cats' 32-year-old coach, Warren Womble, was selected
head coach of the US team. Womble chose seven players, all AAU.
Five were his Cats: Frank McCabe, Ron Bontemps, Dan Pippen,
Marc Freiberger, and Howie Williams; plus two members of the Phil-
lips 66 Oilers: Bob "Foothills" Kurland and Wayne Glasgow. Phog
Allen, named as Womble's assistant, chose seven Jayhawks led by
Lovellette, who was joined by Charlie Hoag, Bill Lienhard, Bill
Hougland, Bob "Trigger" Kenney, Dean Kelley, and John Keller. The

US team won all eight games it played, beating the Soviets, competing in their first Olympics, in that non–shot clock era for the gold medal, 36–25.

The Kansas Board of Regents raised enough money, $1,500 for each man, to send B. H. Born and Larry Davenport to Helsinki as alternates. The board fell short on Smith's behalf, so he had to stay behind, but they did give him the leftover cash, $300, which was legal then, not a violation of amateur rules. Needing another $100 to buy a used 1940 Chevy, Smith's sister, Joan, kicked in the extra money from her savings.

Dean had the car on campus to begin his senior year. Since this was his first car, he knew nothing about maintenance and failed to winterize it with antifreeze. He learned his lesson the sad way while away on a brief road trip to Stillwater, where Kansas played Oklahoma A&M. When the team returned to Lawrence, Smith discovered that the water in the radiator had frozen and the engine block cracked after a subfreezing night. Thus, the car he had wanted so badly was ruined.

For many years, the state of the art in basketball had been Henry Iba's "20 defense" at Oklahoma A&M. Iba's defenders picked up their opponents at the midcourt line and employed nose-to-nose, belly-to-belly pressure in the half-court set. The players had to be in top physical condition to answer Iba's demands: constant movement of the feet and proper defensive positioning. Iba teams generally did not run, preferring to wear down their opponents in the offensive half-court. Iba-coached teams at Oklahoma A&M, which officially became Oklahoma State University in 1957, won 751 games.

Phog Allen's 1951–52 NCAA champions relied on a power game led by Lovellette, a senior, who would go on to great success in the NBA. In 1988—the same year Smith disciple Larry Brown led the

Jayhawks to their next national championship—Lovellette was inducted into the Naismith Basketball Hall of Fame.

Aware he had to retool and rebuild for the 1952–53 season, Doc Allen knew he must adapt to his personnel and drastically change his system. Besides the departed graduates, he suffered a major personnel loss during the 1953 football season. "Charlie Hoag got hurt playing football when he stepped on a water drain and injured his ankle so badly he could not play basketball in the winter," Bill Lienhard recalled.

So Allen and Dick Harp went to work and fashioned a team that would come within a single point of a repeat. For Smith, his senior year was the season he learned what coaching was all about: adjustment, adaptation, thinking a move ahead, and advancing. So he got into coaching, and even took up smoking to act like an adult just like Doc Allen.

Smith's father, Alfred, stressed that bragging was not permitted in his family, nor did he allow profanity—philosophies Smith absorbed and always followed. Alfred also did not allow the use of liquor or tobacco in his household. When it came to his family's aversion to alcohol, Smith wrote in *A Coach's Life*, "that did not make us uncommon. Kansas was old Prohibition territory." Nonetheless, Smith could not adhere to the tobacco and alcohol strictures as he grew older. An avid moviegoer like so many of his generation, Smith observed that nearly everybody on the silver screen smoked. Because his father so avidly frowned on it, Smith rebelled in belief that smoking was attractive, a feeling that was held by millions in this country until the US Surgeon General's 1964 report alerted America and the world to the habit's lethal dangers.

Smith, who did not like people to know that he used tobacco, claimed that he did not start smoking regularly until he got out of college. Close friends of his at KU disagreed, however, saying he was a smoker while he was in school. That included teammates there. "Al Kelley will tell you, Dean always smoked," Bill Hougland said. "He was always hiding his cigarettes," Jerry Waugh said. Bill Bunten agreed. "He smoked a lot for a long time," Bunten said. "Vesta (Dean's mother), said to me, 'Bill, would you talk to Dean about quitting?' I said I would, but I didn't tell her I was a smoker then, too. I quit in 1996."

Once he got going at Carolina, Smith's smoking habit made him a captive in the pressure-filled atmosphere. As Frank Deford and John Feinstein, among others, have written, cigarettes were pervasive. Deford once had Smith alone for a trip in his car and said that the ride was wonderful except for the coach's constant smoking. Friends say his daily intake was three and a half packs. Yet he would cup a smoke when people were around, or snub them out when nobody could see him. Smith did admit in his memoir that nicotine was extremely addictive, and "I succumbed to it and was a pretty poor example for a number of years. I finally was able to quit smoking in October 1988 [at age 57], and it was one of the best things I ever did." Furthermore, his marriage to Ann had suffered and, as it turned out, was broken.

Alcohol abuse has pervaded all aspects of human life seemingly forever, and it certainly has wreaked its toll in the coaching profession. The late Peter Gent told me many times about the smell of booze leaking off the breath of his Michigan State basketball coach, Forddy Anderson, as he gathered his players in a huddle. The same was true for many other Big Ten coaches of that early '60s era, with the possible exception of Ohio State's Fred Taylor, who incidentally had the best record in those years. It had become a tradition of sorts among coaches to visit each other in the prior evenings or even afternoons of a game for a social hour that included raising a glass or two.

Smith was no stranger to alcohol's "medicinal" qualities, and he did love a good glass of Scotch before dinner. In no way was he a heavy drinker, and if strangers showed up, he would stow away his glass of liquor fast and discreetly.

Smith went all out to ensure that any outsider retained a positive impression of him. He was all business, especially when it concerned his profession. When it came to basketball, unlike Iba's half-court pressure, the Kansas defense drawn up by Phog Allen and Dick Harp was their version of the original full-court press designed by Wichita's Gene Johnson in the 1930s and modified in 1950.

Basically, then and these many years later, the press was a display of constant player-to-player pressure. At times, it covered the entire 94-foot length of a basketball floor. At other times, the players picked up their men at the half-court line and forced the action. Allen and Harp did not use the zone press; rather, they had defenders overplay and contest every pass or go for steals. Where some presses apply the heat by the constant semipassive presence of the defenders, the Allen-Harp method tried to force turnovers at all times. They wanted to wear out the offense and force mistakes.

In his memoir, Smith states that "the Kansas defense had a lasting influence on the game." In midseason, Allen and Harp unleashed their press. Kansas went on to win 15 straight games, and they continued their intimidating press into the tournament as they stormed through the Big Seven.

"After the 1952 football season, Phog Allen wanted me to come on and be on his basketball team," Gil Reich said. "He was hurting for experienced players because that whole Olympic basketball team except Dean Kelley, the only returning starter, had graduated. I banged up my hand and dislocated one of my fingers with a slight fracture [during the football season]. Dr. Allen's son Bob was an orthopedic surgeon, so he was taking care of me. He had me in a splint for a while. It was 3 or 4 days before Christmas, and I was going to fly home for the Christmas holidays, then come back afterwards for the January semester."

In the early days of basketball, many colleges built so-called snake pits for their arenas. These impossibly designed buildings became relics in a hurry. Yet many of them still are utilized on campuses, but for purposes other than basketball. They are not regarded with the reverence accorded landmarks like Stonehenge, although they could qualify as ancient in a bizarre sense.

Perhaps the worst snake pit of all was the Notre Dame Fieldhouse, a dump of a place students happily called "the Dungeon" for its unbearable ear-splitting acoustics and, during games, a constantly pounding bass drum near the visitor's bench. The Dungeon was torn down in 1968 when Notre Dame unveiled its modern facility, the Joyce Athletic and Convocation Center, now known as Purcell Pavilion.

Typical of these "monuments" are such weathered arenas still used for basketball as Cameron Indoor Stadium at Duke. Others are now used for other purposes, like Woollen Gym at North Carolina, which was turned over to physical education classes after Carmichael Auditorium, which abuts it, opened in 1965. A cluster of existing, former basketball arenas at several Big Ten schools still are used for other sports. For instance, Yost Field House, built in 1923, was renamed Yost Ice Arena in 1973 when the basketball team moved into the newly built, 12,000-plus-seat Crisler Arena (now Crisler Center); Yost is home ice for Michigan's famed hockey program. Jenison Field House was Michigan State's basketball home from 1940 to 1989 but has been used for volleyball since 1993. The renamed Huff Hall (formerly Huff Gym) at Illinois has been used for volleyball since the basketball team moved into the nearby Assembly Hall in the winter of 1963. Lambert Fieldhouse at Purdue has been an indoor track facility since the basketball team moved next door in 1967 into what is now Mackey Arena. The UW Field House in Madison, a barn of a building built in 1930 that doubles as the south wall of Camp Randall Stadium, has hosted volleyball since the men's and women's basketball teams moved a few blocks away in 1998 to the Kohl Center. Wisconsin's original basketball arena, built in 1894 and known as the Red Gym or Armory, on the shore of Lake Mendota, is still used for various athletic activities.

As for Kansas, Gil Reich even now envisions Hoch Auditorium in his nightmares. That's where KU played before Allen Fieldhouse hosted its first game on March 1, 1955. "Hoch Auditorium opened in 1927 as a multipurpose building, and was designed to hold 'Dr. Naismith's game,'" Reich said. "It was called the 'Hall of Horrors' for the way it intimidated visiting teams. It was an auditorium for theater. They would take out the stands from floor level, the seats at either end. It had two balconies. They would lay down a basketball floor and had bleachers up on the stage. It was a postage stamp. We called it Phog Allen's Mad Opera House." And what a "mad" house it was! "They had an out of bounds close to the walls at the end of the court. So they had to hang mats so you wouldn't kill yourself if you hit the walls," Reich said.

"This was the '52–53 season, and I'm waiting for the team to come from another building for the warmup," Reich said. "We were playing SMU that night at home. I had just been with my fraternity brothers at one of the steak houses and we had a couple of beers. We had a meal, and I'm sitting there in Hoch with my guys ready to watch the game. Phog Allen came by as the team warmed up and saw me sitting there. He grabbed my hand. 'How's it looking? My son says it's coming along,' Dr. Allen said in his best bedside manner before he abruptly asked the clincher. 'When are you going to report?'"

"I'm to go home for Christmas," Reich replied. "When I get back, I'll report for practice. By that time, it will be completely healed."

"Why don't you suit up tonight?" Allen asked.

"Suit up tonight?" Reich said, sensing his coach's pressure tactic.

"Yeah. Right now!" Allen said sharply. "Go get a uniform!"

"I did. I went back to Robinson Gym [razed in 1967], got a uniform, and came back in time to take a few shots," Reich said. "I had not played organized basketball for over a year. Now I was on the bench. Third quarter comes along and we were beating SMU handily. Then Phog says, 'Dean! Gil! Get in the game!' We ran three or four fast breaks and I thought I was gonna die. So I may be the only player in the history of Kansas basketball who ever played in a varsity game without one day of practice. That's how Dean Smith got me involved with Phog Allen and KU basketball.

"Dean was the sixth man on our '52 and '53 teams," Reich recalled. "We in '53 had 6-foot-10-inch B. H. Born, who followed Clyde Lovellette. Dean Kelley was the only '52 starter who came back. This unknown guy from West Point (me) was the other starting guard. I played a lot of high school basketball. First team all-state in Pennsylvania my senior year, and I played a lot at Army my freshman year. Harold Patterson was a 6-foot-3-inch wide receiver in football [who also joined our team]."

"Dick Harp was a big part of it," said former Kansas point guard Jerry Waugh, who graduated before the 1952 championship season and later served Harp as his assistant after Doc Allen retired. "Dick wanted his players to be special people. Good coaches are special for their relationships. We've had many people like that at Kansas in basketball."

Allen and Harp's ace in the hole was Dean Smith. "In '52–53, we played together. Phog Allen and Dick Harp used Dean as an 'assistant coach' who ran the scout team in practice. Dean, never a great player, was a participant," Waugh said. "Dick knew that, and one thing he did was give him the scouting report. Then Dean would take the scout team and set up all the opponents' plays."

"In games, he was a third guard who sat right next to them on the bench when he wasn't on the floor," Reich recalled.

Working hand in hand with coaches Allen and Harp became a finishing school and clinic rolled into one for young Smith. He listened to and absorbed everything Harp and Allen were saying, and he watched what they did and how they did it in a game. "Fundamentally he was very, very sound. He always wanted to be a coach," Reich said.

"We were supposed to be fourth or fifth in the Big Seven Conference because we lost all those great players from the year before. We lost the first game to Oklahoma in Norman," Reich continued. "Dean, of course, had all that experience he took with him. That year, Dick Harp, our assistant coach, and Phog changed our basketball strategy. In '51–52, it was our offense that overwhelmed people. Now, in '52–53, we used the full-court press and defensive maneuvers. We won most of our games by stealing and pressing, forcing mistakes. We went all the way to the national finals. It was defense. All five of us—the Kelley boys, Patterson, me, B. H. [Born]—and Dean as the sixth man could really steal your bacon. We had the fastest hands and feet in the West. All six of us. That's how we won."

Unranked at the start of the season and hanging around the lower sector—closer to 20th than 10th—in the polls by midseason, Kanas caught fire and placed as high as third in the late surveys. Indiana punched its way past Big Ten rival Illinois to gain the second spot in January before eventually overtaking top-ranked Seton Hall in the first March poll and carrying it through to the end of the season. After the 1951 scandal, teams no longer could play in both the NIT and NCAA tournaments.

So Seton Hall, led by All-America guard Richie Regan, opted for the NIT in March and won it. The Jayhawks won the Big Seven and headed into the NCAA tournament again at 16–5. "They call it March Madness now," Reich recalled. "We beat Oklahoma City, Oklahoma State [at the time, Oklahoma A&M] at Kansas State, and [in Kansas City] Washington in the semifinals." Next up for the championship game, 13 years after their title matchup in the second-ever NCAA title game in Kansas City, were the Hoosiers of Indiana and coach Branch McCracken.

Top-ranked Indiana started just one senior, forward Dick Farley. All the other starters were underclassmen led by two All-Americans, 6-foot-9 sophomore center Don Schlundt and guard Bobby Leonard. "Twenty times the score was tied against Indiana," Reich said. "We lost 69–68." Schlundt led all scorers with 30 points. Bobby Leonard, with 12, sank two late free throws for the one-point victory for the Hoosiers. Dean Smith, who played for 6 minutes, hit his only free throw.

"We almost went back-to-back," Reich said. "Dean, Dean Kelley, and I were the three guards. We shared responsibilities throughout that tournament." Kansas's final record was 19–6 to Indiana's 23–3.

Coaches basically are copycats. When someone enjoys success with a new method, they set out to find out what made that new method work. They study film and tape, and they also ask successful practitioners to describe and demonstrate what they did. Thus, Smith wrote, Phil Woolpert, Pete Newell's successor at the University of San Francisco, came down to Lawrence to study the press with Harp. Then he applied those principles in what he called "a hounding defense" to his team, who won back-to-back NCAA titles in 1955 and an unbeaten '56 season. Woolpert did have the presence of the top shot blocker of all-time in Bill Russell and the superb pressuring guard K. C. Jones—both later inductees into the Naismith Memorial Basketball Hall of Fame—but their pressure system has prevailed to this day. Fred Taylor, coach of Ohio State's 1960 national champions and '61 and '62 runners-up featuring Jerry Lucas and John Havlicek, called the press he employed sparingly but quite effectively "the rat game." Hall of Famer Nolan Richardson, whose Arkansas Razorbacks won the 1994 NCAA title, called his pressing tactics "Forty Minutes of Hell."

As Smith wrote, "Almost exactly forty years later in the 1991 Final Four [actually, 38 years later], I couldn't help noticing that all four teams—Carolina, Duke, Las Vegas, and Kansas—used schemes that stemmed from that first Kansas pressure defense."

That 69–68 narrow loss against Indiana for what would have been a back-to-back championship certainly was the touchstone of Smith and Reich's senior year at Kansas—at least athletically. Something else big was happening on the sidelines. "Dean was responsible for my marrying the girl I've been married to for the past 60 years," Reich said.

"[My wife] Kay's from Leavenworth, Kansas, and she was a Pi Beta Phi, a Pi Phi at KU. She was dating Charlie Hoag when I got there," Reich said. "Charlie was an active and I was a pledge. I thought she was awfully cute when I saw her, but you know the rules of the road in a fraternity house. Pledges aren't allowed to ask for a date with a girl an upperclassman is dating. About 6 months later, in early 1952, I was in the room with Bill Bunten, Dean Smith, and John McGilley. By that time, I was an active. We were shooting the breeze. By that time, our interests were sports and mostly girls. Dean said to me, 'Gil, did you know Kay and Charlie Hoag broke up?'

"'Oh, yeah?" I said.

"'Why don't you call her for a date?' Dean said.

"I said 'Oh, no. She doesn't know who I am. I only met her once.'

"'Call her!' he said emphatically.

"So I did, and we started dating," Reich said. "About a year later, we were getting real serious and it was right before Christmas. So we decided to back off a little bit and unwind and see if this was for real. Not puppy love, but the real thing. So New Year's Eve comes and Dean Grogger, one of our fraternity brothers who lived in Topeka, Smith's hometown, had a New Year's Eve party in the basement recreation room. Dean Smith said, 'Why don't you go with me. Stay at our house, and I'll get you a blind date.'

"So I had a blind date, and to this day I don't remember her name," Reich said. "We stayed at Dean's house and went to the party. At midnight, everyone gathered at the mistletoe. And we would wish each other a Happy New Year, etc., etc. Dean was there with Bill Bunten, who asked Kay. Maybe those guys set this up. I still don't know, but she was there with Bill. Kay knew they were aware we had gotten serious the previous year. So, at midnight, I asked Kay, 'Can I give you a New Year's kiss under the mistletoe?' She said yes. We stood there, it seemed, like an hour, embraced. We reconciled.

"The next day, I drove her home to Leavenworth. Her mother, father, and grandmother were there, happy to see me. From that time on, we went steady, got pinned, then engaged, and we graduated together in 1954 on June 6. On June 7, I got commissioned as a second lieutenant in the United States Air Force. Two days later, we were married in Leavenworth, Kansas.

"Dean is a special guy, in my view. My entire career in business, socially, sports, was because I got to KU," the ever-grateful Reich said. "When I was 19, I was shell-shocked because of the West Point incident. I had been the third-ranking cadet in my class at West Point. I always thought I was going to be a general. I was devastated. I had some people who believed in me, gave me a second chance, and when I got to KU all was forgotten. It was a fabulous place to get educated. The people were great. I was able to play two sports under great coaches. I met great friends and was very active. I was national chairman of the Alumni Association. I was on the Athletic Corporation Board. I value what happened there so much. They accepted me with arms outstretched. I have given back time and treasure since then. It's worked out."

People at KU and North Carolina call Smith the most competitive individual they have ever met. Michael Jordan was second to him. "Whether it be golf, Ping-Pong, basketball, whatever, he was a tiger, and he wasn't that big. Only weighed about 160," Reich recalled. "In football, he tried out for the KU team, but he just wasn't big enough.

"When we lived down in Savannah, where we retired to, Dean had those great teams, and he was very kind to me," Reich said. "He used to get me tickets and the royal treatment whenever we wanted to go up to Chapel Hill. It was only a few hours' drive. He'd get me on the bench, and we'd enjoy it. He was in my life a long time. When we were still in [the] New York [area] and living in New Canaan, Connecticut, they had a game at Madison Square Garden on a Sunday afternoon. The team was staying in Midtown New York. The New York North Carolina Alumni Association was honoring Dean with a luncheon at the Plaza. He invited Kay and me, and we sat at the table with Dean and his wife, Linnea. After lunch, Dean got up to say a few appropriate words to the alumni. From the podium, Dean asked me to say a few words. After I finished, Dean said, 'You know I've known Gil a long time. A lot of people have claimed to be my roommate, and few have. *This guy* has!'

"I got back up and took the mike. 'When we were in school, Dean used to brag about rooming with me. Now I do about him.' We set the record straight, and the crowd loved it. His career was fabulous, and we all knew he was going to be a helluva coach," Reich said. "But we never expected the heights he attained.

"I will be eternally grateful to Dean Smith for two things he did for me," Reich said in July 2014. "He introduced me to Phog Allen, and he got me my wife of 60 years."

5 | LEARNING THE BASKETBALL TRADE

BY THE SPRING OF HIS senior year in 1953, Dean Smith knew he had to face his service obligation as an Air Force officer. Word came that his graduating ROTC class would not go on active duty until 1954. By then, his dream of becoming a big-league catcher had entered a fast fade. His baseball roommate and the second-string catcher on the KU team was Galen Fiss, another young athlete whose future lay in another sport, football, although he didn't know it at the time. One day while they were hanging out during a road trip to Iowa State, a man knocked on the door of their room. He identified himself as a scout for the Cleveland Indians, but Smith's heart sank when the man asked, "Is Fiss here?" As Smith noted in *A Coach's Life*, "He [Galen] was not second-string for long."

Like Dean Smith, baseball, too, had been Galen Fiss's dream. Fiss, who was drafted for pro football by the Cleveland Browns in that era before the Major League Baseball draft, signed instead with the Indians. He was hitting .275 for the Fargo-Moorhead Twins of the Northern League when, in 1953, he took a hard pitch to the head and was forced to quit baseball. After he recuperated from the beaning, Fiss turned to the Browns and the NFL. He made Paul Brown's deep and talented roster in 1956, 1 year before Jim Brown arrived from Syracuse to rewrite the league's ground-gaining records and gain recognition as, as he still is, the greatest running back in league history. Fiss excelled at linebacker for years and was captain of Cleveland's fourth and final NFL championship team in 1964. And he stayed close to Smith long after he left football.

Years later, Fiss gave a strong endorsement to Smith's North Carolina assistant, Roy Williams, when he vied for and landed the Kansas basketball job in 1988. Sadly, Galen Fiss died of cardiac arrest in 2006 at age 74 while suffering from Alzheimer's.

Now that he realized his baseball dream was over, Smith knew he had to make realistic plans for his future once he finished his service obligation. He always wanted to be a high school coach and teacher, and his father, Albert, kept after him about getting accredited to become a math teacher. "It's harder for schools to get math teachers than it is for them to get physical education teachers," the elder Smith repeatedly reminded his son.

One day that spring, Smith went to see Phog Allen in his office in a visit he loved to relate all his life, especially after he achieved coaching success. "Doc Allen wanted me to be a doctor," Smith recalled, fully aware that the coach's son, Bob, was a physician. "'Don't go into coaching,' Doc would say. 'Too many ups and downs. Too much heartache.' But I was my parents' son."

As a math major, Smith was well aware of the probability that he was likely to do something else in his adult life other than be a coach. Coaching, though, was the inner siren that drove him. Thus, he designed his plan. He gained his sneak preview as a senior in the 1952–53 season, when coaches Allen and Dick Harp asked him to teach the Jayhawks' offenses and defenses to football players who joined the team after their season ended. Harp let Smith know he was important and that he was saving both Harp's and Allen's time by freeing them from working with the football players. Most important, for Smith, he knew he was gaining practical and valuable coaching experience.

Several of Smith's teammates noticed how he went about his work in those practice sessions. His Fiji brother Bill Hougland, Doc Allen's title team guard and Olympic gold medalist, was still impressed with Smith's youthful coaching ability and drive when we discussed it 60 years later on a summer morning in an office inside Allen Fieldhouse. "It was evident that he was going to be a coach from the way he handled the third team [football players]."

Smith's life after graduation in the summer of 1953 was little different than it would be for thousands of young men waiting to begin active duty with their military units. You can't land a true career-building job, yet you have to make a living of some sort to survive. On graduation night, Smith's friend, Hal Cleavinger, a KU football player, introduced Smith to his twin sister, Ann. Ann was an intern in occupational therapy and was living in Topeka that summer. He and Ann saw each other regularly and soon were making plans to get married.

Later that summer, Doc Allen called Smith into his office and made him two offers. First, he could take a teaching job in Haven, Kansas, that paid $6,000 a year and would let him be a high school coach, or he could stay at the university as an assistant. At the university, he would help Harp with the freshmen and assist Allen and Harp with varsity practices. "I didn't want the money, I just wanted to coach," Smith wrote. Thus, Allen helped land Smith an 8:00 a.m.–to–2:00 p.m. job in the accounting department at the Lawrence Paper Company before he reported to work with the coaches at Hoch Auditorium gym as an unpaid assistant.

That situation lasted until December 1953, when the National Gypsum Company in Parsons, Kansas, offered Smith a desk job in

quality control at what he called "a very good salary" and, most important to him, the chance to play semi-pro basketball on the company's
AAU team. He also was looking at a chance to play for yet another
team being organized by Kansas graduate K. S. "Bud" Adams Jr., the
Phillips Oil heir, that Adams would call the ADA Oilers. This was
the same Bud Adams who, in 1959, would found the Houston Oilers
and, with Lamar Hunt, organize the formation of the American Football League, which began play the following year.

Those various dreams ended abruptly in April 1954, when
Smith's Air Force orders arrived. He reported for temporary duty at
Lackland Air Force Base near San Antonio, Texas, before he was
assigned to duty at Scott Air Force Base for communication school
on the Illinois side of the Mississippi River across from St. Louis.
While there, he and Ann got married. She moved on to finish her
schooling at the Mayo Clinic in Rochester, Minnesota, as Dean
shipped out to West Germany in late September, an often difficult
time to sail the Atlantic as summer gives way to rougher fall weather.
Smith's trip was anything but easy, and when he reached land he
vowed never again to go by water between Europe and the United
States. Ann joined him that December. His main duty in West Germany turned out to be—surprise—playing basketball under the
command of Air Force Major General E. Blair Garland, a man Smith
described as "a passionate basketball fan."

General Garland rose through the Signal Corps during World
War II in the Army Air Corps and moved into the new Air Force
with the National Security Act of 1947, which created the Department of Defense. General Garland wore two big hats in the '50s:
head of airways and communications services for the Military Air
Transport Service at Andrews Air Force Base, and when Smith
arrived in Germany, General Garland became chief of communications at Supreme Headquarters in Europe. More important for Smith,

the general loved basketball, and he showed the young officer the best start to winning was to land the best possible players. Garland "recruited" an elite team for Andrews Air Force Base composed of Kentucky All-Americas (and future Hall of Famers) Cliff Hagan and Frank Ramsey and their Wildcat teammates, C. M. Newton and Lou Tsioropoulos, plus two of Smith's KU teammates, Olympians Dean Kelley and Bob Kenney.

Andrews so dominated service play in the United States that General Garland wanted to fashion a similar model for European basketball. He had Lieutenant Smith assigned to Fürstenfeldbruck Air Base near Munich, where he joined former Bradley stars Dick Estergard and Ron Johnson, who excelled on the Braves' 1954 NCAA runners-up against Tom Gola–led La Salle. Their coach was Captain Jack Schwall, and they won the Air Force championship for Europe. During that tournament, Smith got the call that Ann was about to deliver their baby. He arrived in time to see Ann and greet Sharon Ann Smith. He returned to his team without sleep, but in time to help them qualify for the Worldwide Air Force championship in Orlando, where they lost to General Garland's well-stocked Andrews AFB team led by the likes of Hagan and Ramsey.

In the summer of 1955, General Garland arranged for Boston Celtics coach Red Auerbach, superstar guard Bob Cousy, and Kentucky coach Adolph Rupp, Smith's fellow KU alum, to conduct a series of clinics at Air Force and Army facilities in West Germany. Smith was assigned to take care of Cousy. Naturally they played some one-on-one, and in short order Cousy took him to school, especially when he worked his post moves inside and quickly showed Smith the hook shot that nobody in the NBA could stop. After they finished, Smith, still in sweats, knew he just had to see General Garland to thank him for the assignment to the basketball team duties and for his stay in the Air Force. When he got to the general's table,

where he was having lunch with Rupp and the base colonel, to
Smith's amazement, General Garland asked the base colonel to move
down the table to another seat so Smith could join him at the main
table. Years later, in 1960, when Smith was a rookie head coach at
North Carolina, Rupp still was regaling gatherings with the story of
how General Garland opened a seat at his table for young Lieutenant
Smith. For good measure, Rupp repeated that story years later at a
North Carolina banquet to peals of laughter.

One of the demonstration players Smith and his group brought
in for the clinics was Army private Sid Cohen of Brooklyn, who in
Smith's words "showed a lot of ability." Smith wasn't the only one
there who saw what Cohen could do. Rupp, who had virulently exco-
riated Nat Holman's CCNY team in the 1950 NIT for playing blacks
and Jews, took a more benign look this time at Cohen. He noted his
quickness, leadership, and shooting ability enough to recruit him
heavily for Kentucky when Cohen returned home in 1956 to attend
Kilgore (Texas) Junior College. Another coach who knew about
Cohen through his New York pipeline sources was North Carolina's
Frank McGuire, who told Smith when he joined his staff in 1958 he
was recruiting the ex-GI. When they went to New York to meet
Cohen, they discovered Rupp had gotten there first and already had
signed, sealed, and was delivering him to Lexington for an All-America
career his last 2 years in college.

Late in his German tour, Smith and his teammates went to
France for a game at the Air Force facility in Châteauroux, where he
met their coach, Major Bob Spear. Major Spear had flown a B-54
delivering supplies during the Berlin airlift in 1948. He had also been
a ranked tennis player and assisted Coach Ben Carnevale at the US
Naval Academy. When Smith and his teammates were in France,
Major Spear invited him over to his house for dinner, where they

talked basketball, especially the 1953 Kansas team and its pressure defense tactics.

By then, the spring of 1956, Phog Allen had reached the state's mandatory retirement age of 70 and was forced to step down as Kansas coach, a reluctant retirement if there ever was one. Dick Harp was named his replacement, and Jerry Waugh, just out of service, joined Harp on the Jayhawks bench. Two major athletic events had transpired at KU in the past year. Construction of the Allen Fieldhouse, which began when ground was broken in 1952, finally was completed. Construction had been delayed for some time because steel was considered essential for military use during the Korean War, but Kansas authorities discovered the loophole they sought when they built several rooms in the fieldhouse for gun and weapons storage, giving it the designation of an "armory." The dedication game was played on March 1, 1955, before a record crowd of 17,228, as KU beat Kansas State 77–67 after trailing 44–33 at the half.

The second major occurrence in 1955–56 was the recruitment of the most important and greatest player in school history, 7-foot-1-inch Wilt Chamberlain from Overbrook High School in Philadelphia. Chamberlain was the most heavily recruited player in history to that time. Phog Allen desperately wanted Chamberlain for KU and fervently hoped to coach him. It came down to three midwestern schools: Dayton, Indiana, and Kansas. Chamberlain crossed off Dayton when he learned that the restaurants in that Ohio city were segregated. Indiana, in the words of Allen, lost out because Kansas outworked them and, in fraternity parlance, "they were the worst rushers in the world."

Kansas had prominent African Americans with KU ties take charge of the recruitment and talk up the virtues of a Kansas education to the tall, young Philadelphian. Two were prominent black businessmen: Kansas City newspaperman Dowdal Davis and Lloyd Kerfords, who owned a major limestone quarry in Atchison. Third and most important was concert singer Etta Moten Barnett of Chicago. Barnett was a prominent singer and entertainer who earned a degree in voice at KU in 1931 and went on to star in various musical productions. According to Kansas.com, George Gershwin composed *Porgy and Bess* in 1934, it is said, with her in mind. She starred as Bess when the revival production opened in New York in 1942. The three (Davis, Kerfords, and Barnett) convinced Chamberlain to come to Lawrence.

The recruitment worked, and he enrolled in the fall of 1955. As Allen later admitted, "Of course I used everything we had to get him. What do you think I am? A Sunday school teacher?" Chamberlain's dominance at every level was and remains unquestioned and unchallenged. His incredible strength, agility, and athletic skills were demonstrated in track-and-field events as he threw the shot put and discus at NCAA championship levels, ran the 440-yard (or quarter-mile) dash in 49.0 seconds and the half-mile well under 2 minutes, competed in the long jump, and high-jumped 6 feet 6 inches.

Allen may have secured his biggest ever catch in Wilt Chamberlain, but he never got to coach him at the varsity level. Chamberlain, an aware big-city guy who came to much smaller Lawrence because of Allen and who was angered by segregationist policy there, did his best to ignore the racists as he became the talk of college basketball. In his sophomore season, his first on the varsity, he led Kansas to the 1956–57 title game with a 24–2 record and a number two national ranking. North Carolina, which entered the title game unbeaten at 31–0, was ranked number one. Restaurants in the Lawrence business district north of the campus tried to deny service to Chamberlain, who effectively integrated the establishments by ignoring the owners. "He was politely disobedient," were the words Waugh used to describe Big Wilt's attitude in our interview nearly 60 years later.

Chamberlain provided a look at the future when the freshman overwhelmed the varsity with a 42-point performance in a preseason scrimmage in 1955. Chamberlain's story began in earnest on December 3, 1956, when he scored 52 points against Northwestern's outstanding sophomore center and future close friend, Joe Ruklick, to lead Kansas to an 87–69 victory.

When they met again after the USAFE tournament in Wiesbaden, Germany, Bob Spear asked Smith to consider joining him as his assistant. Smith replied that he planned to return to Kansas as a second assistant to new head coach Dick Harp and his new top assistant, former KU star guard Jerry Waugh. Spear persisted, explaining to Smith that he was about to take over as the first basketball coach at the fledgling Air Force Academy. He urged Smith to join him as his assistant in Denver (the Walter Netsch–designed campus in Colorado Springs was still being constructed) and, true to his word, got Smith extended into an "indefinite commitment," which meant he had to serve at least another year courtesy of the government. Smith saw the opportunity to be on his own and took it.

While in Denver, he and Ann made friends with several junior officers and their wives, among them Lieutenant Tom Brookshier and his wife, Barbara. Brodeshier, his career as a CBS-TV NFL analyst several years in the future, was away from his civilian job as a punishing defensive back with the Philadelphia Eagles, so the Brookshiers and Smiths passed many an hour playing a competitive for sure but far less violent game—bridge. That August, Ann was 9 months pregnant with their second child when daughter Sharon took ill with what doctors diagnosed as pneumonia. That night, when she had trouble breathing, Smith knew they had to get to Fitzsimmons Army Hospital. To his horror, Smith realized his fuel level was so low he was running on fumes. But the baby's breathing was labored, and she was in deep trouble. So he floored it, sped through the Denver streets, and got to the hospital in time for the doctors to perform an emergency tracheotomy. Three days later, Sharon was taken off the critical list.

In his memoir, Smith relates that he had fallen away from religion and the devotionals of his childhood during college and his military service. Then, as Sharon battled to recover in that hospital, he returned to the Bible and prayer. "I prayed. And I prayed for Sharon, and I prayed for her doctors," he wrote. And he stayed with prayer for the rest of his life.

While Smith watched and prayed over Sharon, Ann delivered their second child, daughter Sandra Jo Dean Smith. On her fourth day of life, with grandfather Albert there, Ann, Sharon, and baby Sandy all went home. Son Scott would arrive in 1958.

At the Air Force Academy, Coach Spear gave Smith extra responsibilities. Coaching there came with built-in handicaps: Height and academics. Air Force Academy rules at that time would not allow any cadet to stand taller than 6 feet 4 inches. And academic rules were as stringent as any school in the country. "They made up for the lack of height by getting kids who were smart," Smith's friend Bill Bunten said. "They did things no other teams thought about doing. Change defenses after a basket. Gather together on the floor in a stoppage of play at the free throw line when the opponent was about to shoot. Trapping defense. Get people in the corners and what have you. It was a great learning experience."

Smith came up with other new ideas and innovations as well. He told Spear about his Kansas teammate Al Kelley, who would surprise an opponent who was dribbling toward him by leaving his man and going after the ball handler in an attempt to steal the ball. Often it worked. Smith later imported that technique to North Carolina, calling it the "run and jump" or "30 defense," one of five basic defenses he employed and described in detail in *Basketball: Multiple Offense and Defense*, coauthored with Spear and published in 1982, his 22nd season at Carolina. Another Kansas innovation Smith adopted was the shuffle. The shuffle calls for each man to be able to play any position on the floor, requires fast movement, and features constant cuts.

Air Force went 11–10 in 1956–57, Smith's first year at the academy, and improved to 17–6 in his second season. The important basketball event for Smith during that time was the 1957 Final Four in Kansas City, to which he was invited by his boss Spear. Spear asked Smith to sleep on a cot in North Carolina head coach Frank McGuire's suite, where he was glad to listen to the clinical wisdom of the four head coaches staying there, all friends. They were Spear, McGuire, Navy's Ben Carnevale, and Hoyt Brawner, coach at the University of Denver. McGuire took an immediate liking to Smith and went about recruiting him from the outset to become his assistant.

The four teams competing in the Final Four that year were twice defending champion San Francisco, coached by Phil Woolpert, who had come to Lawrence in 1953 to study KU's pressure defense; Big Ten champion Michigan State, now coached by Pete Newell's successor Forddy Anderson who took Bradley to the NIT and NCAA title games in 1950 against CCNY; unbeaten ACC titlist North Carolina; and Smith's alma mater, Kansas, for whom he was rooting for sentimental reasons if nothing else. Smith still retained tight connections at KU with both coaches and players.

Doc Allen had retired but his top assistant and Smith's mentor, Dick Harp, had been promoted to head coach. Jerry Waugh, Allen's point guard during Smith's first 2 years at KU, was his top assistant. Smith had been freshman coach in 1953–54 for KU's senior starters: shooting guard Maurice King, who was Chamberlain's Kappa Alpha Psi fraternity brother, and cocaptains point guard Johnny Parker and 6-foot-3 forward Gene Elstun.

In 1957, the national championship games were played on Friday and Saturday night, March 22 and 23, at Kansas City Municipal Auditorium. The four contests were truly momentous, as for the first time in NCAA history three of the semifinalists featured black starters. Forddy Anderson's Michigan State Spartans featured sophomore Jumpin' Johnny Green, who didn't play basketball until he grew to 6 feet 5 inches in the Marine Corps while serving in South Korea. He got to East Lansing in 1955, starred on the freshmen team, and came into his own as a sophomore on his way to becoming the greatest rebounder in Spartan history. San Francisco, coached by Phil Woolpert, had lost Bill Russell and K. C. Jones to graduation but still retained his outstanding guard, Gene Brown, and 6-foot-9 sophomore center Art Day from Chicago. KU's two best players were blacks: Chamberlain and guard Maurice King. The only all-white team, ironically, was Smith's future employer, North Carolina, with Frank McGuire's all–New York lineup and major bench substitutes.

The opening game of the national semifinals pitted Big Ten champion Michigan State against unbeaten, top-ranked ACC champion North Carolina. If you wanted to follow your favorite college team in action in those days, you had to find their games on radio, as the national network television contract did not exist. Nothing, though, would prevent an enterprising producer from televising the games in a local market, or even statewide, if he could set up his own operation. Rights were no problem.

Such was the case in North Carolina, where television producer Castleman D. Chesley, known everywhere in the business as "C. D.," noted the building enthusiasm all winter in the Tar Heel State and took charge. Chesley, who ran his business in Malvern, Pennsylvania, a far western Main Line suburb of Philadelphia, knew well and understood what was happening on Tobacco Road. Chesley quickly put together a statewide network to show the Final Four games. He got more than he bargained for on both nights, with two of the most remarkable games in basketball history and the national coming-out party of the biggest star the game had yet seen in Chamberlain.

Michigan State and North Carolina put on a fabulous show in the first semifinal. The Spartans seemed ready to win at two junctures. Jack Quiggle nailed an apparent winner from half-court at the end of regulation, but the officials waved it off, saying time had expired. In the first overtime, Johnny Green missed a potential game-winning free throw. Finally, after three overtimes, North Carolina, led by Lennie Rosenbluth's 29 points, came home with a 74–70 victory.

The second game was a contest only in the first half, as Kansas led San Francisco 38–34 at the break. Chamberlain dominated play in the second half, finishing with 32 points as the Jayhawks pulled away to a comfortable 80–56 win. Back in Frank McGuire's suite, Smith, definitely favoring his alma mater, kept his counsel as the four friends and coaches—McGuire, Spear, Carnevale, and Brawner—gave their postmortem of the games they had witnessed and, in McGuire's case, coached.

The next night, Smith sat with Spear and Carnevale at the beginning of the game, but when they began cheering hard for their pal McGuire and Carolina, Smith had to get out of there. So he joined friends in the Kansas section. Down on the floor, McGuire pulled every psychological trick in the book. "We were on the floor before Carolina. We were directed to the south basket," Jerry Waugh said. "Carolina's team came out and set up their equipment on our bench. By this time, Dick was as tight as a banjo. When Harp complained to Big Seven Commissioner Reeves Peters, the commissioner replied, 'They are our guests.' While Harp and Kansas stewed and waited, McGuire didn't show until game time, when he then sent 5-foot-9-inch Tommy Kearns to jump center with Chamberlain."

In 1991, McGuire told Ira Berkow of the *New York Times* what he was doing with that move. "I told my players that we weren't playing Kansas; we were playing Wilt Chamberlain."

"Carolina opened with a 1-3-1 zone, sagging on Chamberlain," Waugh said. Basically, as Lennie Rosenbluth told Berkow in 1991, all five Tar Heel players collapsed around Chamberlain front and back, leaving the other four Kansans open to shoot at will. Kansas couldn't hit a thing. Carolina, on the other hand, had better luck. "Everything they threw up went in, it seemed," recalled Waugh. "North Carolina took a 10-point lead, but we were patient."

The Jayhawks caught up and appeared to take over the game when Chamberlain, a notoriously poor foul shooter (62 percent in college, 51 percent in the pros), hit a pair. "We took a 4-point lead in the second half," Waugh said. Ten minutes remained. Harp, somehow forgetting that Carolina had endured a triple-overtime game the night before, played into their hands by going into a slowdown. This gave Carolina time to catch a second wind and mount a late rally.

The Tar Heels got another break when, late in the game, Tommy Kearns committed a foul to stop the clock and force free throws so that Carolina could regain possession of the ball. "The referee did not call an intentional foul," Waugh said. "We missed the free throws, and they got back in the game." When Rosenbluth fouled out with

1:47 left, Carolina appeared to be finished. Gene Elstun missed a pair of foul shots though, Carolina battled back, and with 20 seconds left, Kearns sank a foul shot to force overtime at 46–all.

Each team scored a basket in the first overtime. Chamberlain saved the game for Kansas at the end of the extra period when he batted away a Kearns shot. Neither team scored in the second overtime. North Carolina missed all four of its free throw attempts. Chamberlain, sick of being constantly grabbed, had a brief set-to with Carolina's Pete Brennan until Kansas City police took the court to restore order and settle the crowd. That meant for the second night in a row, the game would be decided in a third 5-minute overtime period.

Kearns hit a drive and added two free throws for the Tar Heels. Chamberlain scored a basket and foul shot for a three-point play, and Maurice King and Elstun each hit a free throw to give Kansas a 53–52 lead. Then, with 6 seconds left, King fouled 6-foot-7 Joe Quigg, who answered by sinking two foul shots to give Carolina the 54–53 lead. Sophomore Ron Loneski, from Chicago south suburb Calumet City and Bishop Noll High School across the state line in Hammond, Indiana, was the triggerman on the play that Dick Harp hoped would bring the title to Lawrence. "Ron, a lefty, flashed into the top half of the circle. He was to throw a high pass to Wilt to dunk," said Waugh. "Instead of throwing it high enough, Ron threw it rim high, and Quigg batted it away." Kearns picked up the ball and threw it as far up as he could toward the rafters. By the time it came down, the game was over. Carolina had won its first national title, 54–53.

"It was a great disappointment," Waugh said, echoing Harp, his boss, who never was the same afterward in his coaching career. Chamberlain called it the worst loss of his career, far worse than any he would ever suffer in the NBA.

Those phenomenal games and telecasts not only attracted viewers, they also made rabid fans out of them—rabid Carolina fans. Western Carolina University associate professor Alex Macaulay, writing for the *Tar Heel Junior Historian* in 2011, noted that "one young fan later remembered 'sitting up both nights, watching those two triple-overtime games, and just going nuts in the process.' He added, 'I think my parents got hooked on basketball because of the television. I know I did.'"

To C. D. Chesley's good fortune and delight, airing the most exciting 2 days of action in the history of college basketball caught the notice of big business in North Carolina. Pilot Life of Greensboro soon reached an agreement with Chesley to televise ACC games for the 1958 season, and that was the start of something so big it literally made the game until Eddie Einhorn came up with his TVS network concept a decade later and eventually sold it to NBC Sports.

Back in his suite, McGuire brought in his players before everyone would go out to celebrate, and he asked Smith, who felt as bad as any KU alum could feel, to say a few words. And he did in this first of what would be many victory remarks to a Tar Heel team. "You guys had it at the end," he said. "Congratulations. But I certainly wasn't cheering for you."

McGuire enjoyed the moment and asked Smith to lead the new champions to a good place to eat at this hour. "Eddy's," Smith replied. It was a nightclub two blocks away at 13th and Baltimore, known for its excellent, pricey food, which McGuire figured would work since he had been afforded the luxury of an expense account. "Order anything you want," McGuire told his team and his guest, Smith. When McGuire turned in his expense report, Athletic Director Chuck Erickson questioned the size of the bill. "Can you believe $48 for the Roquefort dressing?" he said. "I'm not paying that part of the bill."

A quarter century later, when North Carolina won its first title for Smith in New Orleans, Carolina Athletic Director John Swofford, who later became ACC commissioner, sent McGuire a $48 check to cover that dressing tab.

That moment was the turning point in Smith's career as well. McGuire had been working on him to come to Chapel Hill. A year later, that's exactly what he did.

6 | THE SOUTHERN
PART OF HEAVEN

THE UNIVERSITY OF NORTH CAROLINA at Chapel Hill was founded in 1789 as the first public university in the United States. Instruction began in 1795 in a single building at the north end of the 729-acre campus known as Old East. Built in 1793 by slave labor, Old East is the oldest building constructed for a public university that remains in use today. At the University of North Carolina, Old East now is a residence hall, perhaps the most prestigious structure at the school. Degrees at UNC are offered in 78 academic majors through 14 colleges and the College of Liberal Arts and Sciences. The university graduated its first woman in 1898 and was racially integrated in 1961, the year Dean Smith became head basketball coach.

The College of William and Mary and the University of Georgia actually are older. William and Mary was chartered as a private school in 1693 but did not go public until 1906. Georgia was chartered in 1785 but did not begin instruction until 1801.

Thanks to North Carolina Governor David Lowry Swain, who persuaded Confederacy President Jefferson Davis to keep the university open in 1861, education continued at UNC during the Civil War.

The state was readmitted to the Union in 1868. The school remained in business but had to endure political change and work through a lack of students and funding, which forced it to shut down from 1870 to 1875, during the Reconstruction.

Its backers love to say the university offers an Ivy League–type education at public tuition prices. In-state tuition was pegged in 2015 at $6,648 per year. Accordingly, the Princeton Review in 2015 rated the University of North Carolina at Chapel Hill as America's best buy in higher education.

For most of the university's history before World War II, North Carolina fielded generally midlevel football teams in the Atlantic Coast Conference and its predecessor, the Southern Conference. Just one coach, Carl Snavely, carved out a truly outstanding record at UNC, going 7–1–1 in 1934 and 8–1 in 1935 before moving on to Cornell, back when the Ivies still were big-time athletic powers. Snavely returned to Chapel Hill in 1945 after a decade of outstanding success at Cornell, and he assembled a series of fine postwar teams led by legendary All-America tailback Charlie "Choo Choo" Justice. Justice came from Asheville in the western area of the state, which also was the hometown of famed writer Thomas Wolfe, another Carolina alumnus and local icon. Football got a big boost again at North Carolina in 1956 when the Tar Heels lured Coach Jim Tatum back to his alma mater from Maryland, where he had won big through the early '50s, including the national title in 1953 and a number three ranking in the polls in 1955, behind Oklahoma and Michigan State.

Basketball, meanwhile, has been the dominant sport at Carolina from its beginning. The school fielded its first basketball team in the winter of 1911 and in its first game defeated Virginia Christian 42–21. In 1924, a decade and a half before the NCAA tournament was created, Carolina finished 26–0. In 1936, the Los Angeles–based Helms Athletic Foundation, the same group that declared back-to-back national titles for Kansas in 1922 and '23, honored the Tar Heels at last for their unbeaten 1924 team. Helms continued naming national champions until 1982, but they mirrored the basketball tournament results.

North Carolina continued to enjoy winning teams but played in virtual national anonymity until 1952, when a charismatic Irish Catholic from New York City named Frank McGuire roared into Chapel Hill. McGuire had just taken St. John's to the NCAA title game against Phog Allen's Kansas Jayhawks, whose benchwarmer and aspiring coach Dean Smith was learning the game from the game's acknowledged founder. "Everett Case at North Carolina State had dominated Atlantic Coast basketball until then," Carolina alum and NBA executive Donnie Walsh said. "Once Frank got there, it changed."

McGuire put North Carolina on the map in 1957 when, as detailed earlier, his unbeaten 32–0 Tar Heels beat Wilt Chamberlain and Kansas to capture their first national championship. The morning after Carolina beat Kansas in that triple-overtime game, the five coaches in McGuire's suite were having breakfast when McGuire told Smith in the company of the others that he wanted him to serve as his assistant. McGuire explained that he had already cleared it with Smith's boss, Bob Spear, and had also gotten positive feedback from the other two men staying there, Ben Carnevale and Hoyt Brawner. All four men believed that Smith was the right man for the number two job at Carolina. McGuire told his coaching friends there that Buck Freeman, his loyal assistant since 1952, was in failing health and was ready to retire, if not this year then in 1958. Freeman was McGuire's coach at St. John's in 1936, and the two had retained a special closeness through the years.

When Smith replied that he was committed to the Air Force until the summer of 1958, McGuire assured him he would wait and that he could get Freeman to stay on until then before he let him retire. "Dean was offered a job at Wyoming but didn't take that," Bill Bunten said. "McGuire called him again, and after the '57–58 season, Dean took the job with North Carolina. Turned out pretty good."

For Dean Smith, seeing that campus in Chapel Hill in April 1958 was love at first sight. The people there gave him the red-carpet treatment, and he was sold. "And," McGuire added, "I will pay you $7,500 a year" (roughly $60,000 today), a salary offer that would make Smith the highest-paid assistant in college basketball. Naturally he accepted, but he did not know then that McGuire still had to clear the offer with his bosses in Chapel Hill.

When word about McGuire's salary offer came back to football coach Jim Tatum, he stormed into the office of Athletic Director Chuck Erickson and complained that the basketball coach was destroying the pay scale on his football staff.

Because he badly wanted Smith and as a point of pride, McGuire, who knew Erickson likely would side with Tatum, pulled an end run on Erickson and Tatum by taking the dispute to the man he considered his real boss, UNC Chancellor William Aycock. McGuire stated that he had found his man and wanted to pay him the money he promised. "Besides, he's a dean as in Dean Smith and an American Baptist."

Aycock said he didn't know about the dean part, but Smith recalled in his memoir that Aycock did say, "There are more Baptists than sparrows in North Carolina." The chancellor immediately approved the hiring at the stipulated salary, and called in Erickson to tell him that he had made his decision. "Frank needs the money to pay this Dean Smith," Aycock told Erickson without further comment.

Smith arrived in August to begin his duties. One of the first people he met on campus was student broadcaster Woody Durham, who was a 17-year-old freshman in the 1958–59 school year. "I got to know Coach Smith in Woollen Gym," Durham recalled when we spoke in 2014. "He was an assistant to Coach Frank McGuire. The educational station had a remote bus that was good. Most of the time he sent Coach Smith to do the interviews, so I got to know him pretty well by the time he became head coach between my sophomore and junior years at Carolina." Durham would become the voice of Carolina basketball and football from 1971 to 2011, a 40-year career.

An early priority for Smith was to find a church and pastor to nourish the spiritual for him and his family. It had to be Baptist, as it had been all his life since his childhood in Emporia. And it had to have an intellectually challenging atmosphere. "I think I was one of the first people in Chapel Hill to know him," the Reverend Robert E. Seymour told me in the summer of 2015. "We were just organizing as a Baptist Church here in Chapel Hill when he came. We wanted to be a liberal church, and we eventually became affiliated with the American Baptist Church, not the Southern Baptist Convention."

Robert Edward Seymour was born on July 13, 1925, in Greenwood, South Carolina. He began his studies at the Citadel, but quickly enlisted in the Navy's prechaplaincy program. That took him first to Newberry College for 2 years and then to Duke University in Durham, where he graduated in 1945 with a BA degree. "I anticipated becoming a Navy chaplain. It was the Navy that sent me to Yale Divinity School," the doctor of divinity said. He was awarded a masters of divinity degree from Yale in 1948. Then he moved on to Scotland, where he earned his doctorate from the University of Edinburgh in 1955 before returning home to the United States.

"It was a pleasure to come back to this part of the country to work," Dr. Seymour said, but his calling came with a caveat. "Sometimes Southern Baptists were suspicious of those people who went outside the fold to get their education. My home was in Greenwood, South Carolina, and I was invited to be an assistant to the minister at Myers Park Baptist Church in Charlotte, North Carolina. My entire career has been in North Carolina." Dr. Seymour also served as pastor at Baptist churches in Mars Hill and Warrenton until 1959, when he moved to Chapel Hill as the first minister of the Olin T. Binkley Memorial Baptist Church.

"As you know, when Dean came here, he was an assistant coach," Dr. Seymour recalled. "He was a very affable young man. He got involved before he became head coach. He was the chair of our senior affairs committee. He took responsibility of various kinds in our small congregation."

And the coach appreciated the close relationship he developed with his pastor. "Bob was brilliant in communicating his intelligent thoughts from the pulpit," Smith wrote. "I was nurtured by the ministry of Bob Seymour for 30 years."

Then came that relationship with his boss at the university. How much did Dean Smith care about Frank McGuire? The feeling is obvious in his memoir. "Frank McGuire was just slightly larger than life," Smith wrote as he described a man who displayed easy confidence and charm, whose clothes looked just right on his body, and, in effect, who was a man who "*looked* like a success." As coach and assistant, their relationship was clear. McGuire traveled first class, ate at the best restaurants, and sent his teams on the court in the most handsome uniforms made with the best equipment. He appeared at games wearing the finest suits and silk ties. Impeccable. Everyone on his staff dressed properly, always ready, if need be, to attend a meeting at any time of day. Smith would follow that lead when he became head coach.

"Dean was doing most of the coaching in the practice sessions,"

Durham said. "Coach McGuire a lot of times would be in New York on recruiting trips." It always had to be New York. It was the one place that the flamboyant McGuire felt right, felt natural. Being in charge when the boss was out of the office benefitted Smith, giving him a chance to gain experience in running a program and knowing how to deal with the many situations, large and mundane, a head coach must learn to handle. He knew the competition in his back-yard in the Atlantic Coast Conference was as tough as any in the nation, as the Tar Heels would have to go up against the likes of North Carolina State and Everett Case; Duke, with Case's fellow Hoosier, former player, and veteran assistant Vic Bubas; Wake Forest, with Horace "Bones" McKinney; and the conference's tough northern-area teams, Virginia and Maryland.

Case brought basketball fever to North Carolina State and the Southern Conference in 1946 when he was named head coach, replacing Leroy Jay, whose teams had finished an underwhelming 28–45 over his four seasons. Case arrived in Raleigh from Indiana, where his Frankfort High School teams had won four state champi-onships in the 1920s and '30s. Case entered the Navy after Pearl Harbor, earned a commission, and served most of the war on the home front as he gained promotion from lieutenant to lieutenant commander while he ran major service athletic programs, mainly basketball, under the guise of building morale. When the war ended, Case, who had investigated trends there, decided that the South, especially North Carolina in and near Raleigh, Durham, and Chapel Hill, represented a mother lode of basketball potential and decided to exploit it. Instead of returning to no positive future in Indiana, he moved to Raleigh to build and run the basketball program at North Carolina State. He brought along a superb guard from Gary, Indiana, named Vic Bubas, who transferred to NC State after playing the last war season at Illinois before the Illini's legendary Whiz Kids returned from wartime service. Case augmented Bubas with more talent from the Hoosier State.

NC State had begun construction in 1941 on the 10,000-seat Reynolds Coliseum, which was designed to be the largest basketball arena in the South. The first thing Case did was persuade the administration to expand the Coliseum plans to 12,400 seats and basically give him the keys to the kingdom. Reynolds Coliseum when it opened was the third-largest college basketball venue in the nation, after Minnesota's 18,000-seat Williams Arena and Butler Fieldhouse, built under the supervision of one-man athletic department—athletic director–basketball, football, and baseball coach Tony Hinkle and later named for him. Hinkle-Butler Fieldhouse seated 14,000-plus, each with a clear view of the floor.

Case brought showmanship to the Southern Conference and showed the folks there how they did it back home in Indiana, with spotlight introductions of players and the celebratory cutting down of nets after championship games. Case also brought an awareness to the Tobacco Road area that his NC State "Red Menace" would totally dominate the other area schools. He served notice on North Carolina, Duke, and Wake Forest that unless they upgraded their facilities and ditched their dilapidated cracker-box arenas, he would own everything there.

NC State administrators gave Case the green light in 1949 to organize and promote an eight-team holiday tournament he called the Dixie Classic. Spread over 3 days between Christmas and New Year's, the Dixie Classic quickly became the biggest midseason tournament in the country. It was all Everett Case. As Bethany Bradsher wrote in her book *The Classic*, "Case designed the Coliseum, selected the field, hired the officials, and used the spectacle as a magnetic draw for recruits." Except for Duke's win in the Classic in 1953, NC

State won all the others from 1949 through 1955. Carolina broke through in 1956, the season before the Tar Heels went on to win their undefeated NCAA championship. The Tar Heels added another Classic championship the following year and won the last Classic title in 1960.

Case made his biggest move in 1953 with help from North Carolina's Frank McGuire when he convinced the six other most important members of the Southern Conference to join NC State in forming a new conference: the Atlantic Coast Conference, better known as the ACC. The Southern Conference had refused to let its member schools participate in postseason play. Now, thanks to Case and McGuire, the new ACC would join the gold rush. The new conference's first seven teams were NC State, North Carolina, Duke, Wake Forest, Clemson, Maryland, and South Carolina. Then the ACC members asked Virginia to join, and Thomas Jefferson's school accepted the invitation to round out the streamlined league at eight.

Case's next bold move was the formation of a postseason conference basketball tournament. The attraction for the fans at this gathering of rival schools and their followers was that there was as much action off the court as there was in the games, and the big prize up for grabs was an NCAA tournament bid. Unlike today's ACC, in which the conference often sends upwards of a half-dozen teams into the "Big Dance," only the winner of the conference tournament would become the ACC representative in the NCAA tournament. Case's ACC tournament quickly became the biggest single event in college basketball outside of the NCAA tournament itself. Other conferences would soon follow suit.

The NCAA tournament was a much smaller event then. Only conference champions could gain admission, along with a limited number of independents that included such major Catholic schools as Notre Dame, Dayton, Loyola of Chicago, Georgetown, Duquesne,

St. John's, and DePaul. Conference runners-up could go to the NIT—if they were invited. That's why John Wooden was so adamant in those years that his UCLA Bruins had to win the conference, as did every other big conference hopeful. No matter a team's rating in the polls, only the conference champion or powerful independents advanced.

The dynamic of the ACC changed again in 1956 with Case's enthusiastic and illegal recruitment of 6-foot-7-inch Minden (Louisiana) High School All-America Jackie Moreland. Bagging Moreland, an outstanding engineering student as well, resulted in 4 years' probation for the Wolfpack. Investigators established that Case illegally promised Moreland's girlfriend a 7-year medical school scholarship. Moreland, who had been sought after by NC State, Kentucky, Texas A&M, and Centenary, went on to star at Louisiana Tech. He played pro basketball for 10 years, 5 with the National Basketball Association's Detroit Pistons and 3 more with the American Basketball Association's New Orleans Buccaneers. In a tragic twist, Moreland took ill in the summer of 1971 with pancreatic cancer. He died that December at age 33.

Until the Moreland fiasco, NC State had dominated the ACC and the ACC tournament. That left it open for McGuire and North Carolina to win their unbeaten 1957 title and for Duke and Wake Forest to join the battle for ACC supremacy.

Two seasons after the unbeaten NCAA title run, McGuire and Carolina had the goods in 1958–59, lacking only a great center to make another run in the first season there for new assistant Dean Smith. The player who might have been the difference was 6-foot-7 center Joe Quigg, who sank the two free throws to beat Kansas for the title in 1957. Quigg suffered a severe left knee injury in a 1958 fall scrimmage that knocked him out for the season. When the doctors removed the cast 6 months later, his leg had shriveled so much he could not play, but the New York Knicks drafted him the following spring, signed him for $7,500, and paid a $1,500 bonus. He went back to Chapel Hill, worked out with the Tar Heels, and helped out Coach McGuire and his assistant Smith. In 2012, Quigg told Deadspin .com's Rob Trucks what happened next. "That year I was just still with the Knicks, getting paid, but I was McGuire's unpaid assistant. And that was Dean Smith's first year, so I was actually Dean Smith's assistant. Back then, you didn't have five and six assistants and all that. It was just Dean and McGuire," Quigg said.

"They were the two guys, and so Dean was the freshman coach. I helped him a lot there. In fact, there was one tournament that I took the freshman team up to Washington, and we won both games, and so I was 2 and 0 in my coaching career with the freshmen."

About that time, Quigg was admitted to UNC's dental school, and he had the money to pay for it, thanks to the Knicks. So he told the Knicks he wanted to quit. Their doctor put him through an examination and agreed he was finished as a player. They cut him and honored his contract. Dr. Quigg enjoyed a lucrative career practicing dentistry in Chapel Hill until his seventies.

In 1958–59, Smith's first season at Chapel Hill as McGuire's assistant, North Carolina finished 20–5. The Tar Heels rose to the top of the polls after walloping Loyola 76–57 to open a Saturday night Chicago Stadium doubleheader on February 14, 1959. Going in that night, Carolina shared top billing with Kentucky, which beat Notre Dame 71–52 in the windup game and, in the process, mysteriously slipped to third in the rankings behind Carolina and Auburn, who ended the season ranked eighth.

Smith's first season at Carolina wound down with a whimper, however, as North Carolina State routed the Tar Heels 80–56 in the ACC tournament final. Navy ended Carolina's season 76–63 in the NCAA round of 32 at Madison Square Garden.

That spring could have been quite eventful for Smith. He received the first of two job offers that would have taken him away from his destiny. First was Wyoming, who was looking for a successor to longtime coach Ev Shelton, who had just resigned. Athletic Director Red Jacoby knew Smith from the Air Force Academy and had promised him the Wyoming job if it ever opened. He had one more candidate to consider, though: Bill Strannigan, a Wyoming alum who had been a successful coach at Iowa State who gained a measure of renown when his defense stopped Wilt Chamberlain for a Cyclones victory during the 1957 season. Jacoby took care of the situation at Wyoming when he called Smith to tell him he had given the job to Strannigan.

The other was Smith's old coach and boss at Kansas, Dick Harp, who called after the 1960 season and told Smith he wanted him to return to Kansas and assist him for 4 or 5 years, then move into the job. Smith told McGuire about the call, and McGuire, who didn't want to lose him, asked Smith to join him on a recruiting trip to New York. When they returned to Chapel Hill, Smith called Harp to tell him he was staying at Carolina.

While McGuire was scouring New York for players, the balance of power shifted west of the Appalachians in 1958. Adolph Rupp's Fiddlin' Five, a team that finished the regular season ranked ninth in the AP writers' poll and 14th by the coaches, got hot at tournament time. Led by Vern Hatton and Johnny Cox, the Wildcats beat Elgin Baylor and Seattle 84–72 at Freedom Hall in Louisville, Kentucky, to deliver Rupp's fourth national championship.

A year later, again in Louisville, Pete Newell's defensively dominant California Golden Bears knocked off Oscar Robertson's Cincinnati Bearcats in the national semifinals and returned in the finals the next night to edge Jerry West's West Virginia Mountaineers 71–70 for the title in a game West called the most crushing defeat of his

Hall of Fame career, college and pro. The Mountaineers blew a 13-point first-half lead and still had a chance to win at the end when Cal missed a free throw with 2 seconds left. West grabbed the rebound, but time expired before he could take a shot.

McGuire, Smith, and Co. thought they would have a fine team in 1959–60, and they did through the regular season, going 17–5 behind ACC Player of the Year 6-foot-7 forward Lee Shaffer of Pittsburgh, one of the few non–New Yorkers on the roster, and two New York All-Americans: guard York Larese and swingman Doug Moe. The Tar Heels opened the conference tournament at Reynolds Coliseum in Raleigh with an 84–63 victory over Virginia. But in the semis, Duke beat the Heels 71–69 and went on to beat Wake Forest for the title the next night 63–59.

At least Carolina would not have to face Ohio State and a remarkable sophomore class recruited in 1958 by their young, brilliant, and superbly organized coach, Fred Taylor. Taylor, who did not play high school basketball in Zanesville, got his basketball start in the Army Air Corps in World War II, went to Ohio State after the war, and starred on a 1950 Big Ten championship team that lost to future NCAA champion CCNY 56–55 in the tournament opener. Taylor, an All-America first baseman, then played for 3 years in the Washington Senators minor league system, including brief late-season appearances for the big club.

The crew-cut Taylor was named Ohio State's freshman basketball coach in 1958 at age 34, with the assurance that he would succeed varsity coach Floyd Stahl, who was due to retire at the end of that season. Immediately, Taylor started recruiting what many at that time would call the best incoming freshman class in college basketball history. He concentrated his primary attention on landing the greatest high school player in Ohio history before the coming of Akron's LeBron James at the start of the 21st century. He was Jerry

Lucas of Middletown, 33 miles north of Cincinnati. A loss in the
Ohio state high school basketball tournament semifinals in his senior
year was the first defeat Lucas ever experienced in his life, after winning unbeaten state titles as both a sophomore and junior. Lucas had
impeccable court sense, was a superb jump shooter from any distance, almost never missed his hook shot, and was a wonderful
rebounder, passer, and defender who involved his teammates in all
facets of the game. To get them involved, he held back on his own
shooting, but he still had the best shooting percentage in all of college basketball. And he wasn't beefing up his shooting percentage
taking mostly layups. When discussing Lucas, Bob Knight for years
has said with as much objectivity that a true friend can muster that
his teammate "Big Luke" was and remains the greatest single player
in the history of Big Ten basketball. Greater, Knight insists, than
Michigan State's Earvin "Magic" Johnson, who led the Spartans to
the 1979 title against Larry Bird and Indiana State, and such other
standouts as Michigan's Glen Rice, Purdue's Glenn "Big Dog" Robinson, and Indiana's Isiah Thomas and Steve Alford.

In the classroom, Big Luke was a straight-A student in the School
of Commerce, blessed with a photographic memory, which he would
use later in life to lucrative acclaim. For Fred Taylor, Lucas was a
coach's dream, a total team player as well as being the country's best
individual player in the early 1960s. He pulled a triple in both the
1961 and '62 seasons, when he was named Player of the Year by the
Associated Press Writers, Basketball Writers Association of America,
and United Press International Coaches polls. Taylor surrounded him
with a superb collection of teammates, all Ohio born and bred, each
a superb student.

Dean Smith's fellow Kansan Adolph Rupp worked as hard to
land Lucas as he had any player he ever recruited. When Big Luke
told Rupp that he was attending Ohio State and not Kentucky, the

floodgates opened for Taylor. Coming out of nearby Columbus East High School, guard Mel Nowell was considered the second best player in Ohio, a great shooter, leader, and a superior ball handler.

Taylor's next elite recruit was 6-foot-5 John "Hondo" Havlicek, from Bridgeport in the eastern Ohio coal-mining country near Martins Ferry. Hondo's boyhood friends were future Hall of Fame pitcher Phil Niekro and his talented brother, Joe, both knuckleballers. Woody Hayes constantly badgered Havlicek, an all-state quarterback in high school, to come out for his football team, but Havlicek chose basketball alone after his freshman year, when he hit .400 for the Buckeyes' freshman baseball team. Havlicek was costar to Lucas in college, an All-American as a senior. As a pro for the Boston Celtics, Havlicek would be regarded as one of the best all-around players in NBA history for his versatility and skills, certainly the equal of his close friend Lucas, if not better. An eight-time NBA champion, he was enshrined in the Naismith Memorial Basketball Hall of Fame in 1984.

Guard Gary Gearhart from Lima was a valuable backup for that team, as was a slow-footed, intense, hard-driving 6-foot-4 forward from Orville, Ohio, the aforementioned Knight. Bobby—or Bob, as he prefers—has called Fred Taylor as fine a man and great a coach as he has ever known and has said he modeled his teams that won 902 games as an extension of his former coach and such honored colleagues as Pete Newell and Clair Bee. Knight coached against Smith five times. North Carolina won the first two, both regular season games, and the last in a preseason NIT matchup. In between, Knight and Indiana beat North Carolina 63–50 in Philadelphia for the 1981 NCAA title and won again 72–68 in a 1984 second-round game in Atlanta, Michael Jordan's last for the Tar Heels.

Upperclassmen included forward and future pro Joe Roberts, who mentored Nowell and other African Americans on the team;

junior guard Larry Siegfried, who went on to an outstanding pro career with the Boston Celtics; and Havlicek. Junior Richie Hoyt, who had started as a sophomore in 1959, the year before the super class became eligible, and senior forward Dick Furry, who gave up his starting slot to Havlicek, sacrificed for the good of the team.

Ohio State averaged more than 90 points a game in 1960, and the Buckeyes went 27–3 to win the national title, defeating California's defending champions and their superb coach Pete Newell 73–55 in a game that never was close. That summer, Lucas and his teammates—including Oscar Robertson, Jerry West, and two Big Ten rivals, Purdue's Terry Dischinger and Indiana's Walt Bellamy—won Olympic gold medals at the Rome Olympics.

Until the final game of the 1961 NCAA tournament a year later, Ohio State was rated by many so-called experts as perhaps the best college basketball team that ever played. The Buckeyes roared through that season, virtually unchallenged except for the Mideast Regional semifinals at Freedom Hall in Louisville, Kentucky, a week earlier, when they scraped past Louisville 56–55 before dispatching Kentucky the next night in the regional final, 87–74. On Friday night, March 24, St. Joseph got caught in the Ohio State buzz saw in the national semifinals in Louisville as the Buckeyes won their 27th game of an undefeated season, 95–69. Jerry Lucas hit 10 of 11 shots, 9 of 10 free throws, and grabbed 13 rebounds as the team shot a remarkable 63.3 percent from the floor. The stage was set to crown the Buckeyes as best ever. It did not happen.

Ohio State basketball of the early '60s is almost forgotten outside the borders of the state because the Buckeyes lost a pair of title games to throw water on the party. This was due to their in-state rival, the Cincinnati Bearcats, who emerged as champions after Oscar Robertson graduated and joined the NBA. Ohio State took a

27–0 record and 34-game winning streak into the 1961 title game in Kansas City. Cincinnati, under first-year coach Ed Jucker, who junked George Smith's breakneck running game for tight defense and sure scoring chances, got the Bearcats moving after a poor 5–3 start before taking them on a 22-game winning streak. Tom Thacker and Tony Yates led a strong backcourt, and wide-bodied strongman Paul Hogue anchored the middle with strong rebounding, accurate jumpers, and short hook shots. In the final, they put the clamps on everyone but Lucas, who led all scorers with 27 points, and the Bearcats and Buckeyes ended regulation in a 61–all tie. Then Cincinnati took over the game in overtime, outscoring Ohio State 9–4 to win the title 70–65.

In 1962, after two noteworthy semifinals—one fateful, the other prescient—the two teams would meet in the first title game rematch in NCAA tournament history. Ohio State entered the Final Four in Louisville rated number one and Cincinnati number two. This time around, Ohio State faced and defeated ACC tournament champion Wake Forest and their two mainstays, All-America 6-foot-8 forward Len Chappell and guard and future TV analyst Billy Packer, 84–68. The Buckeyes romped to a 46–34 halftime lead and apparently were home free when Lucas, who had scored an easy 19 points, went down in the second half with a knee injury that left his availability for the title game in doubt.

The other semifinal was supposed to feature Cincinnati in an easy tune-up for the final. Instead, Final Four newcomer UCLA, in John Wooden's first coaching appearance on the national stage, stole the show and nearly ran off with the tournament itself. Wooden had his Bruins ready. Led by sophomore point guard Walt Hazzard and seniors Gary Cunningham, a future Bruins coach, and John Green, the Bruins played the Bearcats to a 70–70 standoff with 3 seconds remaining thanks in large part to Paul Hogue's 36-point heroics. Bearcats star Tom Thacker, who had been held scoreless to that point, got off a long last shot. It ripped through the net at the buzzer for his only two points in a 72–70 win.

The championship game the next night was anticlimactic. Lucas tried to play on his bad knee, but he was helpless against the strong, powerful Hogue, who led the way in a 71–59 Cincinnati victory. Fred Taylor's Ohio State team featuring Lucas, Havlicek, and Nowell had won 78 games and lost just 6 in their 3 years together. To win that single national championship when three straight were in range seemed almost unjust. At least they had that to remember and savor, while Cincinnati had earned the most unlikely double in college basketball history.

As wonderful as life was on High Street in Columbus, all was not well on many other campuses. Another basketball scandal, in many ways worse than the one that nearly did in college basketball in 1951, was about to erupt, one that would have a direct effect on the ACC and, specifically, North Carolina. This situation would take the mantle of dominance east of the Rockies from the likes of Duke and their innovative coach Vic Bubas and Ohio State and the Big Ten, as the country was helpless against what would begin in 1964 as the super-dominance of UCLA and coach John Wooden that would last for the next dozen years.

7 | ANOTHER FIX
JOLTS COLLEGE
BASKETBALL

THE SECOND MAJOR GAMBLING SCANDAL to erupt in college basketball in 10 years exploded like a detonated bank vault in the winter of 1960–61. In this scandal, 37 players from 22 schools would be arrested for participating in a scheme to rig games. Most, but not all, of the action was focused in the East and with the mastermind fixer Jack Molinas. Molinas, a Columbia All-America forward in the early 1950s and the school's all-time leading scorer at the time, started rigging games when he was still in college.

He was the star rookie of the NBA's Fort Wayne Pistons and had just been named to the all-star team when the league expelled him for life in 1954 for running a fix operation with a bookmaker named Joe Hacken. Molinas, a brilliant student, then became a lawyer and in 1957 applied for reinstatement to the NBA. As Michael Fatale wrote in the *Columbia Daily Spectator*, four owners voted for him, four against. NBA President Maurice Podoloff cast the deciding vote against him. So Molinas resumed his wicked business, working the colleges this time as the leader of a conspiracy that involved 49 players and fixed at least 67 games through the 1961 season.

Molinas caused Tony Jackson, St. John's human pogo-stick forward with a feathery jump shot, to lose a surefire NBA career because he failed to report a bribe offer to authorities. North Carolina's star Doug Moe, whom Dean Smith had tutored in a vain effort to save him from flunking a math course, was dismissed from the school when he also did not report a bribe offer. It took several years for Moe, a Brooklyn native and Smith favorite, to restore his reputation and work his way back into the game. He reached the old American Basketball Association (ABA), where he starred as a player before he became a successful coach from 1972 to 2008 in the ABA and, after the merger, with the NBA's Denver Nuggets and Philadelphia 76ers, employing a run-and-gun attack.

Two of America's brightest high school stars, both playground legends from Brooklyn, got caught up in the Molinas mess. Roger Brown of Wingate High and 6-foot-8 Connie Hawkins from Boys' High were both college freshmen in 1961, back when first-year students were still ineligible to compete at the varsity level. Nicknamed the Hawk not only because of his surname but also because of the aerial acrobatics he exhibited on New York City's playgrounds, most notably at Harlem's famed Rucker Park across the street from the site of the Polo Grounds below Coogan's Bluff, Hawkins was the spectacular forerunner to players like Julius "Dr. J" Erving and Michael Jordan.

Another outstanding Brooklyn-born and -bred player who would become an early favorite of Smith at North Carolina was agile, scrappy, left-handed 6-foot-7 Billy Cunningham, a deadly shooter inside and out and jumping-jack rebounder known as the Kangaroo Kid. Cunningham was all–New York at Erasmus Hall, the high school alma mater of, to name a few, actresses Barbra Streisand, Bar-

bara Stanwyck, and Mae West; singer Neil Diamond; writers Bernard
Malamud, Roger Kahn, and Dorothy Kilgallen; sports figures Sid
Luckman, Al Davis, and Jerry Reinsdorf; and chess grandmaster
Bobby Fischer.

"Wingate and ourselves [Erasmus Hall] were arch rivals," Cunningham said in the summer of 2015 from his home in Philadelphia.
"Hawkins and I became great friends. We actually played on the
same team in different [playground] tournaments when my junior
year was over and their senior years were done" in 1961, Cunningham explained. Both Brown and Hawkins "would have been better
if they had the full opportunity to go to college. They both were
dominant, Brown at Dayton, Hawkins at Iowa. Their freshmen
teams regularly beat the varsity. They were dragged into a mess
where they didn't do anything wrong, but they were dragged into a
mess because they knew somebody [Molinas]."

Because Hawkins and Brown had personal contact with Molinas,
although neither took any bribes, justice was as swift as it was unfair.
Hawkins underwent hours of grilling by New York detectives, who
did not let him seek legal counsel. He always denied wrongdoing.
Nevertheless, both were expelled from their respective schools and
banned from the NBA. Banning the two young Brooklynites without
due process was decidedly unfair and illegal, but NBA President
Maurice Podoloff remained adamant that reputed fixers, even when
not proven guilty, could not participate in his league.

Both Hawkins and Brown sued, and their cases persisted through
the courts for 8 years. "They settled their lawsuits against the NBA
and got to play years later and had fine professional careers," said
Cunningham, who became a Hall of Fame pro with the NBA's Philadelphia 76ers after an All-America career at Carolina.

The 1969 settlement with Hawkins and Brown was approved
by then commissioner J. Walter Kennedy, the NBA's successor to

Podoloff. Hawkins had been a basketball nomad, playing in the short-lived National Basketball League, with the Harlem Globetrotters for 4 years, and for 2 more years in the American Basketball Association for the Pittsburgh/Minnesota Pipers while waiting for a resolution to his case. Kennedy awarded Hawkins $1.3 million and assigned his rights to the Phoenix Suns, where he became an All-Star performer. The Hawk finished his career in 1975 with the Los Angeles Lakers and Atlanta Hawks.

Brown played from 1961–67 in a Dayton amateur league before becoming the first player to sign with the newly formed Indiana Pacers of the ABA. He starred in Indianapolis, earning three championship rings. He later became a Republican councilman on the Indianapolis City Council before his death from liver cancer in 1997. Both Hawkins and Brown are members of the Naismith Memorial Basketball Hall of Fame in Springfield, Massachusetts.

Hawkins and Brown were the two who fared well, as did Moe. Other players caught in that scandal did not. New York University point guard Ray Paprocky paid the price for taking $1,300 from gamblers to shave points in four games, as charged by New York District Attorney Frank Hogan. The scandal also nailed Seton Hall University, whose stars Art Hicks (a Chicagoan who had flunked out of Northwestern his freshman year) and Hank Gunter were both thrown out of school for shaving points.

Bradley, which took a severe hit in the 1951 scandal, had to expel three standout players, all Chicagoans, from their 1961 team. James "Tim" Robinson; a certain future pro from Crane High, Al Saunders; and Saunders' high school teammate from Dunbar Vocational, Leroy Bobo, did not report that they had been approached to do business. Another player nabbed in the so-called Molinas Ring was a top player on the 1961 Columbia team, Fred Portnoy.

The spotlight then smashed down like a fallen klieg light less than a month later onto three mainstays of St. Joseph's 1961 Final Four team: Jack Egan, Vince Kempton, and Frank Majewski. St. Joe's, which beat Utah in a four-overtime shootout in the third-place game, had to forfeit everything they had won in the tournament when New York District Attorney Hogan told the world that Egan, Majewski, and Kempton, the mainstays for future Hall of Fame coach Jack Ramsay, had shaved points in several regular season games. For their troubles in the scheme, the three amassed a total of $2,750. Hogan granted them immunity for their testimony against one of Jack Molinas' partners in crime, Aaron Wagman.

The university expelled the three, who then returned to school to earn their degrees and lead exemplary lives ever after. Molinas was arrested and convicted on five counts of bribery, conspiracy, and perjury. Judge Joseph Sarafite sentenced Molinas to 10 to 15 years in Attica Correctional Facility in western New York. In the sentencing, Judge Sarafite stated, "In my opinion, you are a completely immoral person. You are the prime mover of the conspiracy, and you were the person most responsible. You callously use your prestige as a former basketball star to corrupt college basketball players and defraud the public." Molinas was paroled in 1969 after serving 5 years in Attica. He moved to Hollywood in 1970.

Molinas, always a magnet for trouble, participated in several schemes in California. During his fixing days in New York, he had been involved with mobsters Tommy "Ryan" Eboli and Vincent "the Chin" Gigante. He renewed those connections when he got ensnared in pornography and the fur trade. In 1974, his partner, Bernard Gusoff, was beaten to death and Molinas collected a $500,000 insurance policy because both men had insured each other. A year later, Molinas got arrested again, this time on charges he was trafficking pornographic materials across state lines. The case never got to trial because Molinas was shot in the back of the head in his backyard on August 3, 1975. The crime was never solved.

The fix came in a big way to North Carolina in the winter of 1961. Four NC State players had been participants in a point-shaving scheme, as was North Carolina Tar Heel Lou Brown, a player described but not named by Dean Smith in *A Coach's Life* and identified as "a substitute." As Bethany Bradsher wrote in *The Classic*, Brown's specific assignment was to line up those he believed were potential fixers among his teammates. He never fulfilled his task. The NC State players named in the point-shaving operation were Don Gallagher, Stan Niewierowski, Anton Muehlbauer, and Terry Litchfield. Nobody to this day knows how many games were fixed.

Before those players were indicted, trouble and bitterness hung over the conference. Bad blood was especially evident between Duke and North Carolina. In the wake of the national championship in 1957, Frank McGuire recruited another strong class from the New York area. His two main designated newcomers were Jewish players, tough 5-foot-9-inch point guard Larry Brown from Long Beach and rangy 6-foot-5, hard-driving forward Art Heyman from Oceanside.

Brown and Heyman were supposed to be roommates, but Heyman and three other recruits backed out of their commitments before their national letters of intent came due on July 1, 1959. Brown was the only one left of that original Carolina group. McGuire had added guard Donnie Walsh in 1958. "I owe my career to Frank and Dean," Walsh said in late summer 2015. "Frank was so different. If he walked into a room with a thousand people there, they all would know it. It's like there was a light on him. He was an attraction. Very wise and smart, very loyal."

Walsh would forsake a career in law and, like Larry Brown, become a prominent career basketball man after college as a coach

DEAN SMITH
Football
Basketball
Baseball

Dean Smith, here at 18 years old, was a member of Topeka High's Class of 1949. A math major in high school, young Smith hoped to teach math and coach high school basketball when he graduated from the University of Kansas in Lawrence.
© *Topeka High School Historical Society*

Smith was a backup guard for Kansas in their 1951-52 season when they won the NCAA championship, routing St. John's 80-63 in the final. © *Spencer Research Library Archive, KU*

KANSAS' 1952 NCAA CHAMPIONSHIP TEAM

The Kansas Jayhawks have just beaten St. John's 80-63 on March 26, 1952, in Seattle for the NCAA championship. In the second row, Dean Smith holds the trophy and is standing next to assistant coach Dick Harp, his mentor, and head coach Dr. Forrest C. "Phog" Allen. Coach Allen was considered by many to be the father of college basketball.

© *Spencer Research Library Archive, KU*

Two of Dean Smith's children, daughter Sharon and son Scott, share a warm moment with their father at their home in Chapel Hill, North Carolina. © *Spencer Research Library Archive, KU*

Dick Vitale was a 40-year old ex-coach when he joined fledgling ESPN in 1979. Through his broadcasts, Vitale became a major influence on the game. It started with the Atlantic Coast Conference (ACC) powers as Vitale clicked with their biggest coaching star, Dean Smith. © *Robert Crawford*

North Carolina State University's Jim Valvano (middle) and Smith in a pre-game chat when their teams dominated the ACC. Roy Williams, to Valvano's left, picks up on the banter. © *Robert Crawford*

The joke was on as Valvano entertains Smith and Williams. © *Robert Crawford*

Point guard Kenny Smith, who was one of Dean Smith's favorites, was a brilliant all-around player and All-American on a 1987 team that went 32-4 and lost in the NCAA to runner-up Syracuse. © *Robert Crawford*

Rick Fox, Canadian born, raised in Nassau and Warsaw, Indiana, led the Tar Heels to the 1991 Final Four where they lost to Roy Williams and Kansas despite the efforts of Coach Smith and top assistant Bill Guthridge (right). © *Robert Crawford*

Michael Jordan made his big move in May 1984 when he sat down with Dean Smith (right) as his father James Jordan (left) watched his supremely-confident son make his announcement to go pro. Michael Jordan is acknowledged as the game's greatest player. © *Robert Crawford*

An animated Roy Williams works the sideline in front of Dean Smith and Eddie Fogler behind him. © *Robert Crawford*

A tense moment on the North Carolina bench with assistant Bill Guthridge, to Coach Smith's left, and Roy Williams, two men away, reflecting on the moment. © *Robert Crawford*

Serge Zwikker, a 7-foot-2 native of the Netherlands, came to Chapel Hill to play basketball and gained a measure of fame when he grabbed the game ball after Coach Smith's 877th coaching victory in Winston-Salem, NC. It was Coach Smith's last win in the state of North Carolina.
© Robert Crawford

CBS's Andrea Joyce interviews Dean Smith after North Carolina won 73-56 in the second round of the NCAA tournament at Winston-Salem's Joel Arena. Victory number 877 made Smith the winningest coach in college basketball history, beating Adolph Rupp's 876.
© Robert Crawford

Coach Smith (middle) with two of his favorite people: Bill Guthridge (right) and Phil Ford (left). Ford was considered one of the ACC's greatest point guards and coached for a decade at North Carolina. Guthridge was Smith's friend from Kansas State and assistant coach for 30 years before he succeeded Smith as head coach in 1997 for three more highly successful seasons. © *Robert Crawford*

Dean Smith tosses the ball back to an official after it landed near the North Carolina bench.

© *Robert Crawford*

It was appropriate when Commissioner John Swofford presented Coach Smith with an ACC Legends award. Smith had mentored Swofford through North Carolina as a student, assistant football coach, and athletic director.

© *Robert Crawford*

Dean Smith always considered Charles Scott the most important player he ever recruited. Scott was the first African-American player in the ACC and he became an All-American, Olympian, and NBA player. © *Robert Crawford*

This was a gathering of Carolina legends. Right to left: Larry Brown, Dean Smith, Michael Jordan, Roy Williams, and, at the end, Bill Guthridge. © *Robert Crawford*

Duke coach Mike Krzyzewski became Dean Smith's closest rival and, eventually, college basketball's first coach to win 1,000 games. He is still active in 2017. © *Robert Crawford*

Woody Durham (left) graduated from North Carolina in 1963 and, in effect, never left. He called North Carolina games for 40 seasons, including Dean Smith's two NCAA titles. © *Robert Crawford*

"C'mon ref! Give me that call. I need it." It was that way in all close games. © *Robert Crawford*

Antawn Jamison, with his palms outstretched, was Dean Smith's last great player at Carolina. He went on from All-American to a great NBA career.
© *Robert Crawford*

Dean Smith's final victory, number 879, came against Louisville, a 97-74 win in the NCAA tournament on March 23, 1997. Tournament winner Arizona beat the Tar Heels 66-58 a week later in the semi-finals. © *Robert Crawford*

Dean Smith announced his retirement on October 9, 1997, saying he no longer could give the job the same enthusiasm he always had displayed. © *Robert Crawford*

and, unlike Brown, the president of two teams, the Indiana Pacers and New York Knicks. "I loved Frank, too. Frank was a bigger-than-life personality," Walsh, a senior consultant with the Indiana Pacers, said. "He had a magnetism to him that was bigger than anyone I ever saw."

It seemed that McGuire knew virtually everyone in New York, especially anyone involved with basketball. He especially had pipelines to the police and fire departments that included one of his closest friends, former police commissioner Bill O'Brien. That rang true with the Cunninghams and their well-known basketball-playing son. "I had two options: I would go to a Catholic university or play for Uncle Frank," Billy Cunningham said. "I was the first one in our family to go to college. My family was concerned, my goodness: 'He was going to lose his religion if he goes away.' I delivered papers as a kid in Brooklyn. Frank McGuire's sister was a customer, and I delivered papers to her. I was kind of an easy recruit for him."

When McGuire arrived at the Cunningham's home to sign Billy, he brought along his 30-year-old assistant. "It was a confusing time. I didn't know much about the assistant, Dean Smith, who came to our house," Cunningham recalled. "It was the Frank McGuire Show. My gut told me to stay at Carolina, and everything worked out well, even though we were on probation then."

All the more difficult for the younger guys like Cunningham was McGuire's sudden departure in late summer 1961 after Carolina was placed on 1-year probation by the NCAA that would include no NCAA tournament participation in the 1961–62 season. Carolina did not lose any scholarships.

The NCAA had accused McGuire and Carolina of excessive recruiting, based largely on meal expenses. Only the association never gave a precise definition of "excessive." According to Smith in his memoir, committee member Nicholas McKnight, a former dean of students at Columbia College, questioned McGuire's spending $35 one night for three dinners at a New York restaurant. "I know of many fine New York restaurants where you can get excellent meals for $3," McKnight said, to which McGuire retorted, "I wouldn't eat where you eat." Soon thereafter, the NCAA found Carolina guilty of excessive spending. That was the last straw for McGuire, who started looking for a way out.

Now wrapped up and bound for Chapel Hill was Cunningham, the prized prospect recruited by the charismatic McGuire who never would coach him. Instead Cunningham would have to play for a young coach named Smith who knew nothing about him. It would all work out better than anyone could imagine.

Cunningham was back in Brooklyn finishing his senior year at Erasmus Hall and safely locked up for Smith and the Tar Heels when the North Carolina–Duke rivalry took a violent turn at Duke's Cameron Indoor Stadium on the night of February 4, 1961. Brown and Heyman, who had been friends when McGuire recruited them, became rivals before Heyman renounced North Carolina for Duke after Vic Bubas became head coach in Durham. In a piece for GoDuke.com, Art Featherston wrote that Heyman's stepfather deeply disliked McGuire, and that was the root cause for his estrangement with Carolina.

As for the game that night, an ominous note was struck in the freshman contest before the varsity event when several fights erupted on the floor as Duke's Blue Imps, led by future All-American and pro star Jeff Mullins, pulled away to rout Carolina's Tar Babies 79–52. North Carolina's freshmen had to finish the game with just three players after five men fouled out and three more were ejected for fighting. That was a mere warmup for further trouble.

"Over at Duke, we had the 'YouTube brawl,'" Donnie Walsh recalled, referring to the now uploaded "Duke vs. UNC Basketball

1961" television footage. It was the culmination of a long night of tension and bickering on the floor of Cameron Indoor Stadium.

"They had a fight on television when Larry Brown got knocked to the floor," Woody Durham recalled.

The trouble started in the first half when Heyman got into it with Carolina star Doug Moe. "He spit on me," the Duke star said some time later. "Every time I took a shot, he spit on me. I told him I was not going to take that." When UNC's Dieter Krause ran off the bench and went after the angry combatants, Duke's Doug Kistler stepped in before Duke trainer Jim Cunningham pushed Krause out of Kistler's face. Officials Jim Mills and Charlie Eckman restored order and the game continued. Heyman hit 9 of his first 11 shots, but Carolina still held a 35–34 halftime lead.

Finally, with 3 minutes left and UNC leading 73–70, Heyman scored five of the next six points to give Duke a 76–73 lead. Then, with 15 seconds remaining, Heyman sank a pair of foul shots for an 80–75 edge. Larry Brown took the inbounds pass and raced up court. As Brown went up for the shot, Heyman grabbed him by the shoulders at the basket for a hard foul. Brown threw the ball at Heyman, then fired a punch his way as Heyman flailed back. Walsh raced off the bench near the Carolina basket (benches were behind the baselines in the ACC at that time instead of on the sidelines). He slugged Heyman from behind. Walsh then scooted on the double back to the safety of his own bench. When Heyman got up and tried to follow, Brown and several other UNC players piled on Duke's star.

Fans entered the floor, throwing punches. The battle royal lasted 10 minutes. McGuire was seen standing by adjusting his cufflinks, as was his wont. Heyman was ejected for fighting even though he had fouled out. Brown was not ejected and sank two free throws. Duke then added one more free throw to win the game 81–77. Heyman finished with a game-high 36 points. Perhaps tellingly, as Featherston wrote, not a single Duke player came off their bench at the other end of the floor to aid Heyman.

Duke coach Vic Bubas claimed that Brown threw the first punch, though other observers, including referee Charlie Eckman, insisted that Heyman took the first swing. ACC Commissioner Jim Weaver reviewed the game films and issued a report on Valentine's Day acknowledging that Brown was guilty of starting the fight and that Walsh's "hit-and-run tactics" (as Weaver termed it) turned a brief scuffle into a brawl. Weaver also blamed Heyman for going after Walsh. He then suspended Heyman, Brown, and Walsh for the rest of the ACC regular season. "Larry and I got suspended along with Heyman for the fight, but only from ACC games," Walsh said. "We had to play Duke one more time. I thought it was a good trade. We whipped their ass at Chapel Hill."

That game and fight signaled the coming of closure for Frank McGuire and Carolina. In an attempt to get ahead of the inevitable penalty, the dapper coach convinced the school to withdraw from the ACC tournament after the NCAA placed the school on probation for his recruiting violations. McGuire already was in trouble for his lifestyle and high-rolling "entertainment expenses"—excesses, the powers that be called it. Just about the only bad news Carolina did not get came when the grand jury indictments for the point-shaving scandal failed to name Carolina or any of its players.

When the names of NC State's accused point shavers became known, Consolidated University of North Carolina President William Friday, who ran the entire UNC system, stepped in to take charge. Friday, just 40 years old at that time, had seen enough of a system where too many athletes in his view were getting scholarships without merit. NC State had been disciplined twice, including the Moreland mess, and North Carolina had been placed on probation once.

In that instance, the NCAA placed North Carolina on probation for 1 year and banned the Tar Heels from the 1961 NCAA tournament after investigating McGuire's excessive spending on expenses. Friday, along with Chancellor William Aycock and NC State Chancellor John T. Caldwell, issued a self-imposed penalty on their schools, limiting their schedules to 16 games, just two of them nonconference contests, and banned their coaches, McGuire and Case, from recruiting outside the Atlantic Coast Conference's regional boundaries.

Friday added to the self-inflicted damage on May 22 in a meeting with the combined university trustees. Previously he, Aycock, and Caldwell had decided that they held the power to make the decisions without the trustees' approval. Friday truly could have lowered the boom on both NC State and Carolina. But his solution was to limit scholarships from areas outside ACC borders to just two a year. That penalty, to which Everett Case surprisingly agreed, cooked McGuire, because he had concentrated his recruitment on the New York area since his arrival in Chapel Hill in 1952. But Case didn't get off scot-free. Friday's next move was to do away with Case's great holiday cash cow, the Dixie Classic, that had become a big moneymaker and, more recently, a source of scandal and point-shaving. When Friday presented the fait accompli to the trustees, they had no choice but to accede to his wishes.

Then, as Smith stated in his memoir, Chancellor Aycock wrote a tough letter to McGuire, firmly telling him that things had to change. Aycock reminded McGuire that his contract was up after the 1963 season and its renewal depended on several things, including the result of an NCAA "inspection" of the program that would take place after the 1961–62 season. That move did it for McGuire, who went up to Philadelphia to negotiate with Warriors owner Eddie Gottlieb. Gottlieb acceded to every demand, giving McGuire everything he wanted, including such perks as paid day-off trips to

Chapel Hill to visit his family plus a plush suite at the Cherry Hill
Inn in suburban New Jersey, across the Delaware River from Philadelphia. Best of all for McGuire was the chance to coach Wilt Chamberlain at the unstoppable peak of his career.

Then, in an evening meeting in early August with his wife, Pat,
and assistant, Smith, after he and Smith had run a clinic at Kutsher's
resort in the Catskills in New York, McGuire had a change of mind
and decided to stay in Chapel Hill. This came just a day after he had
decided to move to Philadelphia. But to be certain, McGuire paid a
visit to coaching legend Clair Bee, who convinced him to get out of
Carolina and take the pro job. McGuire told Smith he was going to
Philly, then asked him to come with him as his assistant, warning
him that "things don't look very good here [in Chapel Hill], and it
will be difficult to turn it around."

The 30-year-old coach refused the offer, telling McGuire that
his heart was in the college game and that he believed he had the
fiber to rescue the Carolina program from the troubles McGuire
feared would destroy it. McGuire then drove to Chancellor Aycock's
office and, with Smith waiting in his car, turned in his resignation. A
few minutes later, McGuire emerged and told young Smith the chancellor wanted to see him in the morning to formally offer the job.
"And you won't be the interim, either," McGuire said.

Longtime North Carolina broadcaster Woody Durham's 2014
recollection of what transpired back in 1961 fits Smith's account in
A Coach's Life. "Coach McGuire told Chancellor Aycock he was leaving," Durham said to me. "Chancellor Aycock had great respect for
the way Dean handled himself when McGuire left. We had NCAA
recruiting violations. Carolina could only play 16 games his first year.
Chancellor Aycock said he asked McGuire as he was leaving the
office when he resigned, 'Would it be okay if I talked to Dean Smith
about the job?' And he said yes.

"'Matter of fact, he's outside in the car,' McGuire said.

"'Send him in here,' Aycock said. Within 10 minutes, Dean Smith was the new Carolina coach."

"Frank really wanted Dean to get the job after him," Donnie Walsh said. "Frank told me later that he had no idea Dean would become one of the greatest coaches of all time. He was very proud of that. No matter what, they competed fiercely against each other [on the court]. No matter what, they always retained a very close relationship [off the court]."

The next morning, Aycock formally offered Smith the job at $9,200 a year (approximately $74,000 today) and told him there would be no national search. Saying he believed in him, the chancellor appointed Smith the permanent head coach, as McGuire said he would. They shook hands on the deal. "Give me a team the university can be proud of and don't worry about winning and losing," Aycock told Smith. "If you do the things I've asked of you, you will have a job here as long as I'm chancellor." That was Aycock's way of clearly warning the young man when he said, "Don't cheat, and graduate your players."

That's how Friday handled Smith when he gave him the job. As Frank Deford observed in a 1982 profile for *Sports Illustrated*, a long-forgotten folk tale had it that Chancellor Aycock hired Smith as an instrument to deemphasize basketball at Carolina. Friday's rejoinder to Deford 21 years later was to the point: "I ain't that big a fool." Friday, though, was well aware that Smith provided a drab, rather quiet contrast to the outgoing dapper dandy that was McGuire. "It was obvious to me that he was smart, and there was something strong about this guy."

The first order of business for Smith, who needed to win to keep his first head coaching job now that he had it, was to get some players, any players who could play at all. And he was stuck in his first year. None of the new ones he recruited in 1961–62 could come from New York or anywhere else out of state. Gone from McGuire's last team were All-Americas York Larese and Doug Moe from New York and 6-foot-8 center Dick Kepley from Roanoke, Virginia, who had grown close to Smith as his assistant coach, but who could not play for him as head coach.

"North Carolina was so good and such a great school, and I loved it. I have very great feelings about the school," Walsh recalled from the reflective distance of 55 years when we spoke in 2015. "Going there from New York and the change of cultures taught me a lot."

It also had a profound effect on McGuire's last recruit, Billy Cunningham, who turned out to be a Hall of Famer for Smith, the new Carolina head man. "Dean had his hands full and could not recruit out of the state," Cunningham said, but it was much worse than that in the eyes of a native New Yorker who grew up in an integrated universe back in Brooklyn. "At that time, it was segregation, and all we could recruit were white players. The basketball players we got were not top quality that North Carolina would have. I was a freshman when Dean took over." And Cunningham was a sophomore in the fall of 1962 when he became eligible to play.

NCAA rules in 1961–62 still forbade freshmen from playing varsity ball in any sport. "We were probably better than the varsity," Cunningham said. "Yes, Dean had his hands full at that time."

To make matters worse, Smith lost the services of starters Yogi Poteet and Ken McComb to academic probation. "We lost a couple of our main players due to academics," Walsh said. "That took one of our big men and another good guy off the team."

The two star veterans on Smith's shrunken first Carolina team were point guard Larry Brown and his running mate, Walsh. "I grew up in New York and went to North Carolina. I stayed in Chapel Hill for 7 years," Walsh said.

Smith had to deal with that reduced schedule in his first year as head coach, just 16 regular season games and the ACC postseason tournament. "Because of the scandals that happened, they deemphasized and we didn't play that many games," Walsh said. Smith had to bide his time and struggle through that first year with its truncated 16-game schedule that saw the Tar Heels open with a 6-and-2 record, lose 4 conference games in midseason, and finish with an ACC tournament loss to South Carolina, 57–55, for an 8–9 record, the only losing season in Dean Smith's career as a player or coach.

It was obvious to Walsh, who had seen and admired Frank McGuire's operation, that his replacement was quite an operator himself. "Dean was a good man, a really good man. Specifically, he dealt with his teams in a way that was unique," Walsh said. "He dealt with everybody the same way. His advice to you was the same advice he gave to the star. Except he would tell the star, 'You should go on to pro basketball.' He was open and true to himself. He never cursed, unlike many coaches. He was unique and a great coach."

For the next 32 seasons, Smith followed the rules and Chancellor Aycock's admonitions to a T. As Walsh sees it, Smith was the supreme trendsetter in game preparation and execution, paving the way for the others. "There are a lot of things teams have done for the last 20 years, and he wasn't given credit for being such a great innovator for the game."

The basketball part of it was unique, but there was much more. "The other part of it was he used peer pressure," Walsh said. "He didn't yell at you. When you made a mistake on the floor, he would just say, 'Okay, Donnie is not doing the right thing, and we're all gonna run.' I mean sprint. So you make a mistake, and your teammates say okay. But you make another mistake, and now these guys say, 'Come on.' You make three or four mistakes, and these guys are ready to tear your head off."

Billy Cunningham has always retained vivid memories of Dean Smith's practice sessions. "He was a stickler. Everything had to be precise from the amount of minutes you would go in practice," Cunningham said. "We'd go from one drill to the next. I hear so much today about analytics. He was doing that stuff back in the '60s. Now it's the fad, how to evaluate teams and players. He had all that information at his fingertips. He was a math major, and he had total recall on every bit of information."

That control carried forth off the court, where Smith was a quiet but oh-so-effective whip cracker. Nobody could put anything over on him. "He knew everything that was happening on and off the court," Cunningham said. "We had Bobby Lewis from Washington, DC, when I was a senior and he was a sophomore. We went out to this party one night with our wives of today, and we had a few beers and a good time. We got called into the office the next morning, and I was told I was off the team because I was the captain and a senior and was breaking the rules. Thank goodness he gave me another chance. He knew everything you were doing in the classroom and off the court. I had an awful feeling in the pit of my stomach. It was like you knew it was coming. Begging for another chance was an understatement. Once it was over, it was never mentioned again. It was over and done with, and he knew he didn't have to do it again. Kids are going to do these things, as it is the nature of being a teenager in college. You can't hold grudges."

When Cunningham's playing career ended in 1976, he immediately moved to the bench as coach of his Philadelphia 76ers. In 1983, the Sixers added their best rebounder since Wilt Chamberlain in Moses Malone, and augmented him with Dr. J (Julius Erving), Maurice Cheeks, Andrew Toney, and Bobby Jones to beat the Los Angeles Lakers and capture the franchise's third (and, to date, last) NBA title. Every summer, Cunningham would make a pilgrimage to his mecca in Chapel Hill for some lessons from his college coach. "When I became a coach, I would take my film and Dean would take his. We'd spend 2 or 3 days. We would look at each other's films, go out on the floor, discuss various situations, and talk basketball for 5 or 6 hours, then play a few holes of golf," Cunningham said. "When you hear the word *family*, that's what it's all about. Michael Jordan and 99 percent of the players thought the world of him."

8 | THE FIGHT TO CAPTURE THE ACC

SUDDENLY THAT SUMMER OF 1961, 30-year-old Dean Smith had landed one of college basketball's top jobs and had to begin it with his hands virtually tied. He was also getting off to a late start against the rest of the ACC and his Tobacco Road rivals: Duke, Wake Forest, and the NC State Wolfpack, who remained dangerous despite their own probation. Wake Forest was ready in 1961–62 to make a run at the national title after the Deacons beat Clemson to win the ACC tournament. The next year, Vic Bubas and Duke had the championship ingredients, led by Player of the Year Art Heyman and Jeff Mullins. Carolina was improving, finishing at 15–6 and 10–4 in conference play. But they weren't driving on the glory road. Not yet.

Moreover, like latter-day comedian Rodney Dangerfield, Smith didn't get any respect. Take Ernie Accorsi, a future championship-caliber NFL general manager with the Colts, Browns, and Giants, for instance. Accorsi was a student at Wake Forest late that summer of 1961 when he turned on the TV set at his Theta Chi fraternity house and sat with his fraternity brothers as they saw Smith's introduction to the ACC. "I was watching the 6 o'clock news, and they had the press conference," Accorsi said. "It was on about a minute and a half.

I watched this soft-spoken guy, compared to charismatic Frank McGuire. Here's this guy talking into his tie knot. So I told my fraternity brothers, 'We're not going to have to worry about North Carolina anymore!'

"That's one of the great predictions of all time!" Accorsi said, before roaring in self-deprecating laughter.

For Smith, though, working with McGuire had been akin to matriculating at graduate school for a basketball coach. And, as noted, when McGuire was out recruiting in New York, Smith got to work practices and install game plans as well as his own wrinkles. Moreover, he had a full portfolio of Kansas experiences to supplement and enhance the assortment of plays he had been developing in his stops at KU, Air Force basketball in Europe, and his time with Bob Spear at the Air Force Academy. Defense came first. And he introduced new touches when he got the job itself. One was the "tired" signal a player was to display, because Smith wanted everyone as fresh as possible at all times during a game. "He instructed players to give an uplifted fist to show when they were tired," longtime Tar Heels radio announcer Woody Durham said.

The Tar Heels played their first game under Smith on December 2, 1961, at home in Woollen Gym. It started out inauspiciously, a bit rough around the edges. "Coach had forgotten to get a game ball, properly pumped up and so forth," Durham said, as Smith also confessed in his memoir. The official kindly reminded him that a pumped-up ball was needed to play the game, and Smith sent his manager, Elliott Murnick, to the end of the bench to pick out one of the practice balls. The game went ahead and Carolina moved ahead, but Coach Smith noticed the team was not running the material they had been working on in practice. He called time-out, and they got straightened out. A bit later, he noticed several players pumping their fists into the air. That's terrific, he thought. Larry Brown gave the tired signal, and the coach was so keyed up he forgot he was giving him the tired signal.

"He was trying to get a win," Durham said. As it happened, North Carolina beat Virginia handily, 80–46. The Tar Heels' next game was at Clemson, where they had trouble handling the zone press before escaping with a two-point win.

On January 6, 1962, Notre Dame arrived in Charlotte flat, and Smith had the Heels ready. They opened a 47–15 lead at the half and held an 88–46 lead with 8 minutes to go when Smith called off the dogs and cleared the bench. The final score was 99–80. Irish coach Johnny Jordan, a longtime member of the coaching fraternity, came down after the buzzer and told Coach Smith, "Thank you so much. That won't look bad in the Chicago papers." With that, they retreated to Smith's hotel room to bend their elbows and enjoy some postgame Chinese food.

After defeating NC State 66–56 at home on January 17, 1962, the Tar Heels were a surprising 6–2. Then came four straight crushing conference losses, to Duke and Maryland on the road and to Wake Forest and NC State at home in Woollen Gym. With those four defeats reality set in on Smith, who admitted in his memoir that he had experienced self-doubt about being a basketball coach. What had appeared to be a promising season despite the loss of four starters, two of them to academic ineligibility, had turned sour. When the team lost the ACC tournament opener to South Carolina 57–55, their season record ended at just 8–9, the only time in his coaching career that a Dean Smith team did not finish with a winning record.

Larry Brown, who led the Tar Heels with 16.5 points a game, and Walsh, a 56 percent shooter who averaged 13.4, both made All-ACC second team. "I think I was Dean's first graduate assistant," Walsh said. "So I helped coach the freshman team. My last year, I was on law review. I was all set to practice law, but I got to that fork in the road and decided to stay with basketball. So I didn't take the bar examination my first year out of law school. I went with Frank to South Carolina. It was years later when I took [the bar] in South Carolina and passed it. I was in law school when Kennedy was assassinated. It just didn't fit. In our minds, it happened to Abraham Lincoln, but not in our time."

After that first season ended, Smith got a call from Lexington, Kentucky, from fellow Kansas alum Adolph Rupp. Rupp reminded Smith that both had played for and learned the game from the same man, Phog Allen—Rupp in the Class of '23, Smith in the Class of '53. "Dean, we need to get our schools together and play," Rupp said. He suggested a 10-year series, six games in Lexington, four in Chapel Hill. Smith agreed to take the offer, one-sided as it was, to Athletic Director Chuck Erickson.

As Smith wrote in *A Coach's Life*, Erickson said, "Oh, everybody's calling and trying to schedule us now. We're center cut. We've got a good name and no team." After that discussion with his AD, Smith accepted the Kentucky offer. The two schools signed a contract, and North Carolina won seven of the 10 games in that deal with Rupp.

"He went to Kentucky and won," Accorsi recalled of the game he watched on TV. It took place in Lexington on December 17, 1962, at Kentucky's Memorial Coliseum. With 13 points and 13 rebounds, Carolina sophomore Billy Cunningham controlled the inside, as Larry Brown hit for 19 and Yogi Poteet, back from a year's enforced leave due to academic ineligibility, scored 17 more to stake the Tar Heels to a 68–66 victory. The most lasting impression Accorsi took from that game was a reporter's postgame interview with Kentucky's candid coach. "Adolph Rupp said, 'I've never seen a team run patterns that perfectly in my life!'"

That, of course, was the way it would be for Carolina over the next 3½ decades. Smith would cover all contingencies and run as close to perfect patterns as a person could instill into his team. Game after game. Year after year. A big plus came in 1962 that with the exception of New Yorkers Brown and Cunningham—both of them McGuire recruits—the rest of his starting lineup, unlike McGuire's, was composed of North Carolinians with names like Ray Respess of Pantego, Charlie Shaffer of Chapel Hill (a two-sport athlete whose father was director of development for the university), and Yogi Poteet of Hendersonville, in the western part of the state. That is not to say that he filled his lineup with subquality players. "Certainly Coach Smith went after the best players and didn't zero in on any one area," noted Woody Durham. The truly great ones would come in due course.

Smith explained in his memoir that his ulterior motives for scheduling the likes of Kentucky, Indiana, other Big Ten teams, Houston, UCLA, and Kansas, especially on the road, was to toughen up his charges. "When you play a strong team, your weaknesses are exposed, and then you have time work on them before the tournament starts in March," he wrote. Smith warned against scheduling softies to build up a record and argued that by playing challenging games, the team would learn from their losses.

He also used those games to perfect his delay game, in which the Heels would hold the ball late to lock down victories. The famed four corners maneuver came about when Larry Brown, failing in practice to recognize a zone defense change to man-to-man, drove right by his man and passed to a teammate for an easy layup. "Larry Brown was one of best on the first team and the catalyst when he brought four corners to Carolina basketball," Durham said when we spoke in the summer of 2014. "The big reason for using four corners was to get the big lead, then use the clock with the four corners. It took a long time for other coaches to adjust to it."

"I think he started it in the '60s with Coach Brown," Phil Ford, Smith's three-time All-America point guard of the mid-'70s, told me. "I think I get some credit for it. For the four corners to work, you need five good ball handlers, five good free throw shooters, five good rebounders. We wanted to get them out of the zone. Walter Davis had the excellent short jump shot. Generally, we wanted to run backdoors when we got them into man-to-man. A lot of time, out of frustration, the opposing team would come back and hurry a shot. We would take our time, and by the time we had them down nine, we were on our way."

Smith's accidental discovery of the effectiveness of the four corners worked because from years of experience he knew a good thing when he saw it. "He came up with it here, not from Kansas," Durham stressed. "It came about because he was such a studious coach."

Smith's "Carolina Way" was the practical application of techniques that had been practiced and tried and had become true. The many little things Smith innovated and put into use certainly impressed Durham when he observed them in action, and they still do to this day.

"He did so many things off the court. Players had to thank guys who made assists. Managers had to wipe off the benches after the time-outs before they sat down. He was the unique innovator in the game as far as I'm concerned," Durham said, something that became axiomatic well before Smith retired and, of course, long before his passing.

That 1962–63 team went 15–6 behind Cunningham and Larry Brown, who led in assists. Brown joined the all-amateur US Olympic team a year later and, in Tokyo, became North Carolina's first gold medal basketball player as the United States beat the Soviets 73–59.

The other US gold medalists were Jim "Bad News" Barnes, Bill Bradley, Joe Caldwell, Mel Counts, Richard Davies, Walt Hazzard, Luke Jackson, Pete McCaffrey, Jeff Mullins, Jerry Shipp, and George Wilson. Brown returned to Chapel Hill to assist Dean Smith from 1965 to 1967.

The Tar Heels, though, were operating in the shadow of Duke's well-tuned operation, coached by Everett Case's Hoosier disciple Vic Bubas. "Duke fans don't remember Vic Bubas now," Durham recalled. "They were awfully good when Bubas was there. Bubas recruited unlike any other coach in those days, lining up players before their senior years in high school. He landed two prized catches: Art Heyman from Long Island, after he defected from a pledge to play for Frank McGuire at North Carolina. And [he] lured away Jeff Mullins of Lexington, Kentucky, from Adolph Rupp."

By 1963, Heyman was the national player of the year as Bubas and Duke reached the Final Four in Louisville, ranked number two in the country behind twice-defending national champion Cincinnati. Unfortunately for the Blue Devils, they had to face George Ireland's third-ranked Loyola of Chicago Ramblers in the national semifinal. Loyola routed the Blue Devils 94–75 just a week after they dispatched the all-white Mississippi State Bulldogs in the historic Mideast Regional semifinal on the campus of Michigan State University. The Bulldogs had ignored a court order and left their segregated state under the cover of darkness to fly to East Lansing and face the Chicago-based team that started four black players. Loyola won 61–51 and returned the following night to easily beat Illinois 79–64 and advance to the Final Four.

A week later in the championship game in Freedom Hall, two-time defending champ Cincinnati led Loyola by 15 points with 10 minutes remaining when their coach, Ed Jucker, ordered a stall, not a delay game. The Ramblers, who were so much more than a runaway racehorse team, clamped down, stymied the Bearcats, and battled back. Trailing by two with 12 seconds left, All-America Jerry Harkness nailed a 12-footer from the baseline with 4 seconds left to send the game into overtime tied at 54–all. In the overtime, each team scored four points before Loyola came downcourt and held the ball for the last shot. From the left corner, under pressure, Harkness rose, saw teammate Leslie Hunter open at the foul line, and hit him with a pass. Hunter's shot bounced off the rim and into the hands of fellow Nashville native Vic Rouse, who put it back up off the glass just ahead of the buzzer to give Loyola a 60–58 victory and the national championship. There would be no three-peat for the Bearcats.

A year later Heyman was gone, but Mullins navigated Duke to the title game against John Wooden's unbeaten UCLA Bruins. "Bubas had Chuck Daly as his assistant by then," Durham said. With a short lineup and the tallest starter just 6 feet 4 inches, Wooden employed a relentless zone press led by Walt Hazzard, Gail Goodrich, and Keith Erickson to win going away, 99–83, the first of 10 titles for UCLA in the next 12 years.

Smith and North Carolina also had to overcome Wake Forest and their flamboyant coach, Horace "Bones" McKinney. McKinney, who played 2 years at NC State and finished at Carolina in 1946 after the war, played in the NBA for Washington and Boston before turning to coaching. Led by forward Lenny Chappell, who physically resembled Al Capp's cartoon star Li'l Abner, and future NBC and CBS analyst Billy Packer, McKinney's 1962 Demon Deacons reached the Final Four, where they lost to Ohio State.

Smith saw what he had to do. Wake Forest and Duke were both all-white, typical Southern teams, slow and lacking the quickness Loyola and UCLA utilized to strike from everywhere on the court.

To beat his in-state rivals, he would need to recruit a different kind of player.

That's exactly what he did. After 1961–62, Smith never coached another losing season. He started to bring in his own players, and they began to win the very next year, going 15–6 behind Cunningham's strong play. Then Cunningham let his grades slip and had to leave school. "I was out of school for 6 months. I messed up academically," Cunningham recalled. "Somehow I found a way to get out of there in 4 years. I decided I didn't want to feel the lash from my father again."

By 1965, Cunningham would be named ACC Player of the Year. Equally important was the way Cunningham responded as a leader on January 6 when Wake Forest routed North Carolina 107–85 in Winston-Salem. This was the Tar Heels' fourth straight defeat dating back to December 19. The team arrived by bus outside Woolen Gym shortly after midnight to find an effigy of Coach Smith hanging from a tree. Future baseball writer Peter Gammons "was on that bus going back. He was an undergrad covering the Tar Heels," Ernie Accorsi recalled. "He was there the night the bus got back and the effigy was hanging. That's how bad things were for Dean at that time."

Cunningham confirmed the presence of the student writer covering for the *Daily Tar Heel*. "Peter Gammons, the writer, was on that bus." Another *Daily Tar Heel* guy was Curry Kirkpatrick, who would gain fame covering basketball for *Sports Illustrated*. "Dean was getting killed by getting hanged in effigy in front of the gym and by these great writers of today [Gammons and Kirkpatrick] covering the beat on the *Daily*," Cunningham said. "They said he had no talent to coach."

A furious Cunningham and teammate Billy Galantai—a fellow Brooklyn native—tore down the dummy and let the students who had waited for them to arrive know where the team stood regarding their coach. The two players told the crowd to blame them and their teammates, not Smith. "'He's a great coach. You've got to stop this bullshit,'" they said. "And we went back to our dorms. That was the end of it," Galantai said to WNCN News decades later. "The crowd dispersed, and that was the end of the whole thing."

Future Carolina athletic director and present ACC Commissioner John Swofford was a North Carolina student and football player under Bill Dooley in the late '60s. He, too, recalled that moment of crisis for Dean Smith and the Chapel Hill campus. "That effigy incident's never been forgotten over the years. I think it meant a lot to [Dean] that Billy Cunningham and teammates got off the bus and took it down," Swofford said.

"Billy Cunningham is the most impressive man of that time. Nobody would have thought that in those days," Donnie Walsh said. "Billy is an unusually good man, and competent man."

The effigy episode began an eventful week for Smith and North Carolina basketball. The Tar Heels came back to beat sixth-ranked Duke in Durham 65–62. Then came another tough loss, 65–62 to NC State. Once again, some unknown goof strung up a cloth dummy on a tree branch and lit it on fire. As Smith noted, that second one is all but forgotten, but it led him to consider his life and where it was headed. He went home after that incident and stayed up until the wee hours reading Catherine Marshall's book *Beyond Our Selves*. There he found this passage that he cited in his memoir: "Crisis brings us face-to-face with our inadequacy, and our inadequacy in turn leads us to the inexhaustible sufficiency of God. This is the power of helplessness, a principle written into the fabric of life." From that, Smith rededicated himself to "surrendering his life to the gift of power within."

A few days later, many of the Carolina players were booed during introductions before they played a strong New York University team. That night they clicked on all cylinders and won going away, 100–78.

From that moment forward, Smith writes, "we had turned the corner." The Tar Heels went on to win nine of their next 11 games.

Yet despite their run of success, the Tar Heels arguably weren't even the best team in the state at the time. That team was Winston-Salem State, a black school coached by Clarence "Big House" Gaines whose Rams were led by Philadelphia basketball legend Earl "the Pearl" Monroe. The Pearl led the nation in scoring in 1966–67, averaging 41.5 points a game. In a postseason pickup game in Portsmouth, Virginia, in the early spring of 1967, people who were there claimed that the Pearl rang up 40 points on national player of the year Jimmy Walker, as he held the Providence All-American scoreless. Whether or not Dean Smith heard about that, he did know he could not win big until he made the moves that would define his tenure and place in the lore of the game. He had to land the right sort of players.

As Harvey Araton wrote in the *New York Times* when Smith died in February 2015, Smith made the time to befriend the coaches of the black colleges. He never scheduled Winston-Salem State, as that was not done in those days of Jim Crow athletics below the Mason-Dixon Line, but he did make a lifelong friend in Coach Big House Gaines and his son, Clarence Jr., a longtime NBA scout with the Chicago Bulls in the Jordan era and later with the New York Knicks. "I went back to Chapel Hill and got to meet Coach Smith," Clarence Jr. said. "We talked about my father. You could tell the respect was mutual."

"It was not just what Smith said, more of what he had done," Araton wrote. "Earlier in the decade, Smith had recommended Big House Gaines for board membership on the National Association of Basketball Coaches. By 1989, the senior Gaines was president of the group, a position Smith had already held."

"It was something that my father treasured, being involved in that way after all those years," Clarence Jr. said. "As far as Dean Smith the man is concerned, he's become a role model for what a coach should be," the elder Gaines said on the day before Smith overtook Rupp. It took one to know one.

To get going on his plan, Smith first had to follow Everett Case's admonition and get the basketball team out of Woollen Gym and into a better facility. In 1965, they moved into Carmichael Auditorium, an extremely loud facility where Carolina would go 169–20 over the next 21 years, the ultimate home court advantage. Built on a comparative shoestring because the state refused to fund a totally new arena, Carmichael shared Woollen Gym's eastern wall, and the building's seating capacity was just over 8,000 (later it was bumped up to 9,500 or so). When the men moved into the new Dean E. Smith Center in 1986, the women took over Carmichael. The building was closed for a year for renovations from the spring of 2008 until December 2009 and renamed Carmichael Arena.

"Carmichael was finished just after I left school. It was the 1963–64 team that opened Carmichael," Woody Durham said. Smith still had Billy Cunningham as his cornerstone for a middle of the road team that finished 12–12 and went 6–8 in conference play, but Smith was busy building the sort of team he wanted, thus making North Carolina the dominant team it became.

"Bob Lewis and Larry Miller were his first two great players," Ernie Accorsi said. Those two provided Smith with his start to coaching greatness as they formed the foundation the coach wanted. They starred on his first Final Four teams. Lewis came from Washington, DC, where he became a *Parade* All-American for 1963 at St. John's College High School, averaging 25.4 points a game. At Carolina, Lewis rang up 27.6 points a game in the 1965–66 season and set a school record that stands to this day when he scored 49 points against Florida State on December 16, 1965. Lewis was named

All-American in 1966 and '67, and his number 22 was retired and now hangs in the rafters of the Dean Smith Center.

"I thought Larry Miller was the key in turning the program around," Cunningham said. Miller, like Cunningham a left-hander, was a 1964 *Parade* All-American who led Catasauqua High School outside Allentown to the Pennsylvania state championship. Smith had to battle Duke for Miller, the second-most-wanted high school player in America in 1964–65 behind UCLA-bound Lew Alcindor of Power Memorial Academy in New York. When he won out and landed Miller, North Carolina and Smith had gained the post position for dominance in the ACC.

Once he landed Miller, Smith quickly learned he had to deal with a kid who would push the envelope. That became evident as both Frank Deford and fellow *Sports Illustrated* writer Alexander Wolff noted that when Miller arrived on campus, he told the coach he would *not* attend what had been compulsory chapel services. He explained that if he didn't do it at home, then why should he do it in college? Smith thought about it and agreed with the player. End of what could have been a nasty dispute.

The spring of 1967 also brought down the curtain on Larry Brown's 2-year stint as Dean Brown's assistant. Brown still was in demand as a player and signed on with the New Orleans Buccaneers of the American Basketball Association, owned by seven men including future TV shock host Morton Downey Jr. Brown ran the show on the floor as point guard, joining another Smith favorite, Doug Moe. Brown was league MVP and Moe a first team all-star that year before both were traded after the season to the Oakland Oaks, another ABA franchise.

Brown's departure cleared the way for Smith to hire Bill Guthridge, a longtime friend from Kansas State. Guthridge, who would turn 30 in July, was a guard for Tex Winter's Final Four team in 1958 and joined Winter as an assistant in 1962, 2 years after graduating with a bachelor's degree in mathematics and working a high school coaching job in Scott City, Kansas. Guthridge brought many top qualities to Chapel Hill that included his natural, strong relationship with Smith and the top quality Smith recognized in his colleague: a superb sense of organization. They would be together for the next 30 years, until Smith convinced the athletic director to turn over the coaching mantle to his ally and a man who had become, by that time, his close friend.

Back in Chapel Hill, Larry Miller became ACC Player of the Year and ACC tournament MVP in 1967. "That was the beginning of [Coach Smith's] Final Four teams," Woody Durham recalled. "The first Final Four team was the end of 1966–67 season. They finished 26–6 and won the ACC tournament."

The Tar Heels fell 76–62 to Dayton in the Final Four semifinals and lost the third-place game to Houston, but they had a place at the elite table at last. The next year, they reached the Final Four at the Los Angeles Sports Arena with a 27–3 record, where they handled Fred Taylor's last Big Ten champion Ohio State Buckeyes in a relatively easy 80–66 victory in the opener. Everyone took notice in the nightcap when UCLA got revenge on top-ranked Houston for their midseason loss in the Astrodome with a resounding 101–69 rout.

"To this day, I believe we had the best team in the country that year, player by player," Miller said 37 years later to *Tar Heel Monthly*. Lewis was graduated, but they had sophomore Charles Scott, who was the most athletic player Smith had recruited to this time. Then, Miller said, Smith asked his players if they wanted to run with UCLA, and Miller said he did. "We can beat them." Smith, though, waved them off. Miller continued, "I believe to this day we had more talent than they did." But UCLA got stronger as the game moved ahead and won Wooden's fourth title in five years, 78–55.

Miller went on to star in the ABA, had a long real estate career in North Carolina and Virginia, then went back home. "He's almost a recluse back in his hometown in Pennsylvania, and I don't know of anybody who's seen him in the last 20 years," Cunningham recalled.

"They lost to Purdue and Drake in the 1969 Final Four," Durham said. Needless to say, no more effigies would be hanged on the North Carolina campus.

9 | INTEGRATION COMES TO THE SOUTH

"I'VE NEVER BEEN AROUND ANYBODY else who had such a remarkable ability to remember names," John Swofford said of his friend and former Tar Heel colleague Dean Smith. "He went out of his way in that regard. It didn't matter who it was, from the chancellor to a janitor. He treated everyone so well."

As an assistant coach at the university, Smith continued his work with pastor Dr. Robert Seymour at the Owen T. Binkley Memorial Baptist Church in Chapel Hill, and he stepped up his quest to integrate his team and, with it, the Atlantic Coast Conference. The Reverend Seymour was especially anxious to end segregation in the South.

An early test came with a decision to test the new "public accommodations" required by Title II of the Civil Rights Act, signed into law on July 2, 1964, by President Lyndon Johnson. Bob Seymour asked Coach Smith to join the minister and a black student and future minister named James Forbes for dinner at one of Chapel Hill's best restaurants, the Pines. It was the place where the North Carolina basketball team had eaten its pregame meals since Frank McGuire's time, but it remained a segregation holdout.

In his memoir, Smith wrote that Dr. Seymour was confident that the Pines would serve him, Forbes, and the coach if Smith joined them. "I, of course, agreed to go and did not really consider it a big deal. Years afterwards, some reports have made it sound like I personally integrated every restaurant in Chapel Hill!" Smith wrote. "The truth is, I was just an assistant coach, and hardly the most influential person in town, an unlikely standard bearer for integration. But Bob knew the management, and they valued the business of the basketball team. My presence would make the point. We ordered, were served, visited, and ate without incident. That was it. How ridiculous it all seems now!"

"Dean grew up in a church-oriented family. The church was the center of his life when he was growing up," Dr. Seymour said. Coach Smith's sister, Joan, graduated with a master's in Christian education from the University of Chicago. She lived her final years in the health center at Carol Woods in Chapel Hill.

Away from his office and the basketball community, Smith continued his close relationship with the church. "Dean and I had a very good friendship. I did not interfere with his professional duties," the pastor, now 92, said in the summer of 2015. "He would ask me to review something he had written. During basketball season, he would often call me and ask me to tell him something Martin Luther King Jr. had said that 'I can tell my boys to give something to think about at practice.' Whenever Dean was in town, he was at church."

Again, that was characteristic of Smith's Kansas upbringing. A kind word, consideration, knowing with whom he was speaking, and striving to be the best at whatever he did. Smith had always sought the best players since he became a basketball coach, whether it be as an assistant at KU, in the Air Force, at the Air Force Academy, and as head man at North Carolina, where it was imperative that he land talent that could compete with the best college programs—schools such as UCLA, Indiana, Ohio State, Kansas, Notre Dame, Louisville, Kentucky, and other powers of that era. That held especially true for his own Atlantic Coast Conference, dealing with the likes of Duke, NC State, Wake Forest, Maryland, Virginia, and the rugged Southeastern Conference as well.

Dean Smith in the early '60s would not fool himself thinking that the ACC, SEC, and others schools in the South could measure up year in and year out against the others for one simple reason. They had no black players. None. Smith long had been bound and determined to change all of that for all time. Integration was overdue. The University of North Carolina long had been the most liberal school in the South, one that ranked with such other great public American institutions as Cal-Berkeley, UCLA, Michigan, Illinois, Wisconsin, Texas, Penn State, and Minnesota. There was no doubt that Smith already was as race-aware as any basketball coach in the country. It was a continuum of his upbringing in Emporia and exposure to the changes in education in Topeka when he was finishing college down the way at the University of Kansas.

Carolina's beloved late president, Frank Porter Graham, served briefly in the US Senate in the early 1950s. He was so admired by Illinois's legendary Democratic senator Paul Douglas that he called Graham one of two true saints he'd ever met and known in public life. The other was famed Chicago social worker and activist Jane Addams, the first American woman to be awarded the Nobel Peace Prize. Smith held Graham in equally high esteem. He knew that Graham had wanted to integrate the university well ahead of the Supreme Court's 1954 decision in *Brown v. Board of Education*. Now times were changing in America in both the South and North. "This was the beginning of the civil rights movement. Our congregation had a policy of giving different members certain assignments to work in the community," Dr. Seymour said. "We told Dean, 'Your assignment is to find the best athlete in America and integrate the Atlantic Coast Conference. If you can do that, you will have done well. Your job is to find the top black player.' He took that ball and ran with it."

So Smith went looking for his first black basketball player. He developed a network of black coaches and administrators in the state. He first cast his lot back in 1962 with a Greensboro high schooler of superb basketball ability who ranked third in his class. Unfortunately, Lou Hudson's SAT scores were not quite high enough to gain UNC admission, which was above the ACC standard of 800. Despite his awareness that standardized tests were and are culturally biased, there was nothing Coach Smith could do to change that fact or the university's policy. So Hudson enrolled at the University of Minnesota, where he became an All-American, All-NBA for years with the Atlanta Hawks, then a well-respected businessman in both Atlanta and, after 1984, in Park City, Utah, where he became a real estate investor and served on the city council.

Smith had thought he found the right man in 1964. His name was William Cooper. Cooper wanted to be an achiever, but more so in the classroom than on the basketball floor. He enrolled at UNC, played on the freshman team in the 1964–65 season, and performed well. No frills, no fancy stuff, no undue publicity. In the first week of varsity practice the next fall, Cooper came to Coach Smith and told him he had to quit basketball. He told the coach he wanted to be a business major, but had flunked an accounting exam and had to quit. Smith urged him to think about it. Cooper came back 2 days later and said he would give up basketball to concentrate on his studies. And he did.

Instead of having the first black player in the ACC with Cooper, Smith had to set out again and find someone else, someone strong and capable. Looking ahead to 1965, Smith knew he had to find that high-quality black player and do it ahead of other ACC and southern schools that were ready to make their own moves.

Charles Scott was a 6-foot-5 forward from New York City who was enrolled at all-black Laurinburg Institute, about 90 miles south of Chapel Hill. Davidson College and their coach, Charles "Lefty" Driesell, were leading a pack of suitors that included North Carolina, Duke, West Virginia, and several Ivy League schools chasing after Scott. Scott, who came from a ramshackle apartment in Harlem where he had to care for his alcoholic father after his mother moved out with his three sisters, attended Stuyvesant High School in Manhattan for 1 year, where he was one of the few blacks in the school.

Scott had earned his spurs at the Rucker Park playground in Harlem, playing on the same team as Power High School's Lou Alcindor. He desperately wanted out and had heard of a place in North Carolina that sounded right for him. It was the all-black Laurinburg Institute in Scotland County, just above the South Carolina border, and he landed a scholarship. Scott validated that trust as valedictorian of his class of 1966 and soon was regarded as the top high school player in that section of North Carolina. As Smith wrote in *A Coach's Life*, Davidson coach Lefty Driesell was confident he would land Scott. He had taken him out to eat to a nice place in Laurinburg and all went well. Then, when Driesell got Scott to visit Davidson, the recruit went out to eat with Laurinburg headmaster Frank McDuffie Jr. and his wife. As they took their seats, the waitress walked over, gestured, and said the words that always sting: "This is for whites only over here." Scott and the McDuffies got out of there and he withdrew his commitment.

Smith invited the three Scotts to Chapel Hill for Jubilee Weekend, a spring celebration that would feature a major concert starring Smokey Robinson and the Miracles and the Temptations. Freshman Dick Grubar was Scott's host, and Scott hung around with the players who would be his teammates if he decided to come to school. Smith and Scott talked, and as they did, the coach asked the player what he wanted to be called. He replied Charles, not Charlie. "Coach asked me to go to church with him," Scott recalled in an interview with *Newsday* columnist Greg Logan on February 8, 2015. "When you do that, you're getting into a personal circumstance other than just basketball."

At Binkley Memorial Baptist, Smith introduced Scott to Howard Lee, the first black mayor of Chapel Hill, and his wife, Lillian, both members of the congregation, an experience Scott has savored through the intervening years. "Everything was segregated, but he felt comfortable enough that he could take me to his church without feeling repercussions from the pastor or from the congregation," Scott told Logan. Most important, Scott noted that Smith treated him the same way he treated every other athlete he recruited. Players who would be his contemporaries, not seniors he never would know in school, showed him around. The player felt his treatment was natural and unforced. After church, Scott took off on his own and walked around town unchaperoned. By the end of his visit, he committed to North Carolina.

Then came time to clinch the deal. Smith drove to Laurinburg with Sports Information Director Bob Quincy to sign Charles Scott's letter of intent. "The first person they saw at the academy was Lefty Driesell," Woody Durham said. "Coach Smith went into the office and signed Charles Scott while Lefty was left standing in the lobby."

That was a triumph for Smith to be sure, but he was wise enough to know that things change. In 1969, Driesell signed on as head coach at Maryland and vowed to make Maryland the UCLA of the East. He went on a recruiting spree and landed an outstanding class led by national high school player of the year, 6-foot-11 Tom McMillen of Mansfield, Pennsylvania, a brilliant student and superior player. "Tom's parents didn't like the idea of Dean's being like a father to Tom," said Durham. "Tom had signed the grant-in-aid to Carolina, but his parents wouldn't sign it. When he left for school, Tom sent a telegram to Dean in his office. [It said] 'Going to Maryland for reasons you understand.'"

When we spoke, Lefty Driesell did not wish to discuss his relationship with Smith other than to say he considered him a friend. Of McMillen, though, he was happy to talk. "He was a superb basketball player, a professional, and Democratic congressman from Maryland. Dean Smith thought he had him, but he came to us." Concerning his academics, Driesell said, "The University of Maryland has had just one Rhodes Scholar. That person was and is Tom McMillen, not just the smartest player I ever saw, but the smartest person. Period." McMillen served as a University of Maryland regent from 2007 to 2015 until Maryland's Republican governor, Larry Hogan, caused a stir by refusing to reappoint the popular McMillen in favor of Robert Neall, the man McMillen had defeated in his 1986 race for Congress.

Driesell's 1969 recruits also included Len Elmore, who played in the NBA and who has been an announcer on college and NBA basketball telecasts for years, and Owen Brown of LaGrange, Illinois. Brown was the starting center for Lyons Township's Lions for 3½ years, leading his undefeated team to the Illinois state basketball championship in 1970. Owen graduated with Maryland's Class of 1975. A few months later, he died suddenly of a heart attack, a week before his 23rd birthday.

"Ralph Sampson came to the team banquet the season he was being recruited," Durham said. "The day before the announcement, I am told, he wore a Carolina T-shirt to school. The next day, he announced he was going to play at Virginia. He never did beat the Tar Heels in Chapel Hill."

Looking at the way things are in the 21st century, when black athletes dominate basketball and football in every region of the country, those of us, both black and white, who came of age in the '50s and '60s well remember that the best southern black athletes who were locked out at home—men such as Texan Bubba Smith and South Carolinian George Webster at Michigan State, Bobby Bell from North Carolina at Minnesota, and Illinois superstar backs J. C. Caroline of South Carolina and Arkansan Bobby Mitchell—flocked to northern schools or to the West Coast to play their games in the name of higher education. It is therefore wise to remember that Charles Scott was a true pioneer in the entire South. And for most of that time, he stood alone by going to an all-white bastion there. "Dean always called him Charles," John Swofford said. "That was out of respect. Integration was connecting all around the country. Charles Scott was a trailblazer, and no question that Dean helped him out." As Smith explained in his memoir, Scott stood alone, as he excelled on the court. Joe Lapchick was an Original Celtic with Nat Holman in the '20s, a tall (at that time) center standing 6 feet 5 inches, and the honored head coach at St. John's for a pair of 10-year tenures sandwiched around a decade with the New York Knicks in the fledgling years of the NBA. His son Richard, who helped found the Center for the Study of Sport at Northeastern University, was studying at UNC when Scott arrived in Chapel Hill. He took note when he saw the way Scott dominated play from his first start as a sophomore. In 1967–68, as Richard Lapchick wrote for ESPN.com, Scott "defined the modern-day UNC basketball legacy being built by Smith."

He became an All-American that season, leading Carolina to Coach Smith's first title game appearance as a head coach against the overwhelmingly powerful UCLA team of Lew Alcindor (later Kareem Abdul-Jabbar), Lucius Allen Jr., Mike Warren, and Lynn Shackleford. John Wooden's mighty Bruins cruised to a 78–55 win to claim the fourth of what would eventually number 10 titles in a 12-year span, but Scott had made his mark.

Scott had found a young woman from Durham named Margaret Holmes. They fell in love and eloped on June 1, 1968. As Art Chansky writes in his eloquent book *Game Changers*, trouble signs appeared early in the marriage. Scott still liked to hang out with his friends, male and female, many of them from nearby North Carolina College in Durham. Margaret would fix dinner every night, but he often was late or didn't bother to show up at all. While that was happening on his home front, Scott went to the wild and wooly Mexico City Olympics, where he won a gold medal as a member of the US Olympic basketball team.

Smith was rankled that postseason and again the next year when South Carolina's John Roche was named ACC Player of the Year over Scott, noting that despite Scott's being an All-American and member of the Olympic team, he was denied his conference's honor. ACC's sports information directors and media relations directors who conducted the vote overwhelmingly gave Roche the award. Smith minced no words years later in *A Coach's Life*, saying of the vote, "It was transparently racist."

"That was the only time in college that I felt things were done in a prejudicial manner," Scott told the Greensboro *News and Record* years later. Carolina came back in 1969 with a third straight appearance in the Final Four. Scott saved the Eastern Regional against Lefty Driesell and Davidson at Maryland's Cole Field House with the two most important baskets of the game, in a 32-point performance. He tied it at 85 with 1:30 left. Then, as Davidson was held for the last shot, Carolina's Gerald Tuttle took what Smith called an "epic" charge by Davidson's Jerry Kroll with 13 seconds left. Scott got the ball and from 30 feet out went up with 3 seconds to go and buried it for the 87–85 victory to send the Heels to the Final Four.

A week later in Louisville, Purdue came out smoking and North
Carolina had nothing left in reserve as Rick Mount scored 36 points
on 14-for-28 shooting, mostly from the twilight zone, to lead the
Boilermakers to the title game 92–65 as Scott had to settle for 16 in
his final NCAA tournament game. That was as far as Purdue could
go, as Lew Alcindor scored 37 points and UCLA overwhelmed the
Boilermakers 92–72 over their coach John Wooden's alma mater.

Scott and Smith stayed close long after college, Chansky wrote in
Game Changers. As the fall term at school began in 1969, both Scott
and his coach were caught in troubled marriages. Scott's wife, Margaret, was expecting a child and they still lived together in Durham, but
he was gone most of the time and seldom at home.

Smith was totally immersed in the basketball team. When he got
home from the office, he and Ann had nothing to say other than to
catch up on the doings of their three children. As Smith's sister,
Joan, told Chansky, "The guilt was incredible." The way Joan saw it,
they came from cultures that dictated, "'You stay married, no matter
what.' That ordeal made him search himself even more." Smith
moved into an apartment with assistant John Lotz. Lotz, a stylish
dresser, was an awful housekeeper. It got so bad that Smith felt like
moving back home, and did, twice. Finally, at long last, in 1973, the
Smith marriage ended in divorce. "It was a long, drawn-out, and a
painful thing," his sister said.

Scott tried to stay away from school and hang around Durham as
much as possible to avoid a campus caught up in the Black Student
Movement. The team started out strong and hit the skids, finishing
an 18–9 season with back-to-back losses, 95–93 to Virginia in the
first round of the ACC tournament in Charlotte despite a 41-point
game from Scott, and 95–90 in Madison Square Garden in the first
round of the NIT.

Toward the end of the academic year, area sportswriters named

Scott ACC Player of the Year, despite his failing twice to win over John Roche in conference postseason voting. This award recognized academics and citizenship. Then came the Patterson Medal, considered the most prestigious honor for a Carolina athlete. Scott was the first African American so honored.

Holly Francena Scott was born on May 3, 1970, as her father was about to sign a large contract with the new Washington Caps of the American Basketball Association, who had moved from Oakland. At Smith's suggestion, he followed Billy Cunningham, who left the Philadelphia 76ers for the ABA. The Caps would feature Rick Barry, ex–San Francisco Warriors star and NBA leading scorer; Doug Moe; and his former freshman coach Larry Brown, who said they would move into the NBA. Then, while Scott was on a long-delayed honeymoon with Margaret, the Caps moved to Norfolk and became the Virginia Squires. An unsettled Scott averaged 27.1 points a game but hated being in that league stuck in a southern Navy city. He wanted out of the ABA and his marriage. Margaret, who had it with him, went to Smith, who set her up with his own attorney: W. Travis Porter, a powerful Durham lawyer

Porter put together a separation agreement and sent it to Margaret to have Smith sign it. When Scott saw what Porter wanted, he went to Smith and told him Margaret was "asking for every dime I was making and 50 cents on every dollar I would make after that." Smith went back to Porter and returned to Scott a few weeks later with a settlement he could handle. He then went to Margaret and told her to sign it or face getting nothing at all. She did. It called for $100,000 in three installments—$50,000 up front, and two more $25,000 payments, plus $200 a month in child support for Holly until she finished 11th grade.

Scott played outstanding basketball for the Phoenix Suns and the Boston Celtics in the NBA, retired in 1980, and met and married his second wife, Trudy, in 1986. They had three children who became close to Holly, a Durham school principal. After an import shoe business in Los Angeles failed, Scott, Trudy, and his second family— daughter Simone and son Shaun—moved to Atlanta where he got a second chance, working with Champion Products in marketing. Their second son, Shannon, was born in December 1992. After years attending Dean Smith's Carolina basketball camps where he acknowledged he was treated as another son, Shannon took a scholarship to Ohio State with coach Thad Matta. Scott and Trudy moved to Columbus to give him support and the home life they wanted their son to enjoy.

As for his relationship with his coach, Scott appreciated the life he led with him, especially during that long illness that ended in his mentor's death on February 8, 2015. Years after his last game at Carolina, Scott told *Newsday*'s Greg Logan that late in his North Carolina career, he was walking off the court after beating South Carolina when some student chased after him yelling a racial slur. Coach Smith lost his cool and had to be restrained. "I think more than anything else, it upset him that a person would have to go through the indignity that young man was putting me through," Scott said.

Most important to Scott, his coach was a great human being. "When you played for him," Scott told Logan, "he was your coach, your disciplinarian, your teacher. That was merely the preliminary for life after graduation. He became a friend, a father, and a mentor," Scott said. "Not for just the guys who played professional sports, but every single person who played for him."

Scott, of course, became the catalyst not only for North Carolina basketball and the ACC but for the entire South, which finally recognized the stupidity of exiling your best potential players—players who would bring victories from integration as well as a sense of normality that should be a commonsense way of life at any institution of higher learning.

A shock wave rocked the ACC 2 years later, though, on June 30, 1971. South Carolina, an original member of the Atlantic Coast Conference when it was founded in 1953, announced it was becoming an independent. The people who ran the athletic program there long had felt that the four North Carolina schools dictated the league policy to the extent they no longer could stay with it.

"I felt one of the worst things that happened to the conference was Coach McGuire taking South Carolina out of the conference," Woody Durham said. "That happened [the summer] after South Carolina beat North Carolina in the 1971 ACC tournament in Greensboro. It wasn't a shock because they had been talking like they were too big for the ACC. Carolina had a lead in that [ACC tournament] game, and South Carolina came on to win. It came on a jump ball at their end with 3 seconds left. Kevin Joyce went on to out-jump Lee Dedmon and got it to SC's Tom Owens, who hit a layup to win the game 52–51."

All was not lost that year, however, as Durham notes. "Carolina went on to win the NIT, beating Duke in the semifinal and Georgia Tech in the championship game." Coach Smith was so impressed with that NIT championship that he called it the moment North Carolina graduated from being a team to a program. In 1974, Smith landed point guard Phil Ford of Rocky Mount, the son of two teachers, Mabel and Phil Sr., a history teacher deeply loved and respected by their son. Phil Sr. was the man young Phil emulated, and he also happened to be a coaching friend and contact of Smith's. "I was a daddy's boy," the younger Ford said in 2014. "My daddy was a share-cropper's son. He was in the Army and went to college and became a teacher. He always took me to sporting events. Played all three:

basketball, baseball, and football. My dad started teaching at Frederick Douglass High School. He drove the bus for the basketball team."

Ford grew up with an awareness that education was paramount, but he loved basketball over all the other games. He could see that hope existed for a young African American to play the game at a high level and remain close to home instead of being forced to travel to the faraway, cold places up north. "Willie Cooper was the first black basketball player at North Carolina before Charlie Scott," Ford said. "Scott was so good, and that's when I got interested in basketball."

Ford felt he had a basketball future by the time Scott graduated from UNC. He had already demonstrated the skills and ability to play at a high level. "Not many young guys get that opportunity," he said. "I knew in eighth grade that's where I wanted to go and that Coach Smith was who I wanted to play for.

"I think his recruiting African American players is a part of Coach Smith," Ford continued. "The first time he came to see me in Rocky Mount, the first 35 minutes, we didn't talk basketball at all. We just talked about race relations and what we had to do. My mom wanted to sit in, and she said she trusted Coach Smith. 'He wouldn't have come here if he didn't want you to play basketball,' my mother, Mabel Ford, said after he left. 'He made no promises about how much you'd play at Chapel Hill. A lot of other coaches said you'd do this and do that.'" Mabel told her son, "'You'll play. If you go to North Carolina, when the time comes, Coach Smith won't be promising some other high school All-American like you that he will start.'

"I was the first freshman to start for Coach Smith. I was pretty bad those first couple of games. We won the Atlantic Coast Conference, but we lost to the [other three North Carolina teams—Duke, NC State, Wake Forest—in the] Big Four. We became good enough at the end of the year [1974–75] that we won the tournament," a modest Ford admitted. Ford did not mention that he won the Everett Case Award that year as the most valuable player in the ACC tournament, becoming the first freshman in league history to win that honor.

Smith enjoyed one of the most memorable years of his life in 1976. After the divorce from Ann was final in 1973, he met Linnea Weblemoe, who was studying medicine at UNC after graduating from Whittier College in 1967 with a degree in chemistry. "Dean met Linnea on an airplane going up to New York," Bill Bunten said. "She was in medical school at North Carolina, I believe. I remember Joanne [Mrs. Bunten] and I and another couple went out to Reno at Lake Tahoe, and Dean and Linnea came up to join us. Joanne said they were gambling. Dean was a chance taker. It was time to go to dinner, and we had reservations. He said, 'Will you hold these for me?' He handed her a bunch of chips—$100 chips, and he had a ton of them. He was charitable and always picked up the tab. He liked to take chances. Coaching is such a high-pressure business."

"Dean went through a difficult time when his first marriage ended," the Reverend Seymour said. Smith married Linnea in May 1976, and they had two daughters. Kristen Caroline was born in 1979 and Kelly Marie in 1981, to add to the three older children from his first marriage. "His three older children with Ann go to the neighboring Baptist church with their mother. The two children with Linnea go to Binkley," Dr. Seymour said. "They celebrated Scott's marriage as a family, and that was the beginning of building the bridge between the two families."

The wedding turned out to be a brief time-out from the coach's hectic schedule. In early 1975, a committee composed of veteran basketball people and coaches Henry Iba, Pete Newell, Wayne Embry, and Red Auerbach selected Smith as coach for the 1976 Summer Olympic Games in Montreal. Iba had coached the three previous US teams, in 1964, 1968, and the 1972 Games in Munich, which ended in controversy after the final 3 seconds of the gold medal game were replayed twice after Doug Collins appeared to have sunk the winning foul shots.

British Olympic official William Jones, a man who thought the United States' domination of Olympic basketball was bad for the sport, interceded without standing when the final horn had sounded and forced the timekeepers to wrongly reset the game clock to 3 seconds. On the second retry, after the official forced Tom McMillen to step back from the backcourt baseline to give the Soviets a clear pass, Russian Alexander Belov took a long pass between two defenders, got away with traveling at the basket, and banked in a layup to deal America its first-ever Olympic basketball defeat, 51–50. It was such a blatant case of official misconduct and rule bending that the US team refused to accept their silver medals. They are still being held in a bank vault in Geneva, Switzerland.

Four years later, Smith chose two assistants: his top aide at North Carolina, Bill Guthridge, and Georgetown head coach John Thompson. "I started at Georgetown in 1972. [Dean and I] met when I was coaching at St. Anthony's in Washington. Dean was recruiting Donald Washington, who went to North Carolina," Thompson said. They only had 6 weeks to get ready. That included winnowing down the team to 12 from the 60 who had been invited to try out. One player who stayed just a day and left on his own volition was Bo Ellis of Marquette. Smith wrote in *A Coach's Life* that Ellis came back the next winter to bedevil him and Carolina in the NCAA tournament. Concerning the Olympic team, Smith and his assistants pushed them hard in practice.

"The '76 Olympics was our chance to get back at what happened to the '72 team," Phil Ford said. "We all were college stars, but we had the coach and we got better as a team. We weren't favored to win. We were the youngest Olympic team ever to participate for our country. Tommy LaGarde, Mitch Kupchak, Walter Davis. There were seven of us from the ACC. Quinn Buckner and Scott May of Indiana were there. Phil Hubbard from Michigan."

"Coach Smith's system was disciplined and well controlled. And we had great players," Quinn Buckner said. Buckner, now vice president of communications for the Indiana Pacers, has been a popular basketball figure in Indiana and his home state of Illinois since 1971, when he led his Thornridge High School team to back-to-back state titles. He then moved on to Indiana, his parents' alma mater, to play for Bob Knight. Indiana won the Big Ten title each of the 4 years Buckner was there. The Hoosiers lost only one game in Bucker's last two seasons, to Kentucky in the 1975 Midwest Regional final at Dayton, 92–90, when IU's leading scorer, Scott May, could play only 7 minutes while recovering from a broken left arm. Ironically, 29 years later, May's son, Sean, starred for Smith's successor Roy Williams on the North Carolina team that beat Illinois for the 2005 national title. Buckner was named team captain the next year as the Hoosiers went 32–0 in 1975–76 to become major college basketball's last unbeaten national champion. Then Dean Smith selected Buckner to join the Olympic team. "Kent Benson didn't try out. Bobby Wilkerson did but did not make it," Buckner said of his Hoosier teammates. "It was Scott May and I who did make it.

"Coach Smith basically went for players he was familiar with from the ACC. It was a smart decision," Buckner said. "He took eight from the conference, four of them his own players from North Carolina: Phil Ford, Walter Davis, Mitch Kupchak, and Tom LaGarde. Kenny Carr from NC State, Tate Armstrong of Duke, and Steve Sheppard of Maryland were the other ACC players. Adrian Dantley of Notre Dame and Carr had been high school teammates at DeMatha Catholic outside Washington. Dantley led our team in scoring. Ernie Grunfeld was Tennessee's all-time leading scorer. He's president of the

Washington Wizards. Phil Hubbard of Michigan, Scott May, and I finished the roster."

Of all the players on that team, Duke's Tate Armstrong was upset with Smith, who admired the way the guard made himself into a great college player. According to Johnny Moore and Art Chansky's book, *The Blue Divide*, Armstrong vowed to show the coach he was wrong for keeping him on the bench for much of the Olympics. Armstrong was having a brilliant senior season when he broke his wrist in a 33-point performance in a victory over Virginia. He rehabilitated his injury and was chosen as the top draft pick of the Chicago Bulls in 1977 to augment their 1976 top selection Scott May. Neither of those ACC stars succeeded in the NBA.

In the Olympics, except for an unforeseen scare on July 20 against Puerto Rico, which shot 64 percent from the field, the team enjoyed a relative breeze in Montreal. In that Puerto Rico game, Ford with 20 points and Kupchak with 17 had to make every shot count as Marquette's Butch Lee, a Puerto Rico–born New Yorker who played for Puerto Rico, did everything for them, scoring 35 points. Ford sank the clinching two free throws to ensure a much-closer-than-expected 95–94 US victory. After that, the United States raced through the qualifying games and romped over host team Canada in the semifinal before dispatching Yugoslavia, who had knocked out the Soviets in the other semifinal, 94–74 behind 30 points by Dantley. The Americans had hoped to exact a measure of revenge against the Soviets, but it was not meant to be. In reclaiming gold for the United States, Dean Smith restored order to the world of Olympic basketball.

"I would not have assisted anyone else [but Coach Smith]. I got a lot of insights about coaching being with him at the Olympics, how to strategize and build relationships with players," Thompson said. "We talked all the time. His range of coaching was special.

Some are defensive specialists, some offensive. His range was extraordinary."

"I learned a lot from [Coach Smith] and appreciate the experience," Buckner said. "Later, after it was over, he took me aside and offered me an opportunity, if I wanted to take graduate work, to come to North Carolina and be a graduate assistant for his team. I did not do it, but I certainly was grateful that he made that offer." Buckner went on to play in the NBA for the Milwaukee Bucks, Boston Celtics (where he won a title in 1984), and Indiana Pacers. Only three players in history have played for high school state champions, NCAA titlists, and NBA champions. They are Buckner, Jerry Lucas, and Earvin "Magic" Johnson.

Phil Ford's play for Carolina that post-Olympics winter was so brilliant that it convinced Smith of his point guard's extraordinary talent. "If you ask an honest ACC fan to pick the five best players in the history of the league by position, every one of them would pick Phil as the point guard," Smith wrote in *A Coach's Life*.

The Tar Heels had a 13–4 record early in February 1977. Smith had a mostly veteran roster led by Ford, forward Walter Davis, guard John Kuester, center Tom LaGarde, and forward Mike O'Koren, a rare freshman starter. They went on a 15-game winning streak through the regular season, ACC tournament, and NCAA tournament. Each Carolina NCAA tournament game, in the words of the late Marquette coach Al McGuire (no relation to Frank), was a white-knuckler, close from the opening tip to the final buzzer.

This success was a tribute to the hard work and constant motion Smith's teams put in at practice, as Ford recalled so many years later. "We didn't work long on anything. We had ground to cover," Ford said. "Our practices were hard. I used to tell Coach our practices were harder than a game. I used to see Coach standing on the sideline. Concentration and effort make you tough, he'd tell you. We ran a lot after practice. When I went back on the staff, we didn't run as much. If we had a good practice, we might not have to run."

The Tar Heels opened the 1977 NCAA tournament in the East Region with a 69–66 victory in Raleigh over tough Purdue. Then, in College Park at Maryland's Cole Field House on March 17, St. Patrick's Day, they faced Notre Dame. The Irish had opened up a 10-point lead at the half and were sailing toward victory with their head coach, Digger Phelps, sporting a green carnation. There was no shot clock in those days, and Notre Dame had the game in hand. "Six or 7 minutes to go. Notre Dame up by eight, and Digger was going to shove it to Dean Smith," recalled Ernie Accorsi. "He goes into the four corners. That was Dean's signature. Many steals later, that was the game. Digger Phelps tried to embarrass Dean using an offense Dean and his team practiced every day. I was thrilled. Here's Digger saying, 'I'll show you, buddy.' I don't think Notre Dame got the ball to half-court after that."

Ford, who led all scorers with 29 points, hit a pair of foul shots with 1:16 remaining to break a 75–75 tie. Then, with the score tied at 77–all with 2 seconds left, Ford drew a foul. He drained both free throws to make it 79–77 Carolina. "I wore the green carnation on St. Patrick's Day when we were away," Digger Phelps recalled wistfully when we spoke in 2015. "After we lost that one to Carolina on St. Patrick's, the green carnation never made the road trip again."

"Coach Smith could always figure it out offensively and defensively, and he knew what would give us the chance to win," Ford said. "I call it philosophy, not system. Systems are rigid. Philosophies adapt to situations. Coach Smith could get something out of everyone's talent and put in a wrinkle to bring out the best in our team."

That year's Final Four at the Omni in Atlanta was one of the most exciting weekends in college basketball history. Carolina edged UNLV

84–83 in one semifinal while Marquette defeated UNC–Charlotte in the other when, with 3 seconds left, Butch Lee threw a court-length pass to Jerome Whitehead, who jammed it over and through Cedric Maxwell's hand in front of the rim at the buzzer. That set up the final, which was already bound to be emotional because Al McGuire announced before the game that he was retiring as coach.

"We had played some great teams down the stretch. Notre Dame. Nevada–Las Vegas was one of the best teams I've ever seen. We were fortunate to get through to the final," Ford said. "Marquette played well against us."

With the score tied 45–45 and 12:40 left, Smith, hoping to lure Marquette and their tall lineup out of their zone, ordered Ford to run the four corners. McGuire didn't take the bait and kept his Warriors in their zone. Smith had Mike O'Koren, who had run off eight points in a second-half surge, standing by the scorer's table, but he couldn't do anything with the ball still in play because his coach, who did not believe in squandering time-outs, refused to budge. Three minutes later, Ford found sub Bruce Buckley on a textbook backdoor cut only to see Marquette's Bo Ellis swat it away in midair, and Marquette had the ball. After McGuire bled a minute off the clock, Jim Boylan got a layup for the lead off his own backdoor cut. The Tar Heels could not recover. That elusive first title for Dean Smith at Carolina was not to be.

Marquette won it 67–59 for McGuire in his farewell game in one of the most emotional NCAA championship games ever, in the same rank of Jim Valvano's wild dash around the New Mexico Pit after Lorenzo Charles gave NC State the title against Houston and the two Villanova title wins, over Georgetown in 1985 and against Carolina in 2016. McGuire wept openly on the bench while seated next to his loyal assistants, Hank Raymonds and Rick Majerus. That defeat, though, did nothing to diminish Dean Smith's greatness as a coach and man. And McGuire walked out into the night with his clown paintings and even greater fame as a TV analyst.

From the perspective of a quarter century out of the basketball wars, Digger Phelps had special thoughts when we spoke about his friend Dean Smith and his coaching legacy. "One of the most creative guys the game ever had, and his players, thanks to him, had a life after basketball."

"He's such a good man and I think the greatest coach who ever lived. The University of North Carolina, academically and socially, is such a great place," Ford said. "It's so amazing. When I played professional basketball, I knew an awful lot of fellows who would not go to the same school where they played sports. If I had to do it over, I'd go to the University of North Carolina again."

"Dean's program became a remarkable model of consistency. The family atmosphere he developed is so special. He really nurtured that. I think he was closer to his players in many ways after they left," John Swofford said.

Ford lived in that atmosphere as student, player, and, after pro basketball, assistant coach for Smith. "I think the family situation is because Coach Smith was there so long. We know what we went through and we all enjoyed North Carolina," Ford said. "Coach Smith would always stay in contact with us after we left."

That was especially true in Ford's case. A three-time All-American, winner of the John Wooden Award as a senior in those long-ago days when everyone finished school, his pro career ended after 7 years. In his third year, as AP sports writer Steve Wilstein wrote in 1997, Ford suffered a broken orbital bone of his left eye. It caused permanent double vision, and he turned to alcohol and had to get help. Smith took charge in 1987, found a rehab center, and got Ford squared away. Two years later, he brought his favorite point guard aboard as an assistant. It was a typical example of his loyalty. Ford was an assistant through the end of Smith's career and the tenure of Bill Guthridge, until Matt Doherty took over and cleaned house of everyone from the previous regime, Ford included.

John Swofford is fast to credit Smith for his own future successes. "I was 31 when I became athletic director, and was assistant AD from ages 27 to 31. He could have been difficult, but he wasn't. He stressed a balance between academics and athletics. Any problem or disagreement was behind closed doors. And it wasn't frequent. He could relate to a young AD because he was so young when he became coach."

Smith was a nurturer as well, helping his players think and plan ahead about life after college and athletic competition. It is no coincidence that the commissioners of two of America's major athletic conferences, John Swofford and Jim Delany of the Big Ten, both went to North Carolina and were directly influenced by Dean Smith. "Jim Delany was 2 years ahead of me, a sixth or seventh man. Jim is one of Dean's players who's gone on to great success," Swofford said with pride. "Two commissioners of major conferences from the same school at roughly the same time is so unusual. We both would agree on our experiences there."

10 | THE RIVALS

FROM THE MOMENT OF THAT rumble started by Larry Brown and Art Heyman at then Duke Indoor Stadium on a bitter winter's night in February 1961, the North Carolina–Duke rivalry became perhaps the most intense in college basketball. It remains so to this day. Their meetings are showcase games at either campus in the regular season, and equally, if not more, intense in ACC tournament play. Since that fight, one or both has often been a national contender, many times in the same season. As retired Carolina sports information director Rick Brewer put it in the summer of 2014, "This rivalry is absolutely important to both schools, the conference, and college basketball in general." Partisans believe this rivalry is number one in college sports, on a par with such football battles as Alabama vs. Auburn, Ohio State vs. Michigan, and Notre Dame vs. USC.

Certainly an early igniter in this rivalry's intensity was 1963 Player of the Year Art Heyman who, as earlier noted, intended to play at North Carolina with his then friend Larry Brown, but changed his mind when his father had a bitter skirmish with Dean Smith's boss Frank McGuire and turned to Duke and Vic Bubas.

Heyman led Duke to the Final Four in 1963, became the school's all-time scorer, graduated, and moved on to the New York Knicks, the first of several stops in the NBA and its then rival ABA.

In 1973, now out of basketball and 17 more years before Duke would retire his number 25, Heyman returned to Durham and ACC country for the first time in a decade. According to coauthors Johnny Moore and Art Chansky in their book, *The Blue Divide*, Heyman stood in a runway by the bleachers at the renamed Cameron Indoor Stadium to watch Duke and NCAA title–bound NC State. Heyman did not like it one bit when he saw the Wolfpack's slick, speedy guard Monte Towe, whom he called "that little pissant," drive unmolested down the lane toward the hoop to shoot or dump off a sure bucket to that year's Player of the Year David Thompson for an easy layup. In the time-honored words of a disgruntled old-timer who thinks the kids don't play the game the right way, Heyman carped, "If he tried that against us the first time, someone would have leveled him with a forearm, just knocked the shit out of him. He never would have tried it again."

Heyman then was told that North Carolina was considered the best program in the ACC and Dean Smith the best coach. "Dean Smith!!" he laughed, according to Moore and Chansky. "He was the biggest joke when I played. Everyone wanted him fired!" By then, Smith and UNC had reached four Final Fours in the previous 5 years. Times, indeed, had changed, but the rivalry was just gearing up, and Coach K would arrive in Durham 7 years later.

"I think it's the best rivalry in college athletics," said Woody Durham. "Duke was awfully good when Vic Bubas was there. Bill Foster took them to the Final Four in 1978, where they lost to Kentucky, and Bill went to South Carolina in 1980." That's when Duke hired Army coach Mike Krzyzewski, whose teams at West Point had gone 79–53, a fine record at a place where winning is difficult in championship competition. His mentor was Bob Knight, whose own Army teams went 102–50 over six seasons from 1965–66 through 1970–71.

"Bob had been a friend for many years, and I'd always respected his basketball coaching abilities," former Duke athletic director Tom Butters told CBS Sports. "I told him I was in a position that I had to hire a basketball coach, and he gave me some names. They were all his protégés. Dave Bliss, Bob Weltlich. And I said to him, what about this guy Mike Krzyzewski? And he made a very interesting comment; I will never forget it. He said, 'Butters, you've always liked the way I coach. Mike has all my good qualities and none of my bad ones.' Typical Bob Knight comment." Butters hired Krzyzewski with pleasure and hung on.

By the time Krzyzewski arrived in Durham on March 28, 1980, to take the reins, he had the best of training. Born in Chicago on February 13, 1947, Michael William Krzyzewski (pronounced Zha-ZHEV-ski) went to Archbishop Weber High School on the North Side, where he and best friend Richard "Chico" Kurzawski enrolled in 1961 and, by 1965, pretty well ran it as students and athletic stars.

Kurzawski was a top high school football player in Chicago in 1964 when he led the Red Horde to the city championship over Dick Butkus's alma mater Chicago Vocational 34–13 at Soldier Field. Krzyzewski was the star guard and all-Catholic League for the basketball team. When it came to leadership, Chico was student body president and Mike was vice president. Chico went to nearby Northwestern, where he became captain for Alex Agase's Wildcats and eventually president of Leon's Sausage Co.

Krzyzewski, his pal, earned an appointment to the US Military Academy at West Point, where he refined his game as a 3-year letterman under Army's young coach, still in his twenties, Bobby Knight. When Captain Krzyzewski finished his 5-year service obligation in 1974, he moved to Bloomington, Indiana, to join his old boss Knight as an assistant, at the time he was developing the Buckner, May, Wilkerson, and Benson team that would become the last undefeated national champion. A year later, young Coach K followed in Knight's path when he became head coach at West Point, where his teams went 73–59 over the next five seasons. That was the prelude to the most successful run in college coaching history, as he became the first coach to surpass the 1,000-win mark.

"It took a little time for Coach K to make it go," Woody Durham said. "He had losing seasons his first three seasons. And he is a great basketball coach."

"I don't know if Dean Smith or Mike Krzyzewski could have lasted today," Billy Cunningham said. "Mike K wasn't successful in his early years. There was an AD named Butters at Duke. He called a press conference. It was thought he was going to announce the changing of the guard. He came in and announced he had extended Mike K's contract."

Butters was smart and patient enough to understand in 1983 that Coach K had brought in an elite recruiting class that would feature four future NBA draft choices—Johnny Dawkins, David Henderson, Jay Bilas, and Mark Alarie. They were on their way. Cunningham understood the dilemma all major college and pro coaches face. "Today, we need instant gratification. The Pittsburgh Steelers have had three coaches since the '60s: Noll, Cowher, and Tomlin. [All coached the Steelers to Super Bowl titles.] Dean never would have left Carolina."

Since the first meeting on January 24, 1920, when North Carolina beat Duke 36–25, the two schools just 8 miles apart have gone after each other 242 times through 2016. Carolina leads 134–108 in the all-time series. The ACC schedule always features a Duke Blue Devils–North Carolina Tar Heels regular season finale, which alternates between Duke's Cameron Indoor Arena in Durham and Carolina's Dean Smith Center in Chapel Hill. They couldn't be much closer in their successes. North Carolina is third on the all-time list of winningest NCAA Division I men's basketball programs. Duke is fourth.

Carolina has won five NCAA men's titles, appeared in a record 19 Final Fours, and was awarded a sixth title retroactively in 1942 by the Helms Athletic Foundation for their undefeated 1924 team. Duke has won five NCAA championships, all since 1991 under the tutelage of Krzyzewski. They stand behind only UCLA and Kentucky. North Carolina leads the ACC with 30 regular season championships to Duke's 19, which places them second. Duke leads in ACC tournament titles 19–18. Carolina has been to a record 19 Final Fours; Duke is fourth at 16. They have met just once in postseason tournaments outside the ACC, when North Carolina beat Duke 73–67 in the 1971 NIT at Madison Square Garden. Duke has reached the NCAA's Big Dance 32 times in Coach K's 36 seasons in Durham, the exception being 1995, when he had to take a medical leave of absence to recover from spinal surgery.

There are almost as many explanations for the rivalry's passion as there are people in the immediate vicinity of greater Chapel Hill and Durham. Former *Esquire* editor Will Blythe, a Carolina graduate, suggested in his book *To Hate Like This Is to Be Happy Forever* that it is distinctly southern and is related to "class and culture that surpasses sports: locals vs. outsiders, elitists against populists, even good against evil." Those passions, Blythe believes, "reveal pleasure and even the necessity of hatred." Certainly all those emotions and more are on display in the conduct of the student bodies at each school— the Cameron Crazies at Duke and cooler Carolina Bluebloods.

The list of games over the years that still are discussed is lengthy and better examined in detail by the most passionate followers of each team. No mere inventory can satisfy either side. One that struck home as much as any other was the story of the 1991 Final Four at the Hoosier Dome, where Duke and Carolina could have met in the title game. Duke got revenge for the 30-point pasting they took from UNLV in the 1990 title game as they beat the Runnin' Rebels this time 79–77 in the second semifinal. It was the biggest upset in years, coming off the heels of Roy Williams' Kansas Jayhawks' 79–73 win over Carolina and Dean Smith, his mentor, in the early semi. Duke emerged with their first NCAA championship two nights later when they beat KU 72–65.

Games that defined the series include one on March 2, 1968, when number 10 Duke went after UNC's third-ranked Final Four team in the ACC regular season finale at Duke Indoor Stadium. Vic Bubas was forced to call on seldom-used Duke junior Fred Lind when All-America center Mike Lewis drew his third foul and backup Warren Chapman had a knee injury. Lind scored 16 points, grabbed nine rebounds, and blocked three shots to lead the Blue Devils to overtime. Lind blocked a shot at the end of regulation, hit two free throws at the end of the first overtime, and hit a 15-foot buzzer beater at the end of the second overtime. Duke then pulled out an 87–86 win in the third overtime. The students (pre–Cameron Crazies) carried Lind to the school's main quad to celebrate.

The four-corners offense, especially the way Dean Smith employed it, drove many an opposing basketball coach, player, and fan to the verge of madness. Two such four-corner games stand out in the UNC–Duke series. The first was played on March 4, 1966, in an ACC tournament semifinal at Reynolds Coliseum in Raleigh. After seeing how Duke whipped his Tar Heels by double digits in the two regular season games, Smith had Carolina play an excruciatingly deliberate offense, which they ran throughout the game. They picked away and built a five-point lead, then Duke came to life as well as they could in a game like this. Steve Vacendak hit the tying basket with 2:09 left to make it 20–20. Duke got the ball back and Mike Lewis drew a foul with 4 seconds left. "I was pretty sure I could make one of two," Lewis said in *The Encyclopedia of Duke Basketball.* He missed the first shot but sank the other one. Duke held on and beat NC State in the tournament title game the next day, the third ACC title in four seasons for the Blue Devils.

The second, on February 24, 1979, at Cameron Indoor Stadium, was equally as bizarre. After Duke opened the game with a basket, Smith ordered the Tar Heels to deploy the four corners, which they did for the entire half. Jim Spanarkel was playing in his Senior Day farewell to the campus and scored 15 of his game-high 17 points in the second half, as Duke won 47–40 to tie Carolina for the regular season conference title. After the game, Duke coach Bill Foster wise-cracked to the writers, "I thought Naismith invented the game, not Dean Smith."

Chris Collins lived the rivalry from the inside, as a player at Duke from 1992–96 in Dean Smith's later coaching years and as Krzyzewski's top assistant for 13 years before becoming head coach in 2013 at Northwestern. "Both Duke and North Carolina are so good. The wins are about even. You have two outstanding coaches, and the schools are 8 miles apart," Collins said. "The rivalry was always at the forefront. It's by far the top basketball rivalry in the country."

To Collins, it's the schools and the atmosphere at each one that light up everything about the rivalry. "The home court games are so much better than the ACC tournament [is]," he said. "Cameron is tightly packed and loud. Cameron for the Duke–Carolina game was intense the moment you entered the arena. You could feel it. There was more at stake even in the warmups in both arenas.

"The Dean Smith Center was a sea of Carolina blue. You know you are in Carolina country. We knew so much about each other it didn't come down to much strategy. Both coaches had similar styles. It was about performance, not style.

"I love looking at the history of the game," Collins added. "Coach Smith brought specific things to the game. The four corners, the fast break that is so unique and continues to this day. That transition basketball. The greatest tribute is the way people do things in college and the pros that he introduced at Carolina."

Everyone who knew Smith well is certain they will never meet a more competitive individual. He had to succeed and win at everything he did, and he never gave in regardless of the odds he faced. As Smith wrote in *A Coach's Life*, "It was part of the Carolina philosophy that we were never out of a game."

One such moment Smith savored and loved to detail concerned the Duke game of March 2, 1974, at Carmichael Auditorium, a game he called the greatest comeback in college basketball history. "It seemingly was over when Duke led by 8 with 17 seconds left," Smith wrote. At that point, many Carolina fans started filing out of the arena. Senior forward Bobby Jones grabbed a John Kuester miss and was fouled. Smith called time-out and told the team to go into the 24 defense, a full-court deny press, when "Bobby *makes* these two free throws." Notice that he says *makes*. "Don't let them get the ball inbounds." Jones made the free throws, narrowing the deficit to six. The Tar Heels pressured the in-bounds pass, and when Duke's Rob Fleischer could not find an opening, he threw the ball between the legs of Carolina defender Ed Stahl. Walter Davis intercepted the ball and threw it underneath to Kuester for a layup. Smith called time-out. The deficit was now four. "They feel that they can lose," Coach Smith said to his team over the roaring crowd. Again, the Tar Heels attempted to deny Duke the in-bounds pass, and this time succeeded in forcing Tate Armstrong to deflect the ball out of bounds. Carolina ball. Davis received the inbounds pass, shot, missed, but Jones converted the rebound on a put-back. The Duke lead had been cut to just two with 6 seconds still remaining.

"If they get the ball inbounds, foul immediately," Smith said, and they did. With 4 seconds to go, Duke's Pete Kramer missed the front end of the one-and-one. Carolina used its final time-out. Mitch Kupchak set up for a long pass, Duke thought, for Bobby Jones. But Walter Davis instead set a pick for Jones, then rolled to the sideline where he rubbed off Kuester's pick to take Kupchak's pass. He took three dribbles and fired from past 30 feet. His shot banked, tying the game at the buzzer. In the overtime, Carolina outlasted Duke for an improbable 96–92 win. That's the way it went so many times for Dean Smith throughout his 36 years at UNC.

"Everybody who went through that Carolina program was unbelievably loyal to Dean Smith," Collins said. "I was always impressed with the bond they had and loyalty. We have a bond as basketball players with Coach K. Both men have treated their players like sons."

There were so many outstanding players on both sides, a virtual two-school college basketball hall of fame. An early superstar was Duke All-America guard Dick Groat, who forged a truly great baseball career over 14 seasons as a captain and championship shortstop. With his hometown Pittsburgh Pirates, he won the 1960 batting title hitting .325, was chosen MVP, and led the Pirates to the 1960 world championship over Casey Stengel's New York Yankees that ended with Bill Mazeroski's series-clinching home run. He added one more title in 1964 when the St. Louis Cardinals beat the Yanks in seven games. For all his baseball success, basketball was and remains Groat's favorite and, likely, his best sport. His finest memory came in 1952 when Duke caught North Carolina in Durham and Groat hit for 48 points in a 94–64 victory, the most points any Carolina has scored in the Duke rivalry.

Another moment that saved Smith's career at UNC came in the 1965 season, the game after Wake Forest drubbed them by 22 points and they arrived to find that some goof hanged an effigy on a tree outside Woolen Gym. Billy Cunningham detailed this incident earlier in this book. The follow-up is equally interesting. Smith rallied his troops with a rousing speech three nights later as they knocked off eighth-ranked Duke at Durham 65–62. It was more than just his first victory over Duke. That win saved his Hall of Fame career. To boot, Carolina beat Duke 7 weeks later at home to end the regular season in style.

Smith and Coach K had their moments, especially in the early going in recruiting battles and in tightly contested games. "There were some early disagreements between Coach Smith and Mike," Woody Durham said. "After his [Dean's] retirement, Mike said one of the best things that happened to him was the friendship he and Coach Smith developed after he retired.

"Coach Guthridge and Roy Williams have done so well," Durham said. "Recruiting is so much more competitive these days. I think college basketball is very hard ball. There are more teams capable of winning now than [there] were then."

Chris Collins has a deep sense about the rivalry, not only its intensity but what players and fans feel about it. "It's a great environment, a special place, and the players loved playing for Coach Smith. It's fun to play in that environment. The journey has to be fun. We try to do it here at Northwestern."

"I saw a great thing," Cunningham mused. "When he had these great teams at Duke, Krzyzewski all of a sudden learned and knew what it was like to be Dean Smith. He realized what was expected of him, what it took to handle his time, the expectations. Everything completely changed. He had such a better feeling and respect for Dean. At the end of the day, they were great friends. It's very easy for me to say now. It's only freaking basketball. It's entertainment. That's what it comes down to."

11 | IT TAKES
A CHAMPION

AFTER 20 YEARS AS HEAD coach, Dean Smith's North Carolina Tar Heels had reached the Final Four six times: in 1967, 1968, 1969, 1972, 1977, and 1981. They lost three championship games in those years—78–55 to UCLA and John Wooden in 1968, 67–59 to Marquette in 1977 in Al McGuire's farewell, and 63–50 to Indiana and Bob Knight in 1981. Nobody anywhere in and out of Chapel Hill was about to blame the coach for those defeats.

Now, at last, in 1982, it appeared that all was in order for a run to the top. The road would be tough, though, and the toughest competition would come from John Thompson's Georgetown Hoyas, who were led by Eric "Sleepy" Floyd and 6-foot-11-inch freshman center Patrick Ewing. Ewing, who played for Cambridge Rindge and Latin School near Boston, was considered the top freshman in the country and most acclaimed big man entering college since Wilt Chamberlain went to Kansas from Overbrook High School in Philadelphia in 1955. The Hoyas finished second in the Big East regular season, then took charge in the conference tournament final to beat Villanova 72–54.

Smith's 1980–81 team, which made it to the championship

game before losing to Isiah Thomas–led Indiana in Philadelphia, came back almost intact. He returned four starters from that team, led by All-America forward James Worthy, now a junior; sophomore center Sam Perkins, another All-American; senior point guard Jimmy Black; and sophomore forward Matt Doherty. Smith lost his leading forward, Al Wood, to graduation and the NBA, but in his place along came the single greatest player not only for North Carolina but, with virtually no dissent, in basketball history—Michael Jordan.

Jordan was a freshman from Wilmington, North Carolina, whom Bill Guthridge first saw after his junior year in high school at Carolina's summer camp sessions on campus. Guthridge was greatly impressed. At the end of the camp, Coach Smith met with Jordan's parents, James and Deloris. His assistants, Roy Williams and Eddie Fogler, told them they could get Jordan into Howard Garfinkel's Five-Star Basketball Camp in Pittsburgh. His parents agreed to do that without knowing that Coach Smith feared he would consider other schools when everyone else saw how good he was. The assistants prevailed, saying they needed to see how he stacked up against top competition and that his strong suit was loyalty once he was given the type of confidence Smith could provide, just the way he did with so many players, with Billy Cunningham, Larry Miller, Charles Scott, and Phil Ford as paramount examples. Michael was 6 feet 4 inches by his junior year. Clifton "Pop" Herring, his coach at Laney High School in Wilmington, sensing his ability, made him a guard—not a power forward or center, as most high school players his size get slotted because they can rebound well and work inside. He knew Jordan could use that experience to become a superior college player, even a pro, if everything worked out. All Jordan did was become MVP of the camp, and by then, he wasn't going anywhere else but Carolina. He was that sold, no longer interested in such places as NC State, Duke, or UCLA, which no longer had the mystique it possessed in the dominant era of John Wooden.

As Roland Lazenby points out in his thoroughly researched and superb biography *Michael Jordan: The Life*, many factors came into play that enabled Smith and Carolina to land Jordan with virtually no recruiting competition from other schools.

The late Howard Garfinkel's Five-Star Basketball Camp near Pittsburgh provided the exposure to the best high school players in the nation and the platform to spread the word that Jordan was special. Garfinkel, a lifelong bachelor and basketball guru from New York, knew and loved the game with a well-trained eye. As a superior judge of talent, his camps provided a summertime finishing school for some 10,000 college players and 500 NBA players from 1966 to 2011 that included Jordan, LeBron James, Isiah Thomas, Patrick Ewing, and Carmelo Anthony, among others.

Jordan's unique skills and intense competitiveness showed immediately that summer of 1980. When Garfinkel and his top people saw Mike Jordan, as he was called then, dominate the camp, they tagged him a "one possession" player, meaning that any knowledgeable observer who saw him in action for the first time knew he was special and did not require several viewings to establish an opinion or rating. Jordan's work ethic on a basketball court was unsurpassed, and he quickly rose to the top of all the lists in the camp. One night after a long day, they saw Jordan take the floor and work on his shooting. He explained that he needed to improve his shooting to become a top-flight player. That work ethic was a quality he demonstrated throughout his career with the Chicago Bulls; he became an outstanding three-point shooter and developed high post and wing turnarounds as his game changed when he got older.

He ended up that summer rated the number two player in the

country behind Ewing, but virtually nobody knew about him because he did not have the publicity. His hometown Wilmington, North Carolina, by any stretch, was unknown to most Americans outside of coastal Carolina. His high school, Laney, was not a great athletic power in the state. Thus he flew under the radar. Also, the Amateur Athletic Union (AAU) exposure and constant games young players get today did not exist, and, as scout Tom Konchalski told Lazenby, Jordan's extraordinary competitiveness and desire to win were not tempered by playing one game after another all day long.

Toward the conclusion of Garfinkel's camp in the summer of 1980, Garfinkel called his good friend Dave Krider, editor of *Street & Smith's Official Basketball Yearbook*, THE preseason basketball magazine in the country that mattered more than all others in an era before the Internet and the many websites devoted to scouting reports and the like. It listed 650 high school seniors as top prospects, and Garfinkel wanted to know where he ranked Mike Jordan on his list. Krider checked and did not have any Mike (not yet known as Michael) Jordan on the list. Garfinkel explained: "I called *Street & Smith* to get him ranked first- or second-team preseason All-America."

Krider replied that it was too late, the magazine already had gone to press. In those days, all publications of that nature went to press weeks ahead of time. Garfinkel told Krider it would be an embarrassment *not* to have Jordan on that list. Thus, Mike Jordan is not listed in the 1980–81 edition of *Street & Smith's Basketball*, not even as one of the top 20 incoming seniors in the state of North Carolina.

When they played the McDonald's All American Games that summer, Jordan excelled and set a scoring record in the national game at Wichita with 30 in a 95–94 win for his East team over the West. When the time came to name the MVP, the judges—John Wooden, Philly's Sonny Hill, and DeMatha (Maryland) High School's coaching legend Morgan Wootten—voted for Maryland-bound Adrian Branch and Aubrey Sherrod as cowinners. Jordan's mother, Deloris, was furious, and Michael was sore, giving him motivation to get even with Branch every time Carolina faced Maryland.

By the time Jordan arrived in Chapel Hill, Smith no longer could "stash" him the way the Brooklyn Dodgers tried to do back in 1954, when they signed Puerto Rican outfield prospect Roberto Clemente and assigned him to Triple-A Montreal. Jordan would not be red-shirted, and so he came prepared: to learn, to play, and to excel.

"John Wooden made the statement that Dean Smith overcoached sometimes," Woody Durham said. "When he won the 1982 championship, he used eight guys in that game. It is interesting that when you had James Worthy, Sam Perkins, Matt Doherty, Michael Jordan, and Jimmy Black on the floor, you'd have no reason to change guys unless someone got tired."

Dean Smith noticed almost immediately in fall practice that Jordan had qualities he may have seen pieces of in certain individuals but, in this case, wrapped up in this singular young man. For instances abound: Smith always stressed defense first with all the positioning, footwork, hard work, and technique that are required to play it effectively. When he saw that Jordan had been taught to turn and defend while facing the ball to guard the backdoor play, Smith told him he wanted him to learn how to look over his shoulder and see the man and ball together. The coach knew from coaching North Carolina basketball for more than 20 years that it would take several practice sessions for a young player to learn that technique. But when the drill was run the next day, Jordan had it down perfect, just the way Smith had taught him. The coach quickly discovered that he picked up on everything they taught him, and it became obvious to Smith that Jordan appeared to *enjoy* practice.

It was always that way with Michael Jordan, whose contracts

with the Chicago Bulls had a "love of the game" clause that allowed him to stop wherever he was headed and participate in a pickup game if he thought it was worthwhile or would be fun. Smith had to make a decision whether to start Jordan in the first game. Just three other freshmen had started for Smith: Phil Ford, James Worthy, and Mike O'Koren. *Sports Illustrated* got word that Jordan was a first-teamer in practice and wanted to put him with the returning starters on the cover for their basketball preview issue.

Because Coach Smith did not allow freshmen who never had played a college game to be interviewed, and because he did not want to upset the other players on the team—who might have been offended by an untested freshman getting so much ink and exposure—the coach did not relent in Jordan's case. Smith told Jordan he had to prove his defensive skills before he would get that consideration. So Jordan went out, passed the coach's strict "tests," and won the right to start the season opener for number one Carolina against Kansas in the Charlotte Coliseum. "Mike" Jordan got the first basket of the season with a short jumper from the side. He fit in immediately then, as he always would, scoring a dozen points in a 74–67 Carolina win, the first of 32 for the Tar Heels that season.

The big midseason game came in the Meadowlands in New Jersey when top-ranked Carolina faced number two Kentucky. The Wildcats played a sagging, packed-in zone because Carolina's strength was built around the big men, Worthy and Perkins, and they were not a strong outside shooting team. Jordan's weakest facet then was outside shooting, which he understood and would develop through the years with constant work well into his pro career with the Bulls. Kentucky held him to 3-for-8 shooting in the first half, but he got it going to finish with 19 points on 8-for-13 shooting, coming in behind Player of the Year Worthy's 26 points and Perkins's 21 as the Tar Heels won the battle 82–69.

As Smith noted in *A Coach's Life*, Jordan was afflicted with a throat infection 5 days before the ACC tournament but recovered in time to play. By then, Carolina was top ranked, Georgetown second, and Virginia third. The Tar Heels and Virginia met for the conference championship in a matchup that spawned the changes we see in today's game. Carolina was leading 44–43 with 7:30 left; Virginia had settled back into a zone with 7-foot-4 Ralph Sampson camped under the basket, and they were not moving. So Coach Smith signaled for the four corners, and the standoff was under way. Carolina handled the ball flawlessly and Virginia refused to budge. Finally, with 28 seconds left, Virginia fouled Matt Doherty. Doherty sank the front end of the 1-and-1 and missed the second. With fouls to give to keep Virginia off the foul line, Carolina fouled. Then, with 3 seconds left, Jimmy Black knocked the ball off a Cavalier's knee, and it went out of bounds. Virginia fouled Doherty again, and he made both shots for a 47–43 lead. Carolina stood aside and let Virginia score as the game ended in North Carolina's favor 47–45.

That game forced the two rule changes that made the game better for underdogs and the fans: the shot clock and the three-point arc. It's been that way ever since.

The 1982 season boiled down to the second NCAA championship game played in an indoor football stadium (UCLA had defeated Villanova 11 years earlier in the Houston Astrodome). The Louisiana Superdome in New Orleans was filled on March 29, 1982, with a then record basketball crowd of 61,612 in the first title game not televised by NBC after a 13-year run. "We got it in '82," said Gary Bender, who handled the play-by play for CBS that year and through the 1984 tournament, referring to the broadcast rights.

"We got Billy Packer to come over from NBC," Bender said. "It was the first time we went to a place like the Superdome, with 60,000 seats. I remember Billy Packer and I were standing up at center court looking up at the stands. I asked Billy, 'Do you think any of those folks up there can even see the basketball?' It was an amazing venue at that time."

The game was a matchup of close friends on and off the court. John Thompson, the 6-foot-10-inch, 270-pound coach who defended his own and intimidated opponents, had run Georgetown since 1972 and built it into a major power in ensuing years. He and the Hoyas finally reached the title game after successfully landing Ewing, the most sought-after freshman in the country, from Cambridge Rindge and Latin High School. "We never played against each other when I was at Georgetown (except for the 1982 title game)," Thompson said, noting that was the only way he would go head-to-head with his friend Dean Smith, who had been his boss on the 1976 Olympic team. "It was the championship game. As friends, you feel terrible, but you have to play and do."

"One of the amazing things I had was the Kansas connection with Dean," Gary Bender recalled. "I grew up on a little farm in western Kansas. Dean had the Topeka connection, and he treated me just great. He would bring it up in our conversations. He would ask me about my dad, who was coach at the junior college in Dodge City. He was intrigued by the fact that we both came from the same state. I had worked in Topeka. My first TV job was in Topeka, [at] a CBS station. He knew about that."

That connection between the announcer and the North Carolina coach was cemented by Smith's ties to KU's 1952 championship team. "The '52 team was one I got to know going to Kansas," Bender said. "Bill Hougland, Bill Lienhard, and Dean Kelley. Those guys were remarkable people. I was told they all were Kansas kids. Phog Allen liked it that way. I asked Al Kelley, who was from a small town in southeastern Kansas, 'You guys all hang out together. You must like each other a lot.'"

"'Phog was responsible for that,' Al Kelley said. 'He would make an effort to visit each home, to talk to each parent. He gave them a sense of influence like that.' I never saw them play. I was 12, and I heard that game on the radio. Max Falkenstien called the game. His call was so vivid, and we just beat St. John's so bad for the title."

Pregame jitters are not unusual in any situation, especially before a championship game. Underneath the arena, coaches pace. And in one case, Smith, who didn't want outsiders to know he smoked, was nervously puffing away, slave to the habit he despised and at last would quit once and for all in 1988. Finally, they got the game going. It was superb. It went all the way to the final seconds, with 15 lead changes. Then, with Georgetown leading 62–61 in the closing moments, Carolina got the ball and called time. As Bender recalled, "James Worthy was on fire, the most outstanding player in the tournament with 28 points in the title game. I remember Packer and I were at courtside. During a time-out, we discussed what they would do and figured they would go for Worthy."

So did Thompson. "Worthy was the one person we focused on. He was a difficult matchup for our big men because he was so quick." But instead, Jordan got the ball against the zone, rose, and calmly dropped in a relatively open 18-footer from the left side of the court to give Carolina a 63–62 lead. "I have a picture here in my office of Jordan shooting the ball, and John Thompson is standing in the background with the towel over his shoulder in utter shock. He never figured Jordan would take the shot," Bender said. "[John] never talked to Dean about it."

Still, it wasn't over. Not with 17 seconds remaining. Plenty of time remained for Georgetown to answer. Fred Brown started up court and threw a pass to his right. But instead of hitting teammate Eric Smith, the pass went right into the hands of James Worthy, who had slipped into the spot where Brown thought Smith would be.

Worthy dribbled away and the clock ticked down to 2 seconds before he was fouled. Worthy then missed the first of a one-and-one and Georgetown got the ball, but it was too late to get off a quality shot, and Smith and Carolina at last had their championship.

Worthy was named Most Outstanding Player of the 1981 tournament with a final game where he went 13 for 17 from the field in a 28-point performance. That capped off a season where he shared college player of the year honors with Virginia's Ralph Sampson. He is listed as one of the top 50 players in NBA history for his brilliant career with the Los Angeles Lakers. And when Worthy got arrested for consorting with a prostitute in 1990, Coach Smith supported him, urging Worthy to apologize and move ahead—which he did. He turned pro after the championship and returned to school in NBA off-seasons to earn his degree.

The quality that stood out in Jordan more than any other player was his poise. He knew how to have fun as well. "Michael was not Michael at that time," Thompson said. "Michael is special. He is a special person. I like the way he conducts himself."

"I did a lot of NBA after that," Bender said, referring to his broadcasting duties. "And Jordan would come over to me to talk because he knew I called that shot. It was a remarkable Final Four from Olajuwon to Worthy to Jordan. I just remember that leading up to that we knew we had something going."

Smith wrote in *A Coach's Life* that Jordan stood a shade over 6-foot-4 when he came to Carolina. When Jordan returned to school in the fall, he had grown 2 inches and stood taller than 6-foot-6. And he was faster as well. Smith, who always sought the edge, timed his players' speed in the NFL standard 40-yard dash. Over that one summer between his freshman and sophomore years, Jordan improved from a 4.55 in the 40 to NFL cornerback speed, 4.39. (He was the fastest man in the league when he was a young player with the Bulls, and the best defender.) In every way, Jordan was getting closer to being ready for the NBA. "The shock came the next year when Indiana upset Carolina in Jordan's junior year," Bender said. "It was a good team under Bob Knight. Sam Perkins was gone. Knight did a remarkable job."

The game was played March 22, 1984, at the Omni in Atlanta. Carolina was top ranked, with a 28–2 record, and Jordan, knowing he would likely turn pro, was hungry to win both the game and the tournament. Indiana had lost eight games, but Knight had the Hoosiers ready. He junked the motion offense and spread the offense on the floor, putting freshman guard Steve Alford in charge.

To stymie Jordan, Knight assigned tough Gary native Dan Dakich to stay with him. He ordered Dakich to deny Jordan any backdoor cuts or post-ups and to keep him off the boards on offense. It worked, as Alford scored 27 points. Jordan had to sit most of the first half when Smith invoked his rule that a player with two first-half fouls (and just four points) had to go to the bench. When Jordan came back to open the second half, Dakich held him to 13 points for the game, and Indiana knocked off Carolina 72–68. Two days later, Virginia edged Indiana 50–48 to make the Final Four. In the Final Four, the Cavaliers, led by future NBA head coach Rick Carlisle, lost to Hakeem Olajuwon and Houston in the semifinals. Eventual champion Georgetown beat Kentucky and then Houston for the title.

With the games over, it was time for Jordan to announce his expected decision. "Jordan's parents wanted him to stay," Woody Durham said.

In *Michael Jordan: The Life*, Lazenby writes that former Chicago Bulls general manager Jerry Krause, who succeeded Rod Thorn, the man who drafted Jordan with third pick in the 1984 draft after Olajuwon and Kentucky's Sam Bowie, insisted in 2004 that Smith told Jordan to go. "He was getting bigger than the program," Lazenby wrote.

Billy Packer disagreed with Krause, however, saying Smith played his cards so close to the vest that he would never advertise what he was doing. Instead, he would check his many sources and get the lay of the land before he advised a player about his next move.

Woody Durham remained adamant that Smith did not play games with Jordan and his future. "Coach Smith told him he was ready for the NBA, and that's when he left for the pros and [the] Chicago Bulls." And Jordan lived up to his vow to return to Chapel Hill in the summers ahead to earn his degree, which he did. His loyalty to Carolina Blue has never wavered. He traveled in the spring of 2016 to follow the team to the Final Four and was seen cheering in the stands, then shedding a tear when Villanova hit the final shot to win the tournament.

Every pro basketball executive continuously sought another Michael Jordan, either out there in the gyms, the camps, the playgrounds, or, in the case of Donnie Walsh, who believed he would get an honest evaluation or two from his old coach Dean Smith, on a great lead. "I did talk to him about prospects, and I swore I would never do it again," Walsh said. "I would call Dean up to talk about players on his team. He would always bring up and push a guy who wasn't on the radar screen with the pros. One year, I took one of those guys and I had to cut him and he got mad at me. Finally, I told him, 'Dean, you're always telling me about those guys. Why don't you call me up and tell me when you have a guy like Michael Jordan? Why don't you help me with him?'"

Of course, it never happened.

12 | SONNY SIDE UP

WHEN HE LEFT FOR THE pros, Michael Jordan had far more than a lucrative rookie contract with the Chicago Bulls. He had also become a millionaire thanks to the shrewd business tactics of Nike cofounder and chairman Phil Knight and his marketing wizard John Paul Vincent "Sonny" Vaccaro.

Sonny Vaccaro was born on September 23, 1939, in Trafford, Pennsylvania, outside Pittsburgh. "I went to Youngstown State University, then taught what they now call special education in Pittsburgh starting in 1962. In time, I broke into coaching, working with young people. We had a high school basketball all-star game, the Dapper Dan Classic, and I organized it and ran it."

Vaccaro's Dapper Dan Roundball Classic, which he started in 1965, endured for 43 years. Its alumni include such greats as Calvin Murphy, Shaquille O'Neal, Kobe Bryant, Chris Webber, Alonzo Mourning, Kevin Garnett, Vince Carter, Tracy McGrady, Patrick Ewing, Rasheed Wallace, and Stephon Marbury.

"I quit teaching in 1970, represented George Gervin in his ABA days, and ran summer camps," Vaccaro said. "I became a pseudo-celebrity then. We had the only all-star game. McDonald's didn't start until 1977. I had a friend, an agent in New York who represented Phil Chenier, who was with the Bullets then."

Vaccaro had designed several basketball shoes and sought a company to buy his idea. His agent friend had a connection with a small athletic shoe manufacturer named Nike out in Oregon, near Eugene. Nike was the brainchild of Bill Bowerman, the University of Oregon's famed track coach, and his middle-distance runner Phil Knight, who earned an MBA at Stanford. Knight went to Japan in 1963 and stopped in to visit Tiger, a subsidiary of the Onitsuka Company that made running shoes. He convinced Tiger to make his "company," Blue Ribbon Sports—a name and business he dreamed up on the spot—their American distributor. With $1,200 in the bank and a hustling salesman named Jeff Johnson, they sold Tigers out of Bowerman's car trunk and soon turned it into a million-dollar company.

Bowerman, meanwhile, came up with his special design for running shoes one morning at breakfast when he noticed the grooved pattern his wife's waffle iron created in the morning waffles and thought he could translate it into running shoes. The inventive Johnson convinced Knight and Bowerman in 1971 to use the name Nike, as in the Greek goddess of victory, and they were off and running. Enter Sonny Vaccaro, who was sitting on those basketball shoe designs and several prototypes.

"I paid my way to Oregon. That's how it started. I showed them the prototypes and never saw them again," Vaccaro said. Knight liked the ideas and the man so much he hired the fast-talking Vaccaro as a marketing consultant and put him in charge of the world of college basketball. "I convinced college coaches to take our Nike shoes, and the rest is history. Bill Bowerman and Knight were the Nike guys then. Their business was track," Vaccaro said. "Converse had 99 percent of the business. We had one school [Oregon]." Vaccaro had an idea that Knight, the marketing force behind Nike, bought into. He would pay coaches to outfit their teams in his shoes, and they would give them the shoes. "In time, they started buying from us and turning their schools into Nike campuses," Vaccaro said.

"Converse was the big player then, and Joe Dean was the man who ran it," Vaccaro said. "Dean Smith was the type of man who was loyal to a fault to people like Joe Dean and, of course, his players. He always was there for them, and they knew it and rewarded his loyalty. They knew he would be there for them well after they were out of school, which he was."

The shoe business in the '70s was small-time and certainly did not make coaches rich by any means. The idea, then, for coaches was to make a deal with a school and get shoes for their basketball players. There were no special deals for leisure apparel, sweats, or any other extraordinary garb. College bookstores were in business to sell textbooks and a few extra books they figured students might like to read. They weren't clothing stores.

By the early '80s, Nike had become a major player. Vaccaro was ready to pounce after seeing Michael Jordan play and be honored in 1983–84 as unanimous college player of the year. Jordan also was ready to take the next step. "When it came time for Michael Jordan to turn pro after his junior year, we went to him to get his own brand of shoe," Vaccaro said. "No other shoe company would do that with any other athlete. Larry Bird and Magic were Converse men. Dean Smith and Carolina were Converse. Michael wanted Adidas, but we invited him and his parents to Oregon and they came. I had to talk and talk with Phil Knight to give Michael his own brand, which we finally agreed to do and create Air Jordan. The marketing was and is unique. Nobody else has been able to do that. No other shoes bring in the money the way Air Jordans do. He is so tough and so smart. These shoes have made him a billionaire and made so much for Nike. Jordan landed in the right place at the right time.

"I did not meet Dean Smith until 1985, a year after Jordan left for the pros," Vaccaro said. "Dean had integrity. He controlled the operation and all those great players—Jordan, Worthy, Perkins—and they loved playing for him. I can't say we were close friends. We were not. But he was someone you could trust. His word was good, and his players knew it long after they were out of school."

"Dean never coached for money. Never took a dime. Money was the most insignificant thing in his life," Billy Cunningham said.

"Dean Smith couldn't get hired today. He was too quiet, didn't rant on the sidelines. But he knew the game and taught it so well, like Wooden, Knight, and Krzyzewski," Vaccaro continued.

"He had that basketball camp," Cunningham recalled. "It had to be a lot. Six or 7 weeks of that. All that money went to his assistant coaches. You couldn't get into Dean Smith's camp. You had to know somebody. It wasn't a matter of signing up. It was who you knew to be able to get in."

"It is true, as Billy Cunningham told you," Vaccaro said. "He didn't load up on the extras and camp money, and he let his assistants have it. He was that type of man." Jordan was the star of the 1984 Olympic team, playing as well as he could for the demanding taskmaster Bob Knight. How did the player feel about "the General"? As Roland Lazenby quoted a jocular Jordan, "Coach Smith is the master of the four corners offense, and Coach Knight is the master of the four letter word."

When Jordan got to the Bulls, head coach Kevin Loughery turned him loose on the court. It was so much easier for Jordan to have the freedom he enjoyed in the NBA, plus he had truly big money to live the life any young millionaire would savor. Now he was able to drive his new Corvette with the "JUMP 23" license plates and live well with his own brand of basketball shoes that enriched him and his business associates, agents David Falk and

Donald Dell; his shoe sponsor, Nike; and its chairman, Phil Knight.

Like Jordan in years ahead, Knight would become a billionaire thanks to the magnetic sales ability of this extraordinary athlete. On the other foot, pun intended, coaches and schools raked in the money when they signed on to endorsement deals for shoes, clothing, and logo placement for their programs. Their campuses became outlets for their shoe company of choice, be it for the most part Nike, Adidas, or Reebok.

Vaccaro, the marketing wizard who made Nike the player it became with shoes, took his talent first to Reebok and then to Adidas, where he got Kobe Bryant a million-dollar endorsement deal straight out of high school before he joined the Los Angeles Lakers and a $125,000 consulting deal with Adidas for Joe "Jellybean" Bryant for delivering his son to the shoe manufacturer.

As many coaches were making fortunes from their shoe company deals that ran the gamut from shoes to sweats and leisure wear, Dean Smith remained a creature of his upbringing. Many great coaches have earned far less than was thought, whether they did not know how nor feel confident to negotiate big-money deals in the time before agents stepped up to change the game. While so many coaches have made fortunes in recent years, with huge merchandising contracts, camps, and the like, Smith did not personally cash in the way his contemporaries such as Mike Krzyzewski, John Thompson, and Rick Pitino did. According to AP sports writer Steve Wilstein, Smith in 1997, the year he retired, had a salary from the school of $162,750, veritable chump change already by this time. Wilstein reported that North Carolina's then athletic director John Swofford signed a 4-year, $4.7 million deal with Nike in 1993. It covered 24 of the school's teams. "This easily could have been a contract just for Coach Smith," Swofford said at the time.

Smith, instead, received $500,000 up front. "Smith did something unusual," Wilstein writes. "He gave away half his $300,000 annual Nike salary, distributing it among his assistants and office staff. He also earmarked $45,000 a year of his salary to a special fund to help former players finish their degrees."

UNC and Nike have continued their relationship, the latest renewal in 2009, a $37.7 million extension. In the deal, Nike would provide the athletic department with shoes, uniforms, coaching gear, balls, and other equipment. Nike also gave UNC $2 million to the Chancellor's Academic Enhancement Fund. Nike gave the school's athletic department $1 million to overhaul lighting and sound systems at the Smith Center. Nike also funded bonus payments to coaches based on classroom achievements by their players and in athletic competition. Additionally, Nike entered into individual contracts with Carolina's head coaches.

Under that deal, Nike would pay the university a premium royalty for the sale of merchandise bearing Carolina logos and was awarded the exclusive right to manufacture Carolina merchandise that included jerseys. To stay out of trouble with the government and do-gooders, Nike and UNC reaffirmed a 2001 agreement worth $28.3 million to follow fair labor practices. All this is another way of saying that Nike and other schools were engaged in what had become a quasi-legal form of payola.

Like everything else in sport, the big money called the shots and ruled the day.

13 | A WINNER
TO THE END

LIFE WITHOUT MICHAEL JORDAN, THOUGH, did not mean
Dean Smith would wither on the vine. He did nothing of the sort as
he continued to recruit blue-chip (Carolina blue, of course) talent
and build winners. He did have to adjust to the changing game,
though. There were too many fine players out there at other schools
to run the same systematic plays and patterns that had defined his
term for 3-plus decades. Plus, he had to devote off-hours to fund-
raising, as the money men at the school decided to build a state-of-
the-art basketball facility on a 7.5-acre plot of land on the university's
south campus. Smith protested somewhat in his memoir that he
wasn't pushing for the new arena, that Carmichael Auditorium, with
its 10,000-plus seats, was just fine. "I've always believed that when
you can't get a ticket, that's the best situation for a program," he
wrote. There's a certain logic to that.

Smith knew that state aid to build a new facility was out of
the question and that private financing would have to be secured. The
school and its chief fund-raiser for the project, Hargrove "Skipper"
Bowles, the father of diplomat Erskine Bowles and a powerful state
Democratic Party moneyman, went to work. Skipper Bowles was

especially close to Smith, a fellow Democrat, and he prevailed upon the coach to join him on a 40-stop tour of North Carolina.

According to David Halberstam in his Jordan biography *Playing for Keeps*, Smith did not want the arena named for himself, but the people who count at UNC, from administrators to Skipper Bowles and other financiers, prevailed when they told Smith they feared that without him the fund-raising effort would fail. It did not fail, and $33.8 million later, the newly paid-for 21,750-seat Dean E. Smith Center opened for business on January 18, 1986, with a 95–92 Carolina victory over Duke.

That is not to say that the Dean E. Smith Center—or Dean Dome, as it is universally called—is a thing of perfection. It is not. Smith claimed in *A Coach's Life* that he agreed to supplant Carmichael Auditorium with the new building because more students could go to the game. At least that's what he wrote, knowing the way money was raised at his and so many other schools.

That led to a major hitch. The moneyed backers, who are UNC's athletic boosters—the Educational Foundation, aka the Rams Club—were allocated most of the lower-level seats, virtually all of them season tickets. Scalping long has been prevalent there, as it is at many athletic facilities, college and pro, in this demand economy. UNC now puts any tickets returned by visiting team followers on sale for near face value at 5:00 p.m. eastern time on game days.

Furthermore, as former sports information director Rick Brewer noted, the building needed thorough repairs after some 30 years of use. Brewer reminded anyone who listened that the planners simply did not build enough women's bathrooms in the then new Smith Center. The building is always in use for one event or another, is a focal point of the campus, and, of course, with the name over the door, is a constant reminder of who made it possible.

In November 2015, after Smith's death, North Carolina Athletic

Director Lawrence "Bubba" Cunningham admitted that the school was considering plans to renovate the Dean Dome, a costly project that would involve luxury suites, club seating, or both, and the possible removal of some 4,000 seats—or, depending on the cost (which would be steep), replace it with a new building next door on a current parking lot. Any project would *not* involve state tax money but would be both privately financed and funded with athletic department revenues—meaning basketball and/or football.

Smith for years had to fend off Kansas loyalists who fervently hoped he would return in triumph to create a new era in KU basketball. In effect, he twice closed off such talk when his first point guard and early assistant, Larry Brown, coached Kansas to the 1988 NCAA title and, after that victory over Oklahoma, left town for the NBA's San Antonio Spurs ahead of the NCAA investigators who would soon slap the school with a 3-year probation sentence stemming from recruiting violations. Instead of volunteering to return, Smith instead touted his trusted top assistant, Roy Williams, to replace Brown. Williams reigned in Lawrence for 15 years, leading the Jayhawks to four Final Fours before Carolina called him back for the 2003–04 season.

Dean Smith's success continued onward but not quite to the top over the decade following the 1982 title. The Tar Heels reached the Sweet Sixteen every year and made three Elite Eight appearances but could not reach the Final Four until the 1990–91 team got there, making Smith the first man to coach a team to the national semifinals in each of 4 decades.

One of the referees in that 1991 Final Four was veteran official Ed Hightower, a resident of Edwardsville on the Illinois side of the Mississippi River in metro St. Louis, who became one of the game's most respected officials. Hightower is a retired educator who moved through the teaching ranks to principal and then superintendent of schools in Edwardsville. He earned bachelor's and masters degrees from Southern Illinois University in Carbondale and a doctorate in education administration from St. Louis University. In what passed for spare time, Hightower became a basketball official and worked his way to the top of that profession.

"I worked Division I basketball for 36 years, starting in the Big Ten. I got to know Coach Smith early in my career. I was in my late twenties, age 28, when I broke into the Big Ten," Hightower said in the summer of 2015. "I worked the Big Ten, ACC, and others. They had that contract for years. Well before the Big Ten–ACC Showdown. North Carolina and Duke played teams in the Big Ten. I had the fortune of working those cross-conference games. I would catch North Carolina in the NCAA tournament, including the fortune of refereeing two Final Fours involving Coach Smith."

Officiating at any level is a demanding business and certainly anything but a popularity contest. It takes years of arduous professional work, total knowledge of the rule book from memory with thorough instant recall for each and every situation, and the hard-earned respect of coaches who want favorable calls for certain, but, more important, want the games to be called correctly and accurately. "Coach Smith was always the consummate professional. It was always 'Mr. Hightower . . .' His players always knew the officials. They would *not* say 'Ref.' They would say, 'Mr. Hightower, would you take a look at, say, 21 on the other team. He was holding me as I was trying to cut. He is pushing me on the rebounds.' It was always 'Mr. Hightower.'"

As for Coach Smith himself, Hightower said, "He pushed the line. When he disputed a call, he was always on a professional level. He had that knack of making you say to yourself, 'Maybe I missed that.' Perhaps he was right and he made you take another look, a closer look. He was not ripping us on the sidelines. He was making a case in the professional manner. He was not bombastic. He'd say, 'Mr. Hightower, you missed a travel.' He never said, 'Ed!'"

In the 1991 Final Four, North Carolina faced Kansas, Smith's alma mater, coached by his former assistant, Roy Williams. Williams had the Jayhawks ready, and one of Hightower's officiating partners, Pete Pavia of Rochester, New York, who had worked several other Final Fours, was ready to make a name for himself.

"It was obvious there had been previous experiences involved between Coach Smith and Pete Pavia," Hightower said a quarter century later. "From the time the game started, they were engaged in a conflict. In the first half, there was dialogue. Pavia thought he had crossed the line and administered a technical foul."

The game proceeded toward its conclusion when, with just 35 seconds left and Kansas leading 76–71, Carolina's Rick Fox fouled out and Smith walked substitute Kenny Harris toward the scorer's table to replace him. "There was a continuation of that dialogue," Hightower said. "It ended in my opinion as one of the worst situations I had been involved in as a referee on the on the national stage when you see one of the greatest ambassadors of the game excused with under a minute left." Those who were on the floor, including Smith's assistant, Bill Guthridge, and Kansas's Williams, said Smith asked Pavia three times in these words, "Pete, how much time do I have [to make the substitution]?" Pavia answered with the sign of the T, and Smith was out of the game.

Why? "He left the coaches' box," said Big Ten Commissioner and rules committee head Jim Delany, a former Tar Heels player for Smith.

"I often have wished we could have avoided that situation," Hightower said a quarter century later. "We say as officials, when you get down to the last 2 minutes, unless that coach comes out on the floor and you have no choice, you tell yourself, 'Can I endure this dialogue for the last few seconds of a game?' Coach Smith was not screaming, yelling, or gyrating out on the floor. It was one of the worst situations I have ever been party to. You want to tell your colleague to stay away from the coach and avoid the situation. Confronting it makes it worse. It was so tough, although I had not been directly involved."

For his part, a smiling Smith shook hands with Williams and his team, then left the floor. Kansas won 79–73 to advance to the title game against Duke's Blue Devils, who upset the undefeated defending champion UNLV Runnin' Rebels 79–77 in the other semifinal. Duke then beat the Jayhawks 72–65 for Mike Krzyzewski's first of five titles. Cancer killed Pavia, the official who ejected Smith, a year later.

It took 2 more years for Carolina to return to the throne. An early major test in late 1992 came in the December 29 title game of the Rainbow Classic in Honolulu when Michigan's Fab Five of Chris Webber, Jalen Rose, Juwan Howard, Jimmy King, and Ray Jackson beat the Heels 79–78 on Rose's putback at the buzzer. The following March, Michigan earned the top seed in the West Regional, and Carolina drew the top berth in the East. The Tar Heels faced Kansas again in the semifinal, beating the Jayhawks 78–68 as Michigan beat Kentucky 81–78 in overtime.

That set up a coming-of-age game matching the long-established system way of coaching and playing by acknowledged master Dean Smith vs. the total improvisation and demonstrations of outrageous playground skills handled by Steve Fisher, who played ringmaster more than tutor. Carolina was fundamentals and precise, well-drilled plays and patterns, knowledge of the rules, proper rebounding technique, hands up, tail down, feet moving on defense, crisp passing and picks, no showboating. Smith tolerated no showing up an opponent or yakking at an official, as personified by his well-crafted Carolina Way that he learned through thousands of hours of clinics, reading, practice, film study, and acquired knowledge from people such as his father, Coach Phog Allen, Dick Harp, Bob Spear, and Frank McGuire. It was based on respect.

Michigan's Fab Five athletes were the talk of the country, who considered themselves a fraternity, brothers for life. They mostly came from difficult, inner-city backgrounds, but they each had their athletic skills, and Michigan landed them in 1991. Chris Webber, from Detroit, was a smart, extremely talented athlete who got a scholarship to prestigious Detroit Country Day School in wealthy Oakland County. Webber was a hungry athlete with fluid moves, easily able to play any position on the court. From his junior year in high school, he was rated the best player in the country, so good that he won the Naismith Award for prep player of the year as a senior. Another future Country Day player, Shane Battier, would one-up Webber when he also won the Naismith Prep award in high school then added to it at Duke with the Naismith College award.

The Fab Five starred Webber; his fellow Detroiter Jalen Rose, whom he met when he was 12; Chicago native Juwan Howard; and guards Ray Jackson and Jimmy King, both from Texas. They came out running, jumping, and slam-dunking, each one. Webber was the top star, and Rose, no shrinking violet, had NBA genes. His father was 1965 All-America guard Jimmy Walker, top choice of the Detroit Pistons. Walker, who did not marry Rose's mother, died in 2007 never having met Jalen, who only has seen his father's image in pictures. The Fab Five reached the championship game in 1992 in Minneapolis, losing 71–51 to Duke.

They returned to the Final Four in 1993. Smith got a measure of revenge as Carolina beat Kansas 78–68 to advance to the title game while Michigan had a difficult but winning game, defeating Kentucky 81–68. Hightower would work his second championship game with Dean Smith and North Carolina.

"When you talk about how the game has evolved over the years and pinpoint various aspects of the game, the Michigan team was as talented a young team [of] teenaged freshmen as ever played to that time. In recruiting, everyone got their fair share, but this was a situation where a group of talented freshmen players on the team got together," Hightower said. "They were confident, talented, smart, and [they had] that swagger about themselves that said it will happen. They were the first team that came out there with the long shorts and different socks. When you look at how this talented team changed the game, they will go down in history as much as the three-point shots, reduction of the clock, and other aspects of the game that have changed."

In no way were the Tar Heels as purely talented as the Wolverines, but they had the old fox in their corner. He had landed a unit comprising eight players for the title run, entering and leaving the game as needed, as they had top energy for the effort. Eric Montross, now a 7-foot-tall junior, was the big man Smith had wanted since he was high school All-American at Lawrence North in northeast suburban Indianapolis. The choices in his intense recruitment boiled down to Indiana, Michigan (his parents' alma mater), and Carolina. "I am a homebody, and the familiar feel I got so quickly in Chapel Hill was a direct result of the environment created by the Carolina coaches." After a pro career, Montross returned to Chapel Hill, where he worked on game broadcasts and raised funds for the Educational Association. He checked in with Smith at the office until the coach's illness kept him confined to home.

The main players on this team were Montross, George Lynch,

Brian Reese, Donald Williams (who was named outstanding player of the tournament), and Derrick Phelps.

In a moment of inspiration in the preseason, Coach Smith was looking at a photograph of the 1982 postgame scoreboard in the Louisiana Superdome that read "Congratulations, 1982 champions, University of North Carolina." He had that shot reprinted with the legend, "Congratulations, 1993 champions, University of North Carolina."

A few days later, that new picture was posted in each player's locker. "It was a subtle but conscious reminder," Montross said.

Most observers and experts thought the Fab Five would win. They beat Carolina 79–78 on December 29, 1991, in the semifinals of the Rainbow Classic in Honolulu when Rose made a couple of game-saving plays. The first came when he grabbed a loose ball near midcourt and threw a heave toward the basket that Webber converted with a dunk. Then, when Jimmy King missed a baseline jumper with Carolina up by a point, Rose got the rebound and hit a short jumper at the buzzer for the Wolverines' victory. They beat Kansas the next night to win the Classic.

"That team will go down as a factor in changing the game," Ed Hightower said. "The attitude. Young kids across the country mimicked them: the shorts down below the knees, different shoes and socks. They changed elements of the game as much as any team over the last 20 to 30 years."

That was the challenge Smith and his Tar Heels faced in the championship game. In the finals, Carolina held a 42–35 halftime lead, but nobody in the Tar Heels dressing room was trying on championship hats and T-shirts before their time. "Coach Smith always had something ready. He was selfless, quick to help, a mentor," said Montross in his office at the university's Educational Foundation.

Montross, ironically, was the son and grandson of former Michigan basketball players. "We ran all the time, every game, with the time clock racing, which meant no more four corners," Montross said.

The game boiled down to the final 3 minutes. Michigan had been leading in the second half until Donald Williams put the Tar Heels up by a point. Then with 2:18 to go, George Lynch hit a short turnaround in the lane and Carolina was up by three, 70–67. Carolina had two time-outs. Michigan was down to its last one.

Smith took a chance and put two defensive players in the game, big man Pat Sullivan for Montross and German Henrik Rodl for his leading scorer on the night, Williams. It worked when Michigan turned it over. Smith then resubstituted the originals, Williams and Montross. From the backcourt, Lynch took a pass and hit Montross, who dunked to make it 72–67 Carolina with a minute to go. Ray Jackson countered with what appeared to be a three on television, and Michigan called its final time-out. The referees saw Jackson's foot on the line, corrected their call, and the score stood at 72–69 in favor of Carolina with 46 seconds to play. After North Carolina's Brian Reese stepped out of bounds on the sideline, Webber came back with a basket underneath to narrow the Tar Heels' lead to one. The clock kept running. The Heels' Pat Sullivan got fouled, made the first shot on the one-and-one, but missed the second one and Michigan, trailing 73–71, had the ball and a chance for the tie (or, with a three-pointer, the win) with 17 seconds remaining. That set up the sequence that forever will haunt Michigan and elevate North Carolina into its Blue Heaven.

"You hope as an official you do not become the single factor that determines the outcome of the game," Hightower said. "Just before the extra time-out was called, there was an obvious travel that was missed by the crew as you take a look at it, an unseen traveling call on Chris Webber that was missed by everyone prior to that time.

Not much is said about that. If you look at that tape, which I have a number of times, my colleague was on top of that in front of Coach Smith's bench. He probably had the best look at it."

Now unnerved, Webber dribbled upcourt toward his own sideline, got trapped and, without thinking or realizing his team was out of time-outs, flashed the time-out signal, which resulted in a referee (not Hightower) signaling a technical foul. Carolina's Donald Williams coolly sank two technical foul shots and then added two more as Carolina won Smith's second championship, 77–71.

"We went down the floor and the time-out was called, which Michigan did not have," Hightower said. "That would have become the focus of the game. That was played quite a lot. If Michigan would have gone down and scored, that non–travel call would have been the big focus. The referees missed that travel."

"Even Coach, who knew everything, didn't know that Chris Webber would do what he did at the end of the game," Montross said.

Nobody outside the University of Michigan knew that a booster named Ed Martin had been giving and/or loaning large amounts of money to basketball players for years via money from an illegal lottery he conducted in the Ford plant where he worked. The most prominent player was Webber, who admitted in federal court that he took and repaid just over $38,000 in the scheme. Martin testified that he gave Webber more than $280,000, a figure Webber denied. When Martin died of a pulmonary embolism in 2003, the criminal case withered away. The University of Michigan agreed to sanctions, some self-imposed, that included the removal of banners from Crisler Arena that had honored the Final Four teams for 1992 and 1993, the NIT championship banner for 1997, and the Big Ten tournament title banner from 1998. Four ex-players, most prominent among them Webber, had their names removed from school and conference records. Webber never has admitted that he took money from Martin, a fact his fellow Fab Five brothers say he cannot deny.

Smith's Carolina teams by then, his 1993 title team among them, included several key players who received academic exceptions to gain eligibility to compete. Three of them, George Lynch, Derrick Phelps, and Donald Williams, majored in the since-discredited African American studies program that not only started in 1993 but would continue until 2011, to the detriment of the university. Smith, who had to know that something was amiss in the African American studies program, hung around long enough for his Tar Heels to reach two more Final Fours: in 1995, where they lost to Arkansas, and in 1997, where they fell to eventual champion Arizona. That final team of his featured such players as Vince Carter and Antawn Jamison, the National Player of the Year in 1998 for Coach Bill Guthridge. They followed the likes of Rasheed Wallace and Jerry Stackhouse back in 1994–95. All four had significant pro careers but brought no NCAA title for Dean Smith and their school.

14 | TROUBLE IN
TAR HEEL COUNTRY

THE FOLLOWING OCTOBER, BEFORE THE start of fall practice in 1997, Smith stunned his followers and basketball fans everywhere when he announced that he would be resigning as head coach of the Tar Heels, effective immediately. The coach said he no longer could give the team the enthusiasm the job required. Before the school could launch a national search, and because the timing of the announcement came so close to the start of the season, Smith handed over the program to his capable assistant and friend going back to Kansas days, Bill Guthridge.

John Swofford left his longtime job as North Carolina's athletic director to become ACC commissioner a few months before Smith stepped down. Smith "never was definitive about it. He had some concerns on a personal level on what he would do, which is not unusual when a person has held the same job for so long," Swofford said. "I was a little surprised, but not really, because he always said when it's time to resume practice and I'm not really excited about it, then it will be time to step out of it. Dean loved coaching. It was his classroom, his players and concern about their grades. I think peripheral things like fund-raising got him down, if anything. I never saw any signs of his illness. He had the sharpest mind of anyone I've ever known. Bar none."

Guthridge justified Smith's confidence, going 80–28 as he led the Tar Heels to the Final Four in both 1998 and 2000. They lost in each of those two semifinals, then Guthridge retired in 2000. After Roy Williams, Larry Brown, and Eddie Fogler all turned down the job, Matt Doherty, the head coach at Notre Dame for the 1999–2000 season and the fourth man on the shortlist, was offered the position. He accepted, leaving Smith angry, as Doherty was not the man he wanted in that job. Doherty played on the Michael Jordan–James Worthy–Sam Perkins–Jimmy Black 1981–82 national championship team. Smith's feelings about Doherty soon would become evident.

Doherty brought his assistants with him from Notre Dame; axed the Smith–Guthridge assistants Phil Ford, Pat Sullivan, and Dave Hanners; and fired the secretarial pool. After a winning 26–7 record his first year, Doherty staggered through the worst mark in school history, 8–20 in his second, and came back for a third season with a decidedly mediocre 19–16 record that ended with a loss to Georgetown in the third round of the NIT. That season earned him a pink slip.

This time, with urgent pleas from Dean Smith himself, Roy Williams answered the call, leaving behind 15 years of success at Kansas to return home and "restore the glory," as it were. Williams was able to win a national title in 2005, beating top-ranked Illinois 75–70 in the final and adding another in 2009, when Tyler Hansbrough led the team to an 89–72 defeat over Michigan State for the title.

Over the next 4 years, the glitter washed off North Carolina's glossy program like a cheap paint job. First, Smith's family would reveal the scope of what would be a ravaging, slow-moving terminal illness. His appearances at the basketball office would no longer be routine, let alone a daily occurrence. Then, in 2012, the school revealed that it had perpetrated the most significant and systematic academic fraud any university had ever committed, one that ran for 18 years basically unknown to the public. It started in 1993 and ran until 2011 and directly involved many of the school's basketball and football players and their highly paid coaches. The news would be splashed and splattered everywhere on television and in banner headline stories that started from an investigation by Dan Kane of the Raleigh *News and Observer.* It was blatant enough to merit the firing of football coach Butch Davis. Worst of all, the most prominent name mentioned, but never accused of wrongdoing, was the heretofore sacrosanct Dean Smith himself.

The report from independent investigator Kenneth Wainstein disclosed that during an 18-year period, 1993 to 2011, so-called paper classes were offered to 3,100 students out of 97,500 undergraduates at the university. Student-athletes composed 47.6 percent (about 1,460) of the enrollment in those irregular classes.

News and Observer investigative reporter Kane explained how it worked in a story dated November 8, 2014, after it was revealed in the Wainstein report that several coaches had helped place athletes in the African and Afro-American Studies (AFAM) program over that 18-year period. Many of the classes were bogus, outright frauds. They operated under the guidance of African studies manager Deborah Crowder, who was *not* a UNC professor. Crowder helped the students with classes that required nothing more than a paper that she graded. She did not make quality assessments.

The classes included independent studies, which were listed in course syllabuses as classes that did not meet. Those courses had no academic supervision. Crowder was supposed to issue the paper topics and then collect and grade the papers. Then again, perhaps she didn't even bother to do anything other than issue grades for noncourses.

There were lecture classes that did not meet. They were better known as no-show classes. Crowder treated them as independent studies.

There were bifurcated classes. Those were classes that did not meet, and Crowder allowed some athletes to enroll in them, calling them independent study without undergoing the formality of attending class. All the athletes had to do was turn in a paper that she graded.

Add-on classes where Crowder added students, most of them athletes, were classes that did meet; however, the athletes did not have to attend the add-ons nor turn in a paper. And basketball was right in the maelstrom with football.

When North Carolina reached the 2005 Final Four in St. Louis and beat Illinois for the title, players from the team were enrolled in 35 classes that did not meet. They got through with easy high grades. Star Rashad McCants told ESPN on June 6, 2014, that he took three independent-study classes and one lecture that had no instruction. He walked away with straight A-minuses: a dean's list performance. McCants repeated his story 5 days later after former teammates and Coach Roy Williams disputed his claim.

Other than McCants, who twice volunteered his story to ESPN, the report by the former federal prosecutor Wainstein in May 2014 does not reveal names due to federal privacy law. UNC Chancellor Carol Folt detailed her disappointment in a postreport news conference, lamenting, she said, "the lack of oversight, specifically vital checks and balances that, if in place, would have captured and corrected this so much sooner." Fox noted that the Carolina community would find this report very sobering. "This never should have happened."

Author Ralph Martin published in 1983 a unique, albeit friendly, biography about the late president John F. Kennedy called *A Hero for Our Time*. For people in the Tar Heel State, especially those who religiously follow the comings and goings of the University of North Carolina, Dean Edwards Smith remains the hero for their time no matter the circumstances or even these revelations of academic scandal in recent years. That's the way it's been for almost as long as Smith replaced coaching legend Frank McGuire in 1961.

McGuire's 10-year run that made Carolina a major national power was tarnished at the end after a second major college basketball scandal involving a web of thrown games and point-shaving burst into the public forum. McGuire was not a major figure in the wrongdoing that unfolded that year, but he knew what was going on, and the wise heads who ran the University of North Carolina—men like William Friday and William Aycock—knew enough to encourage his departure ASAP. They also sensed immediately that they could trust his young assistant, Dean Smith, who came from the honored culture of Dr. Forrest "Phog" Allen on the Kansas prairie, had a wife and three small children, displayed an intellectually curious philosophy that fit their liberal institution, and possessed a burning competitive desire to succeed honestly.

When they entrusted Smith with the job at $9,200 a year, Friday and Aycock were certain he would not cheat in procuring talent and would graduate his players in an acceptable curriculum. His graduation rate over the next 36 years turned out to be an outstanding 96.3 percent. Smith-coached teams won 879 games, the most in college basketball history, ahead of Adolph Rupp, at the time of Smith's 1997 retirement. Although his victory mark has been surpassed by Duke's Mike Krzyzewski, Bob Knight of Indiana and Texas Tech, and Syracuse's Jim Boeheim, Coach Smith has remained a "Teflon Dean" and remains beloved among the Carolina faithful.

That he stood for something good and won honestly were primary reasons his name is on the building where Carolina basketball teams play their games: the Dean E. Smith Student Activities Center, as its formal name states; the Dean Dome, as all Carolinians call it.

"There were independent studies going on through AFAM, and he never would have stood for that had he known something had been wrong," John Swofford said. "He would have brought it forward and addressed it. I never had any concerns about his skirting the NCAA rules." Then again, Coach Smith was long honored at the university to the point of naming its most prominent athletic structure after him. People there long have looked the other way when others see clay clinging to their feet.

The coach, when he still was lucid, did confide more than a few troubled thoughts with certain longtime friends and associates, men like the legendary Tar Heels announcer Woody Durham.

Smith told Durham about things that bothered him, including the building that bears his name. "He always called it the Student Activities Center," Durham said. "He didn't want the name Dean Smith on the thing. The other thing about this building that he didn't like at all was the name Dean Dome. He just really didn't appreciate that at all."

After he stepped down in 1997, Smith, as the school's venerated elder statesman, maintained an office in the center and still called many of the shots in Chapel Hill. As mentioned before, he engineered the return of the former assistant he mentored, Roy Williams. Then, by 2007, he was quite ill with the rapacious disease his physician wife, Linnea, termed a "neurocognitive disorder with multiple etiologies."

The illness was a monster that took away everything piece by piece, and did it unreasonably fast once it manifested itself: The man with the photographic memory quickly lost the ability to drive and park a car correctly; to play golf, the game he loved and had played well; to watch a film, analyze it if it concerned basketball, enjoy it if he chose; to read and understand material he loved and thrived upon;

to discuss politics and matters of civic interest; and most telling, to help, and mentor his former players when they sought his help; as well as so many more daily doings. The family never used the words "Alzheimer's disease," even though that term fit the myriad ailments Linnea Smith itemized when she revealed the extent of his illness.

It also is obvious to most of the world outside relatively insular or unseeing Chapel Hill that the once acclaimed University of North Carolina had become a cesspool of intellectual dishonesty thanks to a runaway win-at-all-costs athletics operation. It's a place that lost its so-called Carolina Way and its mission to educate by allowing big money-making intercollegiate athletics, namely basketball and football, to corrupt everything the school's history and reputation was based upon.

Here was a school that was kept alive during the Civil War and then thrived after it, that became a leader in positive activities from coeducation to battling for integration well before the *Brown v. the Board of Education* decision, in a part of the country that far too long had denied racial tolerance and common decency to all—and, in far too many cases, still does. Before that decision took real effect nearly 20 years later (remember the words in the opinion: "with all deliberate speed"), southern schools simply fielded all-white teams as they moved with *no* speed to integrate. The Atlantic Coast Conference began to change when Dean Smith arrived from Kansas and decided that he wanted to win with the best players who not only could play but could legitimately compete in the classroom. All the better, he felt, if they were black, because he had seen African American athletes excel and dominate when he was a young man on the prairie. So he did what he felt had to be done, and until 1993 or so, he made sure they took courses of educational and practical value before he acceded to the new way of doing business, which really was a dishonest way of cheating young athletes out of an education by having them take phony courses to remain eligible instead of academically challenging courses to make them better educated.

Nowadays, too many colleges and universities import the descendants of slaves to entertain their alumni and fellow students in athletic arenas before huge, screaming crowds. It's not gladiatorial combat, because the athletes don't fight to the death. And sure, the athletes are enrolled in their respective universities, but the schools, unfortunately in too many instances, showcase athletic talents without educating the students using their skills to sell team merchandise—such as uniform jerseys—to rake in money for the schools. The little kid at the ballpark who begs his parents for a star's jersey goes home happy to wear a numbered shirt. Meanwhile, the athletes whose names are on the merchandise get absolutely nothing.

Worse than that rip-off, many of these athlete-students cannot read at a grade-school level, let alone grasp collegiate academic study. The schools just do their best to keep the athletes eligible to play their games, especially basketball or football. The schools need the athletes, regardless of their intellectual gifts or lack of them, to win games because those wins help schools rake in huge amounts of money. The really big bucks come primarily from television networks that use the games and the athletes' star power to sell product and make the money so the networks can pay exorbitant "rights fees" to show the games on TV regardless of the time of day.

Has fund-raising been affected by this scandal and the revelations? "The university is reporting record fund-raising," said Dan Kane in August 2016. "I don't know about the Rams Club. It all boils down to whether the university cares if the kids get an education or not."

What UNC created back in 1993 or so is known as a shadow curriculum. As mentioned in the Introduction, former UNC academic advisor and tutor Mary Willingham and her writing partner, UNC history professor Jay N. Smith, described this nefarious system in the 2015 book *Cheated: The UNC Scandal, the Education of Athletes, and the Future of Big-Time Sports*. Their work became known through the enterprising reporting of Raleigh *News and Observer* investigative reporter Dan Kane in a series of articles that exposed the practice beginning in the 2011–12 academic year.

In their book, as well as in Kane's many articles, Willingham and Dr. Smith detail a system in which athletes were steered to courses they called "easy A's." Those courses included dramatic art, philosophy, geology, geography, and French. Also, many black student-athletes were steered into the African and Afro-American Studies curriculum. AFAM was described by ex–Dean Smith player and former basketball coach Matt Doherty as the easiest major on campus.

Deborah Crowder became the key operator in that department. She had been hired in 1979 as the student services manager in the department and sympathized with the plight of the so-called disadvantaged students who, like herself as a UNC student from 1971–75, did not get much direction and support. Crowder also happened to be a sports fan, especially of basketball, and she wanted to help. She had wanted to water down requirements but did not do so until 1992, when Dr. Julius Nyang'oro became chairman of the department. Dr. Nyang'oro, a basketball fan like Crowder, let her design a course of study that was light on student work and easy on the grades.

She devised "paper classes" taught on an independent basis for students and student-athletes Crowder selected. These courses required no class attendance and the submission of a single research paper. Because she wanted the students to succeed, Crowder handled all the work, did not require attendance, and, in time, didn't even bother with a course of study nor worry about the papers, let alone the research part of the assignments. Most egregious under Crowder's purview were courses in Swahili, where she assigned no course of study, just grades that she made up. When courses required research papers, sometimes the work was submitted, other times not. No problem. She always handled the grades and recorded them, usually high Bs or A's. It was that simple.

During Dean Smith's final years as coach, in the period from 1993 through 1997, 54 basketball players enrolled in the AFAM course. Knowing Smith's penchant for absolute control in all facets of the basketball program since Chancellor Aycock hired him in 1961, he had to know what was going on there.

And so it went, from 18 students under Guthridge to 42 under Doherty to 167 under Williams. By 2011, the word was out that the university was running a sham, totally bogus curriculum, granting grades to certain students, mainly basketball and football players, without their having to attend a course, study, write papers, or take any tests. That sham was revealed in detail in October 2014 in the report issued by attorney and university alumnus Kenneth Wainstein, who uncovered the extent of the fraud, as detailed by Willingham and Dr. Smith. Both Willingham and Dr. Smith retain access to the transcripts of those students and went so far as to print one for current Green Bay Packers star and former Tar Heel football and basketball player Julius Peppers, in which he took a large number of paper courses.

Through all this, Dean Smith pretty well escaped blame and scrutiny in the investigation. The investigators were unable to speak with either Smith or Guthridge because of their debilitative medical conditions. In the Wainstein report, former coach Matt Doherty admitted that he inherited the academic support system that Smith and Guthridge developed. Doherty told Wainstein that both Smith and Guthridge, who at that time still shared an office in the Dean Dome, told the younger coach (their former player in the early '80s) that he should not change the system, which he did not.

"Dean Smith is kind of gray in this," Dan Kane added in August 2016. "He's not in the clear, yet he is not named, not guilty. It's a fog. Then he lost his faculties, there was no record, and nothing could happen there."

Williams, on the other hand, said he thought the large number of players in that program made it appear that the athletic department was steering them there. Also, the cat was getting out of the bag, so to speak. It all came down when Rashad McCants's account ran counter to what the coaches had stated. Again, McCants said he took a number of paper courses in his time at UNC, including four paper courses during the 2005 championship season. Furthermore, McCants claimed that Williams was 100 percent aware of all that was going on. And he said all the starters took the paper courses so they didn't have to bother with schoolwork. For his trouble, he made the dean's list. But what he really wanted was an education. McCants did not testify to the investigators.

Williams denied all, calling McCants a liar. This issue continues to fester, and the NCAA has yet to do anything. There may be indications, we are told, that they will *have* to look into it, but skeptics are just not so certain, saying that North Carolina is such a cash cow the NCAA can't afford to go after the school.

Willingham and Dr. Smith told WNCN anchor Sean Maroney in a late January 2015 interview that the situation at UNC was more widespread and pervasive than the Wainstein report revealed. Their book attracted scathing reviews and odium from certain individuals in and close to the university for having the "gall" to reveal that something was truly rotten in the state of UNC's academics. The two were pilloried for being whistle-blowers.

Willingham cited examples in her 2014 research that showed a majority of 180 athletes who took those paper courses could not read at a high school level. In March 2015, Willingham accepted a $335,000 settlement from the university for wrongful termination but did not get back her former job as an academic tutor. In effect, the settlement was made to stop further litigation. Of Dean Smith, Willingham told me, "It's like believing in Santa Claus. We can't prove anything Dean Smith knew. There is no paper trail." Dr. Smith said, "We had access to transcripts, and there are 78 majors at Chapel Hill, Afro-American studies being one of them." Both say the university greatly fears it will have to take down championship banners from at least one tournament, 2005, and perhaps 1993 and 2009 as well. Now that would be a real scandal, every bit as bad, if not worse, than the situation Michigan had to endure with the Ed Martin and Fab Five affair.

In August 2016, Kane told me nothing had changed, except that the university still was stonewalling the NCAA. "The university," Kane said when we spoke, "is saying to the NCAA, (A) it's none of your business, you don't belong in academic business; (B) regular students besides athletes were in those courses; and (C) you had your chance and you failed to act on it because the statute of limitations has run out. That's the argument in a nutshell." There is little if any likelihood that North Carolina will suffer the "death penalty," as the responses and arguments apparently will run well into 2017 and perhaps beyond.

College basketball has yet to deal with "one and done," the modern phenomenon in which players come to college, play for a year, and then declare for the NBA. Kentucky lost seven players from its

2015 Final Four team to the early-departure situation. Carolina's equally self-inflated rival, Duke, has recently lost two top "big men" to the pros, Jabari Parker and Jahlil Okafor, both agile near 7-footers. Both, ironically, are products of Coach K's Chicago pipeline. When the Blue Devils won Krzyzewski's fifth NCAA title in April 2015, two other freshman stars, Tyus Jones and Justise Winslow, joined Okafor in declaring for the NBA draft.

To quote the late Kurt Vonnegut, "and so it goes."

15 | DEAN SMITH'S LEGACY

DEAN SMITH DIED ON SATURDAY, February 7, 2015, with his family at his bedside. Tributes flowed in from everywhere, and perhaps his passing delayed if not deferred any future action against his beloved school. The first person Linnea Smith told outside the school was Dean's best friend from Topeka, Bill Bunten, loyal to the end. "I know Dean Smith well enough that he would not have cheated," Bunten said.

When their mutual high school friend from nearly 70 years ago, former Kansas senator Nancy Landon Kassebaum Baker, got the word, she went to work. As this is written, she and Bunten have raised $50,000 toward a perpetual Dean Smith scholarship fund to be given in $1,000 increments a year each to two worthy Topeka High School students.

What sort of man was Dean Smith? Most who knew him say he was as good a man as any who ever lived. His friend and the longtime Carolina broadcaster Woody Durham was on campus as a student when Smith was hired to replace Frank McGuire. He stayed until the coach stepped down. "Dean Smith could have won the Presidential Medal of Freedom without coaching a basketball game," Durham said. "He recruited Charles Scott and integrated Chapel Hill restaurants. He took the strong stance, and people gave him credit. People get along well unless it's Carolina vs. Duke, or NC State, or Wake Forest. That was Dean."

People loved to talk about Coach Smith's remarkable memory, but what about their memories when it comes to this gentleman? Take retired referee and educator Ed Hightower. "His legacy to the game is more than just basketball. He was an educator. He was a facilitator of change. He was a great humanitarian, treating people with respect," Hightower said. "When I received my doctorate of education, Dean as well as John Thompson sent me a note congratulating me for that. How many coaches would send a referee a note of congratulations as they did? It was such a fine tribute from an educator. He knew I was an educator, a principal, and he and John Thompson were individuals who pushed toward the greater accomplishment from people. Humanitarians."

"I don't think of him in race relations as much as the way he related to me. He was a man who dealt with individuals. He did what was right," John Thompson said. "I appreciate the way he dealt with me, how he was a friend."

"Once I got to meet him, I knew what he did when he first got to Carolina, the civil rights stand, the way he treated his players, all told about his character," Sonny Vaccaro said. "He moved the needle in race relations before anyone else knew what was happening at the hardest of all time in the '60s, '70s, and '80s. He took a stand. He meant more to me than a guy who coached basketball teams."

Smith thrived any and every time he entered the arena, all his life. "The best competitor I've ever been around," Durham said. "He competed in a game of basketball, game of golf. He was most competitive."

Few Carolina alumni have led the outstanding life in basketball and business that Smith's first great star, Billy Cunningham, has enjoyed. Like so many of the others, Cunningham always has been there to laud his former coach for all he did for all. "There were things he did for so many of his players during the course of their lives. You saw the thing he did with his will," Cunningham said. "He sent $200 checks to everybody who participated in his program to go out and have a good dinner on him."

"Whenever Dean was in town, he was at church," said his long-time pastor, Dr. Robert Seymour. "That was the case in the last few years when his wife, Linnea, would bring him to church in his wheel-chair. I'm not sure he knew where he was. His illness was pretty intense. There were times when he had moments of recognition. One of those came when a member of the congregation went down to his home and played some songs and sang them in Dean's presence. Before leaving, this person said, 'One more song.'" As the former coach heard "Hark the sound of Tar Heel voices," the first line of the school song, "Dean sat up, put his hand on his heart, and said, 'Stand up, everybody!'"

"He and Phil Ford had a special relationship. Phil was like a son to him," Cunningham said. "Phil took the program to a special level. They had a truly special and wonderful relationship. Dean was there for Phil through all his issues. He would be there for you. All sorts of great stories about Charles and Lefty in the recruitment. Lefty would have been a great coach [for him], too. Charlie knew what Dean had done for the community, integration. Charlie was there for the memorial service. He knew Dean Smith was more than a basketball coach [because of] what he had done in the community for integration. Dean Smith never spoke about those things. He never wanted the limelight for himself. He truly never did. Dean always pointed toward the players. That was exactly who he was, not an act or show."

"Deep down in his heart, I hope he knew we all cared about him, I hope he knew how much I did and how much he did in our lives," said Smith's personal favorite, Phil Ford.

"In these later years, he was quite interested in theology," Dr. Seymour said. "The one theologian he was especially interested in was Søren Kierkegaard. He respected differences of opinion among people, but he took a stand on controversial issues in a way that I don't think many other coaches would have done. He didn't mind going public saying that we should abolish the death penalty. He would take his players to death row in Raleigh because some of them were his fans. He was publicly against nuclear proliferation and in favor of nuclear disarmament. He belonged to a church that welcomed gays and lesbians and supported that. He won the Arthur Ashe [award] for courage, which was given to him at Radio City Music Hall in New York. He said when accepting it, 'I'm not courageous, I just try to do the right thing.'"

"He was so much more than a basketball coach. He became an institution," Cunningham said. "When you thought of North Carolina, you thought of Dean Smith. His number one concern was what was best for the players."

"He was a great coach, of course, but that's not how I remember him," said Vaccaro. "There are many great coaches. He was something more. He was not a belligerent loudmouth. When he died, I did a lot of radio interviews. He and [University of Nevada, Las Vegas, coach Jerry] Tarkanian had just died. They were special, more human. In my mind, Dean was more than a hall of fame coach. He was a hall of fame human being."

The greatest player and most memorable athlete in basketball history, Michael Jordan, said the things he learned from Dean Smith and treasured most concerned how nervous he was when he left school to turn pro. "He calmed me down with a fatherly attitude, taking me under his wing and teaching me a lot of things about being an adult." In the intervening years since Jordan's father, James, was murdered, he grew even closer to Smith. "I love him," Jordan said. "He's like a second father to me."

ACKNOWLEDGMENTS

I GOT MY FIRST EXPOSURE to organized basketball in 1953 as a 12-year-old boy in Glen Ellyn, Illinois, outside Chicago. A pair of junior high teachers named Don Chase and Ed Boppre were my mentors. They taught me and my teammates the correct way to play the game. They stressed fundamentals: footwork, defense, rebounding, how to dribble, pass, shoot, and how to watch and appreciate a game in detail. It became second nature that has stuck with me to this day.

On my 18th birthday, February 14, 1959, my dad took me to Chicago Stadium for a major college doubleheader. Game one paired Loyola, the host team, with defending national champion Kentucky and its legendary coach Adolph Rupp. After Kentucky won, Notre Dame's Fighting Irish led by Chicagoan Tom Hawkins took the floor to face Frank McGuire's superb North Carolina Tar Heels featuring a host of easterners, mostly from New York.

Carolina won that night, but it took me years to realize that the clue to what that game meant was squirrelled away in a box in our basement. At the time of that game, the name of an assistant coach held little if any interest for a still-wet-behind-the-ears kid. Years later, when I read the program from that doubleheader, I paused when I saw that name with the North Carolina roster—Assistant Coach Dean Smith. Wow. It began to fit.

The rest of America would become aware of Dean Smith in the summer of 1961 when the 30-year-old assistant replaced McGuire, his friend and mentor, to begin his own remarkable 36-year run; develop many of the game's finest players including Michael Jordan, the greatest ever; and gain the utmost regard of basketball fans everywhere by the time he retired in 1997 as the winningest coach in college history, with 879 victories. That record included two NCAA titles, 11 appearances in the Final Four, and the 1976 Olympic gold medal.

This book would not have been possible without the contributions of many men and women who knew and worked with Coach Smith. Smith was terminally ill and unable to speak, let alone receive visitors, when I began my quest in 2014.

I started in Lawrence, Kansas, where Candace Dunback at KU graciously led me to many of Coach Smith's friends and teammates from his time on campus in the late '40s and early '50s as a player and aspiring coach. Candace put in a good word with broadcaster and KU alum Gary Bender, who called Carolina's first title against Georgetown.

I drove over to nearby Topeka, the state capital, on a hot Kansas summer day to see his high school alma mater and to meet with his lifelong best friend, Bill Bunten. Mr. Bunten, a former state legislator and mayor of Topeka, was Smith's friend and teammate at Topeka High School and Phi Gamma Delta fraternity brother at KU. Bunten set me up with their high school friend, former US senator Nancy Landon Kassebaum Baker, who became a valued contributor.

Back home in the Chicago area, I met and interviewed Gil Reich, another KU teammate and Phi Gamma Delta fraternity brother, who developed another enduring friendship with Smith.

Then I traveled to Chapel Hill in beautiful North Carolina, where I obtained the leads I needed to interview many Smith friends and associates. Among them were Atlantic Coast Conference Commissioner John Swofford, veteran basketball announcer Woody Durham, and two of Coach Smith's greatest All-Americans, Phil Ford and Billy Cunningham.

I called and interviewed famed basketball referee Ed Hightower in suburban St. Louis, who was a fountainhead of valuable information and memories. After Smith's death in 2015, I connected with the coach's pastor and mentor, the Reverend Robert Seymour from the Olin T. Binkley Memorial Baptist Church. Dr. Seymour guided the coach through uncharted territory as he advised him on integrating the previously all-white North Carolina team and the ACC itself.

Special thanks are warranted for Sonny Vaccaro, who changed the dynamics and direction of the game with his knowledge of human nature and ability to bring money to the sport in many ways as he helped make Michael Jordan, many other black athletes, and coaches become wealthy.

The writer Roland Lazenby has been an invaluable help, as has Bill Orr of TelRa Productions in Philadelphia. The support and memories from my friend Ernie Accorsi were invaluable, as were Dan Kane, the Raleigh *News and Observer*'s superb investigative reporter, and Mary Willingham, who has stood tall among people who have trouble dealing with the truth in what she saw and reported as an academic tutor and counselor at UNC.

I was fortunate to have the backing of my patient and understanding editor, Mark Weinstein of Rodale, who understands what a project of this nature entails, and my agent, Paul Bresnick, who knows and has seen everything.

ABOUT THE AUTHOR

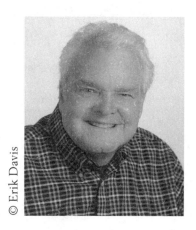

© Erik Davis

JEFF DAVIS IS A CAREER journalist and lifelong Chicagoan. A graduate of Northwestern University's Medill School of Journalism, Davis served nearly 4 years as a junior officer in the US Navy on an Atlantic Fleet aircraft carrier and saw much of Europe north and south before he and his family came home, where he broke into broadcast journalism and gained his first experience in the tumult and shouting of the wildest year ever: 1968. He wrote and produced news, sports, and documentaries and contributed reports to NBC Sports and the *Today Show*. He has been cited for excellence in journalism, including receiving AP and UPI awards, and has been honored with five Emmys for television production.

BIBLIOGRAPHY AND SOURCE NOTES

Interview Subjects

Ernie Accorsi, retired NFL executive; Wake Forest University, class of 1963

Nancy Landon Kassebaum Baker, former US Senator from Kansas; friend of Smith at Topeka Kansas High School and KU (University of Kansas)

Gary Bender, former CBS Sports broadcaster

Rick Brewer, retired sports information director, KU

Quinn Buckner, Indiana University All-American, 1976; Olympic basketball team gold medalist; NBA player; NBA broadcaster

Bill Bunten, former Kansas State senator; former Kansas State Representative; mayor of Topeka; lifelong best friend and basketball teammate of Smith at Topeka High School, KU; fraternity brother

Chris Collins, basketball coach, Northwestern University, 2013 to present; player for Duke, 1992-96; assistant coach at Duke, 2000-2013

Billy Cunningham, All-America at UNC 1962-65; All NBA with the Philadelphia 76ers; former 76ers coach

Charles "Lefty" Driesell, former coach, Davidson U., and U. of Maryland

Candace Mason Dunback, senior director of K Club and Traditions at KU

Woody Durham, retired play-by-play broadcaster for UNC, 1971-2011; friend of Coach Smith

Max Falkenstien, retired play-by-play broadcaster for KU, 1946-2006

Phil Ford Jr., UNC All-America point guard, 1974-78; 1976 Olympic basketball team gold medalist; NBA player; assistant coach for Smith at UNC

Ed Hightower, educator; former NCAA referee

Bill Hougland, KU teammate on 1952 NCAA champions; Olympic basketball team gold medalist, 1952 and 1956

Dan Kane, investigative reporter with Raleigh *News and Observer*

Dick Kepley, KU player when Smith was assistant coach

Steve Kirschner, associate athletic director at UNC; senior sports information director at UNC

Roland Lazenby, author of *Michael Jordan*

Bill Leinhard, KU teammate on 1952 NCAA champions; Olympic basketball team gold medalist in 1952

Doug Moe, UNC player; NBA coach

Eric Montross, UNC player; 1993 NCAA champion; NBA player

Bill Orr, Tel Ra Productions, Inc., Wayne, PA

Digger Phelps, former coach at Notre Dame

Gilbert Reich, teammate, classmate, and fraternity brother of Dean Smith

Joe Ruklick, former Northwestern and Philadelphia Warriors teammate of Wilt Chamberlain

Dr. Robert Seymour, retired pastor, Olin Binkley Memorial Baptist Church Chapel Hill, NC; Smith's spiritual mentor

John Swofford, ACC commissioner; former UNC football player; former UNC athletic director

Professor Jay M. Smith, UNC historian

John Thompson, former basketball coach Georgetown University; assistant to Smith on 1976 Olympic basketball team; radio announcer-analyst

Tommy Tomlinson, Charlotte *Observer* columnist; ESPN columnist

Donnie Walsh, player on Smith's first UNC team, 1961-62; NBA executive with New York Knicks and Indiana Pacers

Jerry Waugh, KU player and assistant coach

Mary Willingham, former tutor and reading instructor, UNC

Books

Anderson, Rob. J. *Tarnished Heels.* Rock Hill, SC: Strategic Media Books, Inc., 2014.

Bradsher, Bethany. *The Classic: How Everett Case and His Tournament Brought Big-Time Basketball to the South.* Houston, TX: Whitecaps Media, 2011.

Brown, Gerry and Michael Morrison, eds. *ESPN Sports Almanac, 2009.* New York: Ballantine Books, 2009.

Chansky, Art. *Game Changers: Dean Smith, Charlie Scott, and the Era That Transformed a Southern College Town.* Chapel Hill, NC: The University of North Carolina Press, 2016.

Feinstein, John. *The Legends Club: Dean Smith, Mike Krzyzewski, Jim Valvano, and an Epic College Basketball Rivalry.* New York: Penguin Random House, 2016.

Lazenby, Roland. *Michael Jordan: The Life.* New York: Little, Brown, and Co., 2014.

Moore, Johnny, and Art Chansky. *The Blue Divide: Duke, North Carolina and the Battle of Tobacco Road.* Chicago: Triumph Books, Inc., 2014.

Smith, Dean, with John Kilgo and Sally Jenkins. *A Coach's Life.* New York: Random House, 1999, 2002.

Smith, Dean. *Basketball: Multiple Offense and Defense.* Englewood, NY: Prentice-Hall, Inc., 1982.

Smith, Dean, and Gerald D. Bell with John Kilgo. *The Carolina Way: Leadership Lessons from a Life in Coaching.* New York: Penguin Books, 2004.

Smith, Jay M. and Mary Willingham. *Cheated: The UNC Scandal, the Education of Athletes, and the Future of Big-Time College Sports.* Lincoln, NE: Potomac Books, 2015.

Taaffe, William and David Fischer. *Sports of the Times: A Day-By-Day Selection of the Most Important, Thrilling and Inspired Events of the Past 150 Years.* New York: St. Martin's Press, 2003.

Whittingham, Richard. *The Final Four: A Pictorial History of the NCAA Basketball Classic.* Chicago: Contemporary Books, Inc., 1983.

Articles

Crothers, Tim. "Column: 'Thank you, Dean Smith,'" *Sports Illustrated,* February 9, 2015.

Deford, Frank. "Long Ago He Won the Big One: Dean Smith's Best Victory." *Sports Illustrated, the Vault,* November 2, 2015.

Dodd, Dennis, on the UNC Scandal, May 1, 2016.

Jauss, Bill. "Lights Out." *Chicago Tribune*, June 19, 1999.

Lapchick, Richard. "Scott and Smith Gave New Look to Tobacco Road." *ESPN*, February 28, 2008.

Logan, Greg. "Charles Scott Recalls His Journey with Dean Smith to Desegregate ACC." *Newsday*, February 8, 2015.

Smith, Timothy W. "College Basketball; Smith Ejected on 2 Technicals." *New York Times*, March 31, 1991.

Wilstein, Steve, "Smith Is Dean of College Hoops," *Washington Post*, March 15, 1997.

Wolff, Alexander, "Man of the Year," *Sports Illustrated*, December 23, 1997.

Many internet items including articles from *CBS Sports, Go Heels.com, Tar Heel Times.*

And *"Webber's Timeout"* in the 1993 NCAA championship game.

Newspapers and Periodicals

Chicago Tribune, ESPN Magazine, Newsday, New York Times, Raleigh News and Observer, Sports Illustrated, Tar Heel News, Topeka Capital-Journal, Washington Post

INDEX

An asterisk (*) indicates a photo shown in the photo-inserts.